I Sing the Body Electronic

To Dee & Chuck,
who run an awesome
loadstar —
With all the
things in my best —

Fred Moody

I Sing the Body
Electronic

A Year with Microsoft on the Multimedia Frontier

Fred Moody

VIKING

VIKING
Published by the Penguin Group
Penguin Books USA Inc., 375 Hudson Street, New York, New York 10014, U.S.A.
Penguin Books Ltd, 27 Wrights Lane, London W8 5TZ, England
Penguin Books Australia Ltd, Ringwood, Victoria, Australia
Penguin Books Canada Ltd, 10 Alcorn Avenue, Toronto, Ontario, Canada M4V 3B2
Penguin Books (N.Z.) Ltd, 182–190 Wairau Road, Auckland 10, New Zealand

Penguin Books Ltd, Registered Offices:
Harmondsworth, Middlesex, England

First published in 1995 by Viking Penguin,
a division of Penguin Books USA Inc.

1   3   5   7   9   10   8   6   4   2

Grateful acknowledgment is made for permission to reprint excerpts
from the following copyrighted works:
"We Die Young," lyrics and music by Jerry Cantrell. © 1990 Buttnugget Publishing (ASCAP).
International copyright secured. All rights reserved. "Man in the Box," lyrics by Layne Staley,
music by Jerry Cantrell. © 1990 Jack Lord Music/Buttnugget Publishing (ASCAP).
International copyright secured. All rights reserved.

LIBRARY OF CONGRESS CATALOGING IN PUBLICATION DATA

Moody, Fred.
I sing the body electronic / by Fred Moody.
p.   cm.
Includes index.
ISBN 0-670-84875-1
1. Microsoft Corporation—History.   2. Computer software industry—
United States—History.   I. Title.
HD9696.C64M5357   1995
338.7'610053'0973—dc20   95-1919

This book is printed on acid-free paper.

(∞)

Printed in the United States of America
Set in Bodoni Book
Designed by James Sinclair

To Dick Moody,
my brother

This is one of those very peculiar cases where what seems to be a somewhat natural definition leads to extremely puzzling behavior: chaos produced in a very orderly manner. One is naturally led to wonder whether the apparent chaos conceals some subtle regularity.

—*Douglas R. Hofstadter*

In this head the all-baffling brain;
In it and below it, the makings of heroes.

—*Walt Whitman*


```
BOOK*aWeirdBook;

        if ( aWeirdBook = new BOOK)
        {
                a WeirdBook-> setTitle("I Sing the Body Electronic");
                aWeirdBook-> setAuthor("Fred Moody");
                aWeirdBook-> setCharacter("Kevin Gammill");

                WriteBook(aWeirdBook);
                PublishBook(aWeirdBook);
                cout < < "Great book\n";
        }
        else
        {
                cout < < "Book sucks!\n";
```

—*Kevin Gammill*

In Lieu of a Glossary

Technical terminology and arcane computer-industry slang have been kept to a minimum in this book, except when absolutely unavoidable or irresistibly entertaining, and all such words are defined when first used. Even so, there are a few software terms and social conventions that the reader unfamiliar with personal computers would do well to learn before beginning this story.

Much of the dialogue and business at Microsoft is conducted on electronic mail, or *e-mail*. Everyone at Microsoft has an e-mail name, called an *alias*, that usually is an abbreviated form of the person's name. Kevin Gammill's e-mail alias, for example, is keving; Bryan Ballinger's is bball; Carolyn Bjerke's is cbjerke. Sometimes there are group aliases—Gandalf, mmpcore, and soc are three among the hundreds at Microsoft—and mail addressed to such an alias is copied automatically to all registered members of the group. E-mail generally is written in haste, and it is understood among all correspondents that there is no need to worry about spelling or grammar. E-mail quoted in these pages is quoted verbatim, with spelling and grammar mistakes left intact and unmarred by unsightly [*sic*]s.

The software product that vaulted Microsoft into its position of dominance is *MS-DOS*, which stands for "Microsoft disc operating system." An *operating system* is a computer's consciousness—the software that turns a set of chips, wires, boards, and other components into a functioning brain. Microsoft also manufactures *Windows*, a software *platform* that sits on top of MS-DOS and makes computers easier to use. (The latest generation of MS-DOS/Windows, called Windows 95, has Windows fully integrated into the operating system, with the result that the system is faster and more powerful.) Software *applications*—word processing programs, spreadsheet programs, solitaire games, flight simulators, and so on—work by sending *calls* to Windows, which in turn sends calls to MS-DOS, which in turn makes the computer behave like a typewriter, a spreadsheet, a calculator, a television set, a deck of cards, or the view from a moving airplane's cockpit window.

Windows is a *graphical user interface,* intended to make MS-DOS personal computers look and behave like Apple's Macintosh, the first commercially available personal computer with a graphical user interface. Anything on a computer screen that allows a user to interact with a computer program is part of the interface. An interface is graphical when it employs metaphorical pictures, or *icons,* upon which the user can *click* with a *mouse* to activate computer programs or functions rather than having to activate them by typing cryptic commands, as one must do on an MS-DOS computer without Windows. (The mouse is a pointing device, connected by cable to the computer, that controls a *cursor,* which usually looks like an arrow, on the screen.) If a user wants to print something from a graphical–user interface computer, he or she might use the computer's mouse to move the cursor to a small picture—an icon—of a printer, then click the mouse's button. The computer would respond by activating its printer.

A common feature in graphical user interface is a *dialog box*—a *window* that suddenly appears, or *opens,* in the foreground of a computer screen to ask the user a question or offer an array of options. A window is a square or rectangular portion of a computer screen, contained in a frame. A dialog box might ask the user to type in his or her name, or it might present a list of alternative actions, one of which is chosen with a mouse-click.

Most of the products discussed in this book are stored on *compact disc* for use in a *multimedia personal computer* with a *CD-ROM drive.* A compact disc, which stores as much information as can be stored on 1,000 conventional floppy discs, looks exactly like the compact discs sold in music stores. A multimedia personal computer displays text, pictures, animation and video, and plays sound—all of which can be stored on compact discs. The term *CD-ROM* stands for "compact disc–read only memory," the ROM meaning that the information stored on the disc cannot be altered or replaced.

In this book, readers often will be told that a user's mouse-click opens a window containing a *stack* of *pop-ups*. This window opens when the user clicks on a *hot spot*—any part of a computer's display that responds to a mouse-click. The pop-up window contains blocks of text and pictures that are shown in sections rather than all at once, just as pages in a magazine are stacked on top of one another rather than displayed on a single long piece of paper. A given pop-up window might have six or seven such sections. When the user is finished reading the first section of text, a mouse-click on the appropriate icon will make that section vanish, to be replaced by the next section. Since the visual impression is of a pile of printed cards or pages, the product's designers refer to these sections as parts of a stack. As with many computer terms, use can be inconsistent: Sometimes *pop-up*, as used in this book, means the window itself and sometimes it means one of the cards in the window's stack.

In any event, the visual image readers should keep in mind when reading this book is that of a program that presents detailed pictures on the computer screen—of nature scenes, street scenes, interiors of furnished rooms. The user clicks on individual elements within these pictures to cause windows containing text and pictures about them to pop up. Other mouse-clicks on hot spots or icons will trigger the playing of music, speech, or other sound, and still others will trigger the playing of animation or video sequences.

The animations are of two types: *animations* and *sprites*. An animation performs an action while standing in one place; a sprite moves about on the screen.

A final word: the term *cool*, as used at Microsoft, is roughly analogous to the Russian *khorosho*. Depending upon the context in which it is used and the tone of voice with which it is uttered, *cool* can mean perfect, phenomenal, awesome, ingenious, eye-popping, bliss inducing, pretty, clever, enchanting, fine, adequate, acceptable, okay, or any of hundreds or so other such words. The opposite of cool, in all of its meanings, is *random*.

Acknowledgments

Among the many people deserving my thanks for making this book possible are, first and foremost, the young men and women at Microsoft who tolerated my presence among them for so long: Kevin Gammill, Carolyn Bjerke, Jayleen Ryberg, Sara Fox, Bryan Ballinger, Lindsey Smith, Bill Sproule, Len Dongweck, Sandy Dean, Abigail Riblet, Meredith Kraike, Meg Nyland, Susan Denning, Ralph Barton, and Kim Emery. Craig Bartholomew gave me everything I asked for by way of information and perspective, and more. Phil Spencer patiently answered hundreds of my questions, as did Amy Raby and Richard Hobbs. Susan Boeschen and Tom Corddry, at considerable personal risk, took me under their wings and found a splendid place for me at Microsoft. Other company executives proved unfailingly cooperative; chief among these are Bill Gates, Rob Glaser, Nathan Myrhvold, and Jabe Blumenthal.

Indispensable help was provided by Microsoft's Nancy Hutchinson, Sheila Geraghty, and Mary Dieli. I am indebted to Carrie Seglin for furnishing me with no end of insights. Pam Edstrom and Alison Obrien, at Waggener Edstrom Public Relations, secured interviews and answers to my questions, as did Karen Meredith and Julie Larkin, in Microsoft's corporate communications department.

John Verzani gave the technical sections of my manuscript an expert reading, and Katherine Koberg labored long and hard to correct its excesses of language.

Andrew Ward, Glen and Jean Moehring, John Moehring, Jane Steinberg, David Brewster, Sally Hewett, Dave Jackson, Jesse McFarlane,

Richard Holt, Kathryn Robinson, and Sam Hudson all provided essential advice, solace, care, feeding, and inspiration. I am also beholden to the incomparable Ronnie Sue Stangler and to those masters of forbearance, Kathy and Rick Countryman.

I am blessed with a wonderful and hard-bitten agent, Nat Sobel, and with two gifted editors: Kathryn Court, with her keen eye and gift for motivating feckless writers, and Marion Maneker, who is possessed of pep, verve, wit, intelligence, and insight.

Finally, my wife, Anne, and my daughters, Erin, Caitlin, and Jocelyn, suffered through this project with provocative grace and patience.

I Sing the Body Electronic was composed on a low-end Macintosh LC with 12 megabytes of RAM, a 40-megabyte hard disk, and a Prometheus Home Office fax/modem. Its words were processed with Microsoft Word 5.1. I also made use of an antique Compaq Deskpro 386/20, running Windows for Workgroups 3.11, and a Macintosh Quadra 800. All writing and thinking was undertaken while under the influence of Pegasus French Roast coffee, Redhook Extra Special Bitter Ale, Ballard Bitter, and the music of Nirvana, Rage Against the Machine, Mudhoney, Alice in Chains, Soundgarden, Screaming Trees, Tad, Primus, and Johann Sebastian Bach.

Contents

Introduction

By the beginning of 1993, the Microsoft Corporation had long since been living one of the most dramatic success stories in American history. It was entering its eighteenth year with a market value pegged at $26.78 billion, having recently surpassed both General Motors and IBM in that category. Microsoft's 1992 earnings, $3.5 billion, were equal to those of its next seven competitors combined. Its 1992 net income of $800 million was more than double the combined income of those same seven competitors, and analysts at Dean Witter Reynolds expected 1993 net income to exceed $1 billion.

Among the world's 120 million personal computers in use at the end of 1992, one would have been hard-pressed to find a single one that did not include at least one Microsoft product. Eighty-one percent of the 22 million PCs manufactured that year left the factory with Microsoft's operating system, MS-DOS, already on them. Microsoft was cranking out five new software application titles per month and had hundreds more in the works.

Cofounded by Bill Gates and Paul Allen in 1975 as a two-man startup company supplying computer languages to a single hardware manufacturer, Microsoft had from the beginning grown faster than the personal-computer industry in general. It had become formidable enough to attract the attention of the Federal Trade Commission (FTC), which was investigating the company for a variety of pricing and other commercial practices. (Eventually, the FTC, deadlocked, would turn its investigation over to the Justice Department, which would spend nearly two more years investigating Microsoft before finally arriving at a settlement that called for minor concessions: technical changes in the company's agreements with applications companies and personal computer manufacturers.) Now often referred to as Big Green, just as IBM, computer colossus of the 1970s, was known in its heyday as Big Blue, Microsoft found its competitors in the 1990s looking ever more desperately for a way to bring the company down.

Microsoft, in short, was a juggernaut—universally feared, loathed, and revered. Undaunted, it continued to extend its reach in areas where it already dominated—most notably in computer operating systems, word processing programs, and spreadsheets—and to look relentlessly for new markets. Consequently, the work and the growth never slowed at Big Green's headquarters. The place had grown from a one-building campus housing 100 people in 1982 to 1993's 24-building (with two more under construction), 260-acre campus in Redmond, Washington—a suburb east of Seattle—where 6,000 of the company's 12,888 employees worldwide worked.

Computer programming and its related interface design work is painstaking and frustrating even in the best of circumstances. When undertaken in the circumstances described in the following pages—in an intensely competitive company that develops personal computer software for the corporate and consumer marketplaces and is run by a man who is determined to remain number one in the world forever—the work can reduce people to rubble.

This book chronicles a year in the life of a Microsoft design and development team. The team was working in the company's Multimedia Publishing division at a time when multimedia software was newly emerging and still in search of a definition for itself. The team's efforts took place against a backdrop of almost infinite corporate suspense. The product of its labors played a crucial role in Bill Gates's plan to dominate the emerging multimedia computing field. Gates hoped to command multimedia as thoroughly as he had the computer operating systems, word processing, and spreadsheet markets since the 1981 introduction of the personal computer.

With the somewhat bemused blessing of Microsoft, I lived with this team, attended all of its meetings, shared an office with its lead developer, read all of its electronic mail, and exhaustively discussed with team members their experiences in the context of the broader Microsoft culture.

Seen from the inside, Microsoft differs markedly from its public image. Living among Microsoft employees, I felt a little like Luke Skywalker unmasking Darth Vader in *Return of the Jedi*. Take away the company's monolithic facade and you come upon a completely unexpected, nearly indescribable creature.

The Microsoft approach to corporate organization is to form small teams around specific products and leave them alone to organize and work as they wish. It is a risky approach, for these crews are left unsupervised to a degree unthinkable in standard American corporations. Yet Microsoft management regards this approach as the best way to avoid the kind of gigantism and bureaucratic paralysis that brought down both its chief rival, the IBM Corporation, and many of the previous generation of large American companies. Gates and those who help run his company are determined to keep it small and agile, like determined startup companies, no matter how big Microsoft's numbers become.

The resulting atmosphere, combined with the company's rapid growth and the youth of its employees, makes for a casual and frenzied workplace, rich in informality, individual freedom, and excruciating psychological pressure. It is, in short, an ideal place for a writer to conduct unsupervised research on an exotic corporate culture. Because people move through Microsoft so quickly and in such large numbers, mine was seen as just another new face on the campus, and it seemed that within a matter of days the characters in my book-to-be forgot that I was a spectator rather than a fellow-sufferer.

At the same time, my credentials as an outsider and my constant interest in their lives and work made my companions uncommonly willing to talk about their quest. The presence of a writer among them lent credence to the vague notion in their minds that there was something fundamentally odd—both weird and special—about the way they were living and working. They soon fell into the habit of reflecting on their experiences as they went along. I often found myself engaged in long conversations, particularly after stressful meetings, in hallways, vacant conference rooms, cafeterias, offices, taverns, and on paths through the campus and the forest on its eastern edge. It was as if my companions were trying not only to complete their project on time, but also to divine its meaning and purpose.

Many of the team members' most poignant observations and asides came to me through e-mail, a medium that combines distance and intimacy in a way that can only be compared to traditional Catholicism's old confessional booth—that dark and cozy place in which sinners used to pour out their hearts to a barely discernible silhouette on the other side of a screen.

While there may well be no such thing as a typical design team at Microsoft, as each defines its own mission and structure, all teams are so imbued with the company's vision that they give uniformly vivid expression to Microsoft's culture. While each team in many ways is a separate company within the larger whole, each also is a Microsoftcosm, sharing with all others a set of founding principles and aspirations that come from the office of Chairman Bill Gates. So an intimate look at the small group in this book is also an examination of the ingredients—psychological, technical, and situational—in the company's potent corporate mix.

This is not to say that I understand what exactly is going on at Microsoft. For the sad fact of the matter is that I left the company's campus more confused than I was when I entered. And looking back over these pages now leaves me even more perplexed, as I still cannot manage to tell whether they contain a story of success, of failure, of success disguised as failure, or of failure disguised as success. Yet I am convinced that the solution to the puzzle is woven into this narrative somewhere, waiting to be discovered.

I Sing the Body Electronic

December 17, 1992

From behind the office door, which is resolutely closed, can be heard the thumping torpid rage of Alice in Chains, the Seattle band known for its ballads of dread and drug addiction. The bass is pounding hard enough to rattle the door in its frame, and the begrunged voice of lead singer Layne Staley is declaiming:

I'm the dog who gets beat
Shove my nose in shit
Won't you come and save me . . .

Inside, the small office is cluttered. The blinds are drawn shut and the lights are off. There are six computers in the room—four on an L-shaped desk, one perched atop a bookcase, and one down on the floor in front of the desk. All but the terminal on the bookcase are turned on. The desk is littered with discarded soda cans, papers, and books: *Future Crime*, *The New Peter Norton Programmer's Guide to the IBM PC & PS/2*, Raymond Queneau's *The Blue Flowers*. Stereo-system components, connected by wires running along the floor and the walls, are scattered around the room. A mangled Homer Simpson doll, a cigar protruding from its torn mouth and a golf ball embedded in its face, stands on the desk, propped against the wall. A framed picture depicting a wall on which a graffitist has written "Hardcore Software" hangs above the book-case. Next to it hangs a poster depicting one of the Our Gang kids as an exuberant grade-school Jimi Hendrix brandishing an electric guitar and

1

dressed in 1960s rock-and-roll garb. Its caption reads, "Buckwheat Say . . . Rock 'n' Roll . . . O-Tay!" Several computer mice, each with a mousetrap snapped shut on it, are hanging by their cables from the ceiling.

The floor of the cave, covered with discarded papers, books, children's toys, a pacifier, a pillow, a blanket, and two chairs, is all but unnavigable.

A boyish twenty-five-year-old wearing a T-shirt, blue jeans, and boat shoes without socks sits at the desk, his attention directed at the largest of his computer screens. He is conventionally good-looking, with spectacles, an athletic build, and hair hanging nearly to his shoulders. He sports a three-day stubble on his face, grimy skin, and glittering brown eyes that never blink. His shirt is drenched in sweat.

Furiously tapping one foot, typing in blazing short bursts, and muttering imprecations to himself, he sits rigidly upright; with each tap of his heel on the floor, his body bounces up from the chair. Windows open and close frenetically on the screen in front of him. In one of them—black background, white text—he types:

```
void main()
{
     char chTemp;
     for (chTemp=0; chTemp <=MAX_CHAR; chTemp++)
     {
          printf("chTemp is: %d-%c\n", (unsigned int)chTemp, chTemp);
     }
     printf("All done!\n");
}
```

Kevin Gammill, a software development engineer at the Microsoft Corporation, is in the final stages of a years-long project. He has been working sixteen hours a day, seven days a week for so long that his supervisor has been pleading with him for weeks to take a day off. He neither allows visitors in his office nor speaks to people on his rare trips outside of it.

South of Gammill's office, down a labyrinthine hallway decorated with two Jacob Lawrence prints, four people work quietly in a conference room. One of them writes notes on a whiteboard mounted on the wall as they lay out the preliminary blueprint for the next two years of Gammill's life.

The group is discussing two projects, code-named *Sendak* and *Charles*.

The first—the one to which Gammill will be assigned—is a children's encyclopedia; the second, an atlas of the world. Both will be stored on a compact disc for use in a multimedia personal computer, and both are being produced in Microsoft's Multimedia Publishing division. Although work has barely begun on either project, it is clear from the discussion that their production will pose significant and possibly insurmountable problems.

From the board, Carolyn Bjerke, lead designer for *Sendak*, is alternately lecturing and questioning the two young men and the woman seated before her. The seated woman looks vaguely like Loretta Lynn: her hair is long in back, with bangs plastered into an arc of huge curls arranged around a freckled face. One of the men is wearing a rumpled long-sleeved button-down shirt under a green T-shirt decorated with the black-and-white dairy cows that are the semiofficial symbol of the state of Vermont. His cohort wears a T-shirt, two rings in his left ear, and a haircut that looks like a soufflé. The back of his shirt displays a huge globe enfolded by two hands over the caption, "Shaping the World." The front of the shirt shows a smaller version of the globe, framed by the words, "Microsoft Consumer Division."

At thirty years of age, Carolyn Bjerke is the oldest person in the room, the others all being twenty-four. After earning bachelor's and master's degrees in fine arts at the University of Oregon, she came to Microsoft in 1988, lured there by a fellow alum who told her that the company was looking for artists who could design for computers. Now, nearly five years later, she is a few months away from seeing the first tangible product of her labors—Microsoft *Encarta*, a multimedia encyclopedia—hit the marketplace. *Encarta*, the project Gammill is working so feverishly to complete, is now in its final development stages, and Bjerke is able to turn her attention to *Sendak*, a more technically ambitious young children's product that Microsoft hopes to position as a stepping stone to *Encarta*.

Bjerke is a tall, athletic woman. She has luminous pale blue eyes, brown hair with blond highlights, and wears stylish outfits—an anomaly at Microsoft—that are color-coordinated down to her earrings and one of the twelve watchbands she owns. Attention in meeting rooms tends to gravitate toward her, as she speaks with an air of natural authority that, in part, is a function of her tenure at Microsoft: by company standards, she is a grizzled veteran.

The conversation in the business meeting is laced with adolescent slang, as in, "It costs $152,000 to get something really really cool," or

"His combination is really neat." The Loretta Lynnish woman, to whom the team turns often for answers of one sort or another, is particularly given to kidspeak: "So she, like, says, 'How are you going to get this effect?' And I'm, like, 'Sprite engine!' And she's like, 'No way!' and I'm, like . . ."

Hundreds of these meetings take place each day all over the Microsoft Corporation campus. Every time I sat in on one of them, I felt like I was watching a gang of adolescents who had sneaked into some corporate headquarters after hours, taken over its boardrooms, and were playing at being businesspeople. Everything about the buildings here, and their offices and rooms, testifies to corporate success and wealth. And everything about the people who inhabit them exemplifies youthful rebellion, irreverence, and barely governable zest for rock 'n' roll music—which can be heard issuing from Microsoft offices at all hours of the day and night.

The atmosphere on the campus is one of unrelenting anxiety and constant improvisation. Microsoft is ceaselessly assembling and reassembling its recruits into small teams of engineers, designers, and editors, turning them loose to dream unsupervised, then eventually calling them on the carpet and demanding that they produce something.

The seven years since the 1985 establishment of a multimedia division at Microsoft had seen the production of virtually nothing. Aside from the publication in 1987 of *Bookshelf* (a reference title, with sound and color pictures, containing *Bartlett's Familiar Quotations*, *The Concise Columbia Encyclopedia*, *The American Heritage Dictionary*, *Roget's II Electronic Thesaurus*, *The World Almanac and Book of Facts*, and *The Concise Columbia Dictionary of Quotations*—all stored on a single compact disc) and the 1992 publication of *Cinemania*, a comprehensive film reference that includes sound, video, animation, and printed text, the company had little to show for the approximately $21 million it had invested in multimedia. Microsoft's attempts at multimedia publishing added up to little more than a long research-and-development project. Mostly, the company had racked up huge losses as it began and abandoned a series of projects, stopping occasionally to reorganize its multimedia division in an attempt to get some titles out the door. Asked late in 1992 what his division was up to, Tom Corddry, general manager of Microsoft Multimedia Publishing, said, "We have four product units that are sitting around trying to figure out what to do next."

Management nonetheless continued to pump money into what it called

"MM Pubs." At a time when Microsoft had instituted a companywide growth cap of 5 percent per year in employee headcount, trying to keep costs down and profit margins up, Multimedia Publishing was growing at 60 percent per year. Microsoft was driven by the belief that the emerging marketplace would be dominated by the competitor who got there first. "There's a sense within the management team in this department," said Craig Bartholomew, manager of the product unit in which *Encarta* and *Sendak* were being created, "that the time to grow is now. If we don't grow now, people like Sony will be in the market. It will become harder and harder and harder to compete. Our goal is to really get out there with a series of beachhead products now, that hopefully will give us presence in the market."

Bartholomew and others were convinced that their goal was at hand and that Microsoft at last was on the verge of simultaneously creating and taking over the multimedia market. Going into 1993, Microsoft had fourteen multimedia titles in the works, the first of one hundred to be published over the next three years. In offices throughout Building 10—headquarters of MM Pubs—developers like Kevin Gammill and designers like Carolyn Bjerke were laboring mightily to fulfill a vision that none of them could define, but in which all of them passionately believed.

The *Encarta* Years

The *Sendak* core design team comprised, for the moment, five Microsoft employees and a handful of freelance editors and artists. The team had come together, more or less haphazardly, during the last two years of the *Encarta* project—a monumental and pivotal effort that had spanned the entire history of Microsoft's multimedia division—which was now only three months from completion.

The design-and-development process that had evolved in Multimedia Publishing began with designers, editors, and at least one representative from marketing sketching out a rough plan for a product. Eventually the product would have enough definition for its designers to build a tiny prototype on a computer. This prototype would then be used to demonstrate the product to developers, managers, and potential users. Once the fundamental design was worked out, the team began amassing content and designing specific features. Eventually, the lead designer would write a detailed specifications document, describing every feature in detail. That document was then handed over to the product's developers, who could begin writing its code.

Generally, designers and editors worked six months or more before the project's developers began code-writing. Then the entire team would work simultaneously and more or less separately for another six months or more. Finally, designers and editors, their work done, would move on to another project while the developers spent several more months finishing their work.

In creating *Encarta*—a nine-million-word encyclopedia on a single compact disc—Microsoft had taken the text of the *Funk and Wagnalls Encyclopedia*, edited and updated it, and supplemented it with an 83,000-word dictionary; a 40,000-entry thesaurus; 100 animations and video sequences; 7,000 photographs, charts, and maps; 700 computer industry–related articles and terms; an interactive knowledge-adventure game called MindMaze; and seven hours of sound, which included the national anthems of more than 170 countries, spoken samples from 46 languages, recordings of authors reading their works, historical speeches, nature sounds, and samples of music.

By putting an encyclopedia on a compact disc, Microsoft made its information accessible in ways impossible through print. A user had only to type in a single word—*plant,* say—and *Encarta*'s screen would instantly produce a list of all articles in the encyclopedia containing that word. *Encarta*'s 250,000 *see* and *see also* references—ten times the number found in the *Funk and Wagnalls* print version—allowed users to browse briskly through the text, traveling, in a matter of minutes, through innumerable related topics on a journey that would take hours in a set of printed volumes. Users could copy sections of a given article into a word-processing document and include the passage in a report they were writing. They could reprint pictures from *Encarta*, record its sounds, and fashion customized charts and graphs from the encyclopedia's printed information.

Microsoft's drive toward publishing multimedia encyclopedias had its origins in the company's first tentative explorations into multimedia itself—an exploration inspired by the invention of the compact disc, which stores 1,000 times as much information as can be stored on a conventional personal-computer floppy disc. Bill Gates, who makes a habit of looking at emerging hardware inventions and trying to foresee what will drive people to buy them, looked at the compact disc and decided that the first CD titles to sell would be encyclopedias, "because," he said, "the searching and linking and touring and quizzing are all very leveraged in that kind of context—and helping your kids stay ahead is a good buying theme." Accordingly, he established a CD-ROM division in 1985, directing it to find a way to get reference titles into the marketplace.

The CD-ROM division first demonstrated a mock-up of a multimedia encyclopedia in 1986, calling the effort its "proof-of-concept work"—an exercise in demonstrating the viability of such a thing. The division couldn't manage to advance beyond the prototype stage until 1989, when

Microsoft hired Tom Corddry, an advertising–media–public relations consultant who had been a consultant with Microsoft on a series of projects since 1981.

Corddry teamed up immediately with Carolyn Bjerke, and the two initiated the Merlin encyclopedia project, which began putting the *Funk and Wagnalls* text into electronic form and working up specifications for the electronic storage of photographs and sound. Bjerke worked at designing the encyclopedia's interface, trying to come up with an aesthetically appealing design so coherent that people could figure out how to use the encyclopedia simply by looking at the screen and intuitively understanding what all its words, menus, and commands would do when activated. Bjerke was further charged with creating a technically feasible design—one that could be implemented in spite of the shortcomings of the computer hardware and software of the time.

Merlin moved along in fits and starts for a year, getting nowhere, then was put on hold for six months. Microsoft bought a share of Great Britain's Dorling Kindersley Publishers with the idea of publishing electronic reproductions of DK titles, which are known for their lavish graphics and high production values. (Dorling Kindersley is best known in this country for its popular Eyewitness Books series of children's reference titles—issued in the United States by Alfred A. Knopf—which feature breathtaking color photographs and drawings, and very little text.) Gates was determined to start producing multimedia titles in large numbers, even if he couldn't produce them from scratch.

In November 1990, the company came back to Merlin. Craig Bartholomew, from Microsoft's marketing department, sent Gates a memo outlining his plan for producing a bookshelf encyclopedia—a scaled-back version of Merlin that Bartholomew thought could be done by using Microsoft's Multimedia Viewer 1.0, an "authoring" program developed to help artists and writers create multimedia titles. By using Viewer, Bartholomew reasoned, Microsoft could add pictures and sound to the *Funk and Wagnalls* text without having to write much of anything in the way of new computer code.

The Microsoft board of directors was reluctant to pursue Bartholomew's initiative, but Gates persuaded the board to go along, and Bartholomew was put in charge of the effort the following March. Now code-named *Gandalf*, the bookshelf encyclopedia, the project was to be finished by September 1992.

When Bartholomew took it over, the encyclopedia was a political hot potato. By designating it as Microsoft's most determined, high-profile attempt to leap into multimedia computing with a product of such power that the company would instantly be the world leader in that market, Gates had made the stakes monumental for Bartholomew. *Gandalf* was to "define the bar" in the encyclopedia category; that is, it was to be the standard against which all other encyclopedias would be found wanting. Gates wanted *Gandalf* to "own the market": to be the first multimedia encyclopedia out and of such high quality that competitors would be scared off. The consensus at Microsoft was that the encyclopedia would never be completed because Gates's vision was far too ambitious ever to be realized. Few dared take on such a project; for all of Gates's willingness to experiment, he was merciless to managers who couldn't deliver on his enthusiasms. Many believed that Bartholomew and his project were doomed.

At first glance, Bartholomew seemed an unlikely prospect for managing tough propositions. Bespectacled, with soft eyes and an almost inaudible voice, he is meekness personified. Sitting at his computer, looking up at its screen, he has the wistful look of a kid before Santa Claus. He had, however, come to Microsoft from the book publisher Addison-Wesley, thus bringing to the software company's multimedia venture an understanding of the nuts and bolts of publishing and marketing text. More important, he enjoyed a reputation at Microsoft as an able and highly organized manager and had what Corddry called the kind of "arrogance" that the *Gandalf* project needed.

Bartholomew spent nearly a year testing programming methods and interface designs before even beginning to build a product. *Gandalf* did not begin to take shape and make progress until October 1991, when Bartholomew hired a young editor named Sara Fox.

At twenty-seven, Fox had come to Seattle from Los Angeles after she and her husband decided they wanted to move to the northwest, where her husband had been raised. Stanford-educated, with a master's degree in education and teaching credentials in English and biology, she had worked as an editor both at Addison-Wesley and at Davidson, a software company, where she helped produce *English Express*, a videodisc and CD-ROM English-as-a-second-language teaching title, and *Math Blasters*, an extremely successful children's educational title. After an interview with Corddry and a few freelance editing assignments on *Gandalf*, she was hired by Bartholomew, who wanted an editor with expertise in children's education to direct work on both *Gandalf* and on future Microsoft multimedia titles for kids.

Bartholomew was taken with Fox's energy, intelligence, organizational skill, and ability to make decisions quickly. She could take in small amounts of information and immediately marshal a strong argument for or against a given proposition. But Bartholomew most wanted Fox aboard because she brought a rare and precious bit of experience to Multimedia: she had actually *shipped a software product.* In hiring someone who had seen a project through all the way to retailers' shelves, Bartholomew was adding to his R&D lab a person who understood the importance of meeting deadlines when developing something tangible for the consumer market.

Slender, blond, and blue-eyed, Fox has the gentle mannerisms of someone born to teach preschool. Her voice is high and soft, and has a tranquilizing effect on the listener. The emotion that comes most naturally to her is reflexive sympathy; she seldom makes a decision or carries out an action without fretting over the consequences to other people.

Yet Fox also is possessed of strong opinions and firmly held beliefs about education and multimedia. She immediately imposed an overall editorial vision on *Gandalf*, establishing and defining the level of its prose and the depth of its information. She carefully analyzed the strengths and weaknesses of its text, set about hiring freelance editors, and began updating and improving the encyclopedia's content.

With that under way, other elements of *Gandalf* began to fall into place. Bartholomew got Jayleen Ryberg, Multimedia's producer, working full time on the encyclopedia. As producer, Ryberg was charged with finding the talent and equipment, either within Microsoft or from freelance artists and other media studios, to manufacture *Gandalf*'s multimedia elements—its animations, videoclips, recorded sound, and still images—and to coordinate their production within the constraints of *Gandalf*'s schedule and the schedules of other projects.

The following March, Bartholomew's team was completed when two programmers, Kevin Gammill and Jay Gibson, finished up their work on an update of *Bookshelf* and went to work full time on *Gandalf*.

March 1992 also saw the elimination of the CD-ROM division and the creation of Multimedia Publishing. Enough work on enough different titles was then underway for the group to organize into four subgroups, called product units. Bartholomew's was dubbed the Gandalf product unit; the other three were called Jurassic, Mercury, and Variety. Each group was instructed to define its own product line and lobby Microsoft's upper management on its own for resources. Gandalf staked out reference titles as its specialty, while Jurassic began work on a series of multimedia renditions of Dorling Kindersley books, the first being a book on dinosaurs. Variety opted to work on entertainment titles, the first being *Cinemania*, and Mercury took on a mixed bag of more specialized reference works, from travel companions to a medical encyclopedia.

Before long, the *Gandalf* team had taken on a full roster of freelance artists and editors, bringing the team up to 135 people, and work on the encyclopedia proceeded at a frantic pace.

Even so, for every advance the team made, it seemed that there was an equal and opposite retreat. By May, Bartholomew and his team knew that their September 1992 deadline was hopelessly unrealistic. Viewer 1.0 proved inadequate, and Gammill and Gibson were constantly writing new code either for features it could not provide or to eliminate unnecessary or unappealing features that it forced on them.

In addition, every editorial or design enhancement to *Gandalf* seemed to bring with it a new set of problems requiring massive amounts of time to correct. When *Gandalf*'s editors, for example, decided to include more cross-referencing than had ever before been attempted in an encyclopedia, they sent their text to a Professor Gerard Sultan at Cornell University, who was famed for having written a "relatedness algorithm" that could analyze text and automatically spit out cross-references. Sultan sent back a list that included a number of howlers, among the most memorable being a "*see also* concentration camps" cross-reference from an article on camping. It took Fox's team months to ferret out all the unintentional word play.

Even as simple a task as naming the encyclopedia turned into an endless and expensive quest. Focus groups shot down *Electronic Encyclopedia*, and the company floated such names as *Mindbridge*, *Crystal Cubed*, *Helper*, *Exploratorium*, *Discoverer*, and *Discovery Trek* before finally hiring Seattle consultant Terry Heckler, who had come up with the names *Redhook*, *Starbucks*, and *Cinemania*. For $10,000, Heckler conjured up, among other names, *CyQuest*, *Cyclodome*, *Cogitour*—and *Encarta*.

As the encyclopedia's deadline neared, it was still little more than a collection of incomplete, barely functional components, and those parts that had been finished were failing test after test. The software was loaded with bugs—improperly or inefficiently written code that caused the computer either to fail outright or perform the wrong task. Inexplicable error messages would pop up on the screen in response to the simplest of commands. Sometimes the encyclopedia program would abruptly shut down when testers tried displaying some of its media elements. Other times, computers loaded with *Encarta* would respond mysteriously or helplessly to a request: ask it, for example, to print italicized words, and it would print them instead in standard type, with an extra space before and after each letter.

In addition, there were thousands of errors in *Encarta*'s displays of content. One of the more horrifying to the team showed up when the encyclopedia displayed an article on Bill Gates, featuring a captioned photograph of the chairman. Above the caption was a picture of Hank Williams. By the time *Encarta* was finished, 2,100 such problems would be discovered—many requiring hours, if not days, of a developer's time to correct—along with an additional 5,100 content bugs, or mistakes in the text.

Still, Bartholomew and his team pressed on. Partly out of fear of confronting Gates with bad news and partly out of the wishful hope that they could somehow find a way to bring *Encarta* in on time, they did not tell Gates that they would miss their deadline.

At Microsoft, Gates's pyrotechnics are the stuff of legend. It is considered a mark of great personal progress for him that, as Carolyn Bjerke says, "He only beats up on his managers now. He leaves us peons alone." Indeed, no matter how close a personal relationship a given manager may enjoy with Gates, he or she is never insulated from his attacks. Microsoft's early years were punctuated with frequent shouting matches between Gates and cofounder Paul Allen, his closest personal friend at the time. Jabe Blumenthal, an eleven-year Microsoft veteran in whom Gates has tremendous faith, was once brought up short in midpresentation when Gates began banging his head on the table, shouting, "You think I'm an idiot! Don't use that logic on me!"

Rob Glaser, an executive at Microsoft for eleven years, who served as the company's vice president in charge of Multimedia Systems until his retirement at age thirty-two, insists that the present-day Gates is a far mellower version of his former self. Yet Glaser also acknowledges, somewhat euphemistically, that "people are sometimes challenged at communicating with Bill, because of that question of, 'If I take a nanosecond more to explain something, will Bill get impatient?' He's quite a combination of persistence and impatience. I think a lot of the time when Bill's rude, it's persistence coming out, and it's impatience coming out . . . or it's probably just metabolic."

Gates nearly always reduces his audiences to wretchedness, no matter how thoroughly they have prepared themselves for his tantrums. A group developing software to drive network printers once got no more than two minutes into a presentation I was watching before Gates started shouting. Their voices soon were quavering, their sweaty hands dropping transparencies on the floor and inserting them into their overhead projector upside down and sideways. The more frightened they grew, the angrier Gates grew. "You've studied it and you've seen that it's turning bits on and off!" he shouted at one point. "And it's a brilliant insight! That's basically the presentation I've seen so far!" A few minutes, later, snorting, he burst out with, "Ah, they think that's the best way. . . . Well, they're just wrong! That's the silliest thing I've ever heard!" From then on, his interjections were constant: "It's nonsense!"; "This bullshit thing with no definition"; "This is where you guys have really gotten confused, okay?"; "Let's just say there were never any printers! Wouldn't that be nice? We could actually make money on this work!"

His head full of images from such scenes, Bartholomew finally went before Gates in early September, when it was no longer possible to deny the obvious, and told him that the encyclopedia would not be finished until March 1993—six months late, well after the all-important Christmas shopping season, and after two competitors, Grolier's and Compton's New Media, would have released multimedia encyclopedias.

Gates lit into Bartholomew with a harangue that Bartholomew later, with characteristic understatement, would describe as "a really unpleasant thirty-five minutes out of my life." Gates was incensed not so much at the missed deadline (although anathema at Microsoft, missed deadlines are a fact of life there, as no new product in company history has ever been finished on time), but at the fact that no one involved seemed to have anticipated that the deadline could not be met. In Gates's mind, that apparent lapse in judgment defined Bartholomew and virtually everyone connected with *Encarta* as people not to be trusted. "If you promise too tight a schedule here," says Tom Corddry, Bartholomew's supervisor, "you pay a terrible price. It wasn't so much that we didn't ship it that bothered him, it was that we didn't know it wouldn't ship until so late. That to him is a major red flag."

Bartholomew believed he had seriously tarred himself by taking on a title of importance and committing such a critical error with it. The experience left him morbidly preoccupied with the image Gates had of him. He developed the habit of reading into the slightest of clues profound evidence of peril to his prospects. Gates's body language at meetings, chance comments from peers, the context in which *Encarta* might be mentioned by the chairman or anyone else in his hearing, were all imbued with significant meaning in Bartholomew's mind.

So when Bartholomew convened a year-end meeting of his Gandalf product unit just before Christmas 1992, it came as a surprise to no one that Gates was the first item on the agenda. Where they stood with the chairman was of considerable interest to all of them, as Gates's opinion of individual workers or product units played an important role in determining how many resources they would be given and what kind of titles they would be given to develop.

The week before, Bartholomew had spent two hours with Gates, explaining in some detail what had gone wrong with *Encarta* and presenting him with a plan and list of positions he needed filled in order to do future multimedia products better and faster. Now, as he recounted that meeting, his subordinates snickered and smiled whenever Bartholomew alluded to Gates's anger, for they knew he was sparing them an abundance of gruesome details by opting for understatements like "not all that happy," "made a pretty big point," "wasn't too thrilled," "seemed to be ticked off." Then, as if to underscore how seldom Gates parcels out praise, Bartholomew concluded his recitation with an earnest, "By and large, it was a pretty good meeting."

Gates had not only been exercised over *Encarta*'s deadline slipping, but also over a more vexing problem: the constant need to reinvent the "tools" with which multimedia titles are built. Herein lay an enormously complicated problem that has forever dogged software developers. The term *tools* can mean either authoring programs, which help developers and designers build other software programs (Viewer 1.0 being intended as the primary tool for building *Encarta*), or it can mean sets of engines, which are contained within programs. All applications programs, whether they be word processing programs, spreadsheets, games, or multimedia encyclopedias, are essentially collections of engines: a search engine, a text layout engine, a user-interface engine, an indexing engine, and so on. These engines are sections of code written to make a computer perform specific tasks. If someone writing on a computer, for example, wants to search for a specific word in a document, he or she strikes the keys that activate the computer's search function; in carrying out the search, the computer follows the instructions in its search engine.

Because many of the basic functions a computer performs are similar, developers writing code for new programs prefer to lift as many engines as possible from other programs, in order to save themselves months of work. Gates had established his multimedia division with the idea that part of its systems group would write tools for developers of all multimedia products to use, rather than having ten different product development groups, working on ten different projects, writing ten different but essentially identical search engines, text layout engines, animation engines, and so on. To cut down on the development cost of new titles, Microsoft planned to use the same code in all programs for such functions as the display on the screen of printed text, video, and animation—functions that all titles would have in common.

If the use of Viewer 1.0 by the *Encarta* team was any indication, Gates's vision was too ambitious. By the time *Encarta* was finished, its developers had written over 100,000 lines of code—34 percent of the total lines of code in the encyclopedia—in order to get functions Viewer could not provide. This was hardly what Gates had hoped for some seven years before, when he began his hefty investment in multimedia. "I want to see this come down to a system where it doesn't cost a million dollars to build every product," he said to Bartholomew, "and where we're not constantly inventing the wheel on code."

To that end, Gates agreed in December 1992 to give Multimedia Publishing a core tools group consisting of five software developers who would write code for an authoring tool and set of engines to be used in all multimedia titles. Under this scheme, each design team would have assigned to it only one or two developers, who would write only the code for features unique to their product. For such widely used features as text layout engines or animation engines, a team would simply retrieve the appropriate block of code from the library of code written by the core group. Product designers and artists would use core group–developed authoring tools to create their parts of a given title. "We got these developers," Craig Bartholomew said, "with the caveat that they will make core reusable software."

Bartholomew considered the formation of the tools group to be a significant political coup not only for Multimedia in general, but for his product unit in particular. In his view, headcount was a sign of Gates's esteem. "Bill seems particularly interested in products from this product unit," he said, commencing a kind of chant. "He sees definite potential from the product unit. He sees the revenue potential from this product unit."

At Microsoft, there is nearly as much competition between individual product units as there is between the company and its competitors. So Bartholomew sounded as if he was rehearsing for future arguments. As he saw it, the tools group, while nominally for all of Multimedia, was in effect almost exclusively a resource for Gandalf. "*Encarta* is Multimedia's biggest product," he said, "the children's encyclopedia is its second-biggest product, *Atlas* stands a good chance of being its third-biggest product, so the three biggest products in Multimedia will come out of this product unit in the next two years." As he saw it, Gandalf would be doing the best and biggest titles, and would require the most developer time.

Of course, with the increased attention such products would attract from Gates would come the greater risk of being raked over the managerial coals. Looking ahead to his next projects, Bartholomew was determined not to repeat the mistakes that had delayed completion of *Encarta*. As his product unit meeting wound down, he passed out a document written by eleven-year Microsoft veteran Chris Peters, entitled "Shipping Software on Time." "This document," Bartholomew said, "comes down to the interesting concept that your job here pretty much boils down to shipping products on time. And it's kind of an interesting concept. I think if you went around and asked everybody here what their job was, they'd say, 'My job is to make animations,' or 'My job is to make interfaces,' or to do this or that. . . . What it really comes down to is that your job is to ship products on time, because that is how you get a competitive advantage in the market, that's how we make money, that's pretty much what makes Microsoft click."

As his audience looked over Peters's writing, Bartholomew invoked *Encarta* yet again, recalling a piece of vociferous e-mail from Gates. "We got some pretty rude mail from Bill one time, back when *Encarta* slipped," he said, "saying, 'You guys cannot convince me that you can make a business of this until you can ship products on time, because every day you don't ship once you've announced a product, your competitor knows what your features are, and your competitor's out there getting the sales that you aren't. Let's say we sell 10,000 units a month of *Encarta*. We just lost four months of sales. So we just lost 40,000 units.' "

Bartholomew continued in this vein for awhile, his soft voice fairly drowned out by the shrieking tone of Peters's document. "Everyone in the business unit has the same job," he had written. "That job is to SHIP PRODUCTS. It doesn't matter if you are in development, test, program management, user education, or product management; your job is not to code, not to test, not to manage, not to go to meetings. The job description of everyone is the same 'ship products.' An expansion of this statement is 'ship products EXACTLY ON TIME.' Every day you should do what you can to maximize that goal."

"I Have a Bill Meeting!"

Sendak, scheduled to hit the market in February 1995, was to be Gandalf's next showcase product. Targeted at children somewhere between the ages of five and eleven, the encyclopedia was envisioned as a family's first substantial purchase of compact disc–stored multimedia software. So from the time it first was conceived, *Sendak* was seen by Microsoft's upper management as a crucial strategic initiative.

Thus it was with a certain sense of pride and urgency that the *Encarta* team, nearly freed from its labors, began turning its attention to *Sendak*. Team members were seized with new vision and zeal. "We're in the very first position of doing things we want to do," Sara Fox, *Sendak*'s lead editor, told me in one of our first conversations, "and in ways that have never been done." Defined by pallor—pale blond hair, pale skin, pale blue eyes—she spoke in a soft monotone, the intensity of her emotions coming through in the way her sentences piled up like cars in a cartoon traffic accident. "It's our job to figure out how to make something open-ended, that you want to go back to, that's really rich, that's useful, that's got something, that's got a reason to live, a reason to be made. We have a vision here that goes beyond just taking a book and slapping it on a disc. In general, we all want to make something that's pretty unique. We're making something that doesn't exist yet. There really is nothing to compare it with, because there are no other products that are trying to do what ours is trying to do, so we're really breaking new ground, which is very cool."

As envisioned by Fox and lead designer Carolyn Bjerke, *Sendak* was to be a comprehensive package incorporating a full-scale printed reference source for children—based on the *Dorling Kindersley Children's Encyclopedia*—along with an array of entertainments, and the look, feel, and interactivity of a game.

Led by Bjerke and Fox, the *Sendak* team designed a prototype in which a goofy, plump, cartoonish kid in sloppy clothes, whose most noticeable physical feature was a set of asymmetrical, bulging eyes, appeared on the screen when the encyclopedia was loaded into the computer. The kid, code-named Troy, after Bjerke's two-year-old son, acted as a guide for the user, leading him or her onto a spaceship on which they traveled through a universe of information.

Once Troy was on the ship, the child using the prototype was presented with four possible destinations: Nature, Geography, History, and Civilization. If the child then clicked with a mouse pointer on Nature, a series of sound effects would go off and the picture on the screen would dissolve and fade, reconstituting itself as a nature scene rendered in the style of young children's books. The user could summon up information about given creatures in the scene by clicking directly on them. Clicking on a beaver, for example, brought up a pop-up of text and pictures from the Dorling Kindersley book. When the user clicked on the beaver's teeth in one of the pictures accompanying the text in the pop-up, there popped up a smaller window of text and illustrations about them; a click on the tail conjured up text about the uses of its tail, and so on.

Not all of the information was printed. A click on the prototype's spider, for example, triggered the playing of an informative song about spiders by Tickle Tune Typhoon, a Seattle performing group for children:

Arachnids are 8 legged

Very hairy spiders are arachnids,
A spider is a spider if it's 8 legged.
They are a hungry carnivore
With poison fangs they're hunting for
Insects, worms they eat fresh meat!

Arachnids are 8 legged

With 6 joints a leg that's 48 knees
Four pairs of eyes that's a lot of eyes to see

Their spinnerets make silk and spin
A web to trap their dinner in
Insects, worms they eat fresh meat!

Arachnids are 8 legged

Spiders spiders, you'll find
35 thousand kinds.

Other clicks would trigger questions, with clues about how to search through the encyclopedia's landscape for answers. Still others would activate video clips, animations, recorded speech, or puzzles. Children, it was hoped, would be further engaged by a variety of tools to be designed for Troy's backpack: crayons for recoloring scenes on the screen; a camera for copying text and pictures, which could then to be taken back to the ship and printed out on the computer's printer; a notepad on which could be typed notes or reports; a remote-control device for playing video clips; a lookup tool for finding specific topics in the encyclopedia rather than navigating through it more or less at random; a beeper for beaming Troy back up to the ship so he could take the user on to a new landscape.

This was a considerably more ambitious project than originally mandated back in January 1991, when Multimedia editors penned a document describing a "Children's Multimedia Encyclopedia" for "children from eight years and upwards," which was little more than the Dorling Kindersley book transferred verbatim to a disc and augmented with video, animation, and sound. That encyclopedia was to have been organized thematically along Dorling Kindersley lines ("The Living World," "The Story of Humankind"), with the material also accessible alphabetically. On the screen, it would have looked very much like the book.

Bartholomew, Bjerke, and Fox wanted *Sendak*, by contrast, to combine the look and feel of television and video games with the information content of a book. Over the previous two years, each time they had turned their attention to *Sendak*, they had built a little more into it. Now, they believed, the *Sendak* screen would offer the visual quality and entertainment value of television without turning the user into a passive spectator. The pursuit of *Sendak*'s knowledge and information, as in a video game, would call for the user to navigate through a landscape in pursuit of a goal—in this case, a piece of information. And concealed under the skin of the landscape would be the full text of a print encyclopedia.

Carolyn Bjerke saw *Sendak* as a one-size-fits-all encyclopedia. It would take full advantage of every conceivable technical advance in personal computing hardware. Children would be able to manipulate *Sendak* in various ways, changing it to fit their mood and exploring to whatever depth they wanted. Young or low-achieving children could confine themselves to narrations, videos, and animations if they chose, while more capable ones could dive into the far reaches of printed information either by navigating through the landscape or by going directly to an article by means of the encyclopedia's searching and indexing functions. "I envision it to be something that's extremely deep," Bjerke said, "and not merely deep in the sense that there's a lot of content in one area." It was to be a far more ambitious project than anything yet undertaken in MM Pubs. "You can sort of react to whatever your mood or your abilities or your interests are, and it's customizable in a new way. We want you to actually change its nature, based on what you set it to be."

In the beginning phases of Microsoft projects, team members tend to regard their distant products as powerful weapons for social good. Whenever I asked its team members about *Sendak* in the early going, I was treated to the declamation of a dream. Bjerke saw it as a supertext that could reach children who could not be reached by standard texts and teaching methods. "I think we can help all those kids out there to want to learn, to learn even though their environment is not conducive to that," she said. "They may not have a strong family or anyone to inspire them to learn. And if somehow they get exposure to this product and they can get excited about information also, we can help them to go down a path they would not otherwise have taken."

Bjerke further hoped to incorporate features designed to "bring family members together—like, 'Mom and Dad, come over and help me,' or even have activities where the computer says, 'Go get your brother or sister or mother or father or best friend or something,' thereby having the computer point up unity between families that oftentimes don't do anything together. We have parents who would sit down with their kids—if the activity is educational—and take as much time as they want."

Since the previous September, Craig Bartholomew's subordinates had been developing such vague outlines and dreamy notions for the encyclopedia, but the sense now was that the time had come to get to work in earnest. In his latest performance reviews with Bjerke and producer Jayleen Ryberg, who had been named *Sendak*'s program manager, Bartholomew told them that they were not as far along in the project as he had hoped. When I asked him about the team's work as 1992 drew to a close, he answered crisply: "They have to start showing some progress pretty quickly."

December, then, saw the *Sendak* team working hard at determining exactly what form they wanted the encyclopedia to take. At a meeting convened by Bartholomew with Bjerke, Fox, and Ryberg a few days before Christmas, the four tried to lay out a month-by-month production schedule covering the next two years. They wanted to do something Microsoft had never done before: finish a project before its deadline arrived. "Projects always drag on longer than expected," Bartholomew explained, "because our quality standards are very high, and because we try so hard to be feature-rich in our products. Eventually we are forced into unpleasant tradeoffs—what do we give up to stay on schedule?"

Summarizing his notes from previous meetings, Bartholomew told the three women that their team was to "create a discovery learning product that is rich in content. It is to be fun to play with, to play around in, to move through, but it is also to be a valuable learning tool." He ended the meeting by reluctantly agreeing to the two-year production schedule they wanted, although he warned them that upper management would likely insist that they finish at least six months sooner.

After nearly an hour, Bartholomew and Ryberg departed, leaving Bjerke and Fox behind to begin hammering out a more detailed production plan. Instead, they passed the time in a rapid-fire exchange of hopes, dreams, fears, speculations, and analyses of Bartholomew. He was no sooner out of the room than the two began worrying aloud—about Bartholomew's nerves, about the schedule, about their ambitions for *Sendak*, about the expectations of parents and children, about Gates, and about their own abilities to realize their ambition. "Craig seems to be getting general cold feet about this whole thing," Bjerke said. "We'll have to attribute all of his input to stress."

They began planning for "the mad scramble" that January promised to be. The scramble would be made all the madder by Fox's absence, as she was due to deliver a baby on December 31 and would be gone on maternity leave for the following three months. The *Sendak* team was slated to make a February 8 presentation to Gates, at which they would have to justify everything about *Sendak:* its cost, its features, its schedule. They would have to have facts, figures, features, and arguments firmly in hand by that time. "We have to focus everything in on that meeting with Bill," Bjerke said, "and we have to answer the problems and objections we know he will have now rather than later." To that end, they planned to devote the next month to hammering out an exact description of *Sendak* and a solid marketing argument for their approach, as Gates was notorious for demanding thorough "business cases" for all Microsoft products.

Adding to the pressure on Bjerke and Fox was their dawning sense that the time had come for the Multimedia Publishing division to justify its existence. As the corporate computer market was showing signs of slowing growth, Microsoft was looking for new markets. Gates was convinced that multimedia-capable computer sales were about to take off. So it was critical to Microsoft's continued growth and dominance that the company develop products in time to be properly positioned to profit on the coming demand for multimedia software.

Not only were the *Sendak* team and the other teams in Multimedia Publishing racing to develop splendid new products, but the division in general had been directed by Gates to develop an overall business strategy based on division director Tom Corddry's description of where the industry would be a few years hence. Corddry's plans could meet with Gates's approval only if the division could demonstrate impressive new products to justify his projections—a circumstance about which every product designer and program manager in Multimedia Publishing was painfully aware.

The more Bjerke and Fox talked about the upcoming meeting with Gates, the more uncertain they felt about their work on *Sendak*. Bjerke fretted that the wider they tried to make the age range, the less coherent and more feature-filled the encyclopedia would become. Fox felt that the current *Sendak* prototype looked so much like a game that its educational value would be lost on potential purchasers. "Is this thing going to be education or entertainment?" she asked. "A game or an encyclopedia? It can be hard to distinguish ourselves from games if we look like games." On the other hand, she wanted "kids to turn to it in the 'you're-at-home-competing-with-the-television' situation."

They vacillated constantly between bluster and fear. One minute Bjerke would be saying, "We always blow competition away"; the next, she would be fearful that Disney would suddenly enter the multimedia business and blow Microsoft away. One moment Fox would say confidently, "We just have to make a plan and get done what we need to do"; the next, she would wonder if anything they were planning was feasible.

The two decided to convene an "education summit," for which they would bring some of the nation's top experts on early childhood education into Microsoft for consultations on *Sendak*'s design. The summit would help iron out their own theories on what form the encyclopedia should take, and would give them solid, expert, credentialed evidence to present to Gates. The only problem with their plan for the summit, Bjerke pointed out, was the timing. They were late in getting under way, and it was unlikely that they could make the necessary arrangements for such an event far enough in advance of their presentation to Gates for it to do them any good. "What's your strategy," Bjerke asked Fox, "for getting these people in here on such short notice?"

The two women stared thoughtfully across the table at one another. For a few moments, neither spoke. Finally, Fox said, with a laugh, "I'm just going to call them up and scream, 'I have a Bill meeting!' "

January 7, 1993

The Bill in question is referred to at Microsoft variously as Trey (the nickname bestowed upon him in childhood by his mother), as Bill Gates, Bill G, Bill, or billg, this last being his moniker on Microsoft's electronic mail system. Only two emotions seem to surface among Microsoft employees when Gates's name is mentioned. One is awe, the other is fear. He is revered as an unrivaled genius both at technology and at business strategy. Employees called before him know they will be grilled mercilessly not only on the technical details of their project, but on its market potential and profitability as well. No one ever hopes to slip an unresolved issue past him. Over and over again, you hear it said that you have to "do your homework" before meeting with Gates, that you have to be thoroughly prepared, that he has an unerring instinct for gaps in a presenter's knowledge even when the subject is something unfamiliar to him, and that if you don't have ready answers for all of his questions he will destroy you.

Microsoft employees believe that the best you can hope for is to do work barely good enough for Gates. Kevin Gammill, walking with me through the central square of Microsoft's campus one day, stopped and pointed up at an office window. "See that?" he said. "That's Bill Gates's office. And see that sidewalk there, that goes nowhere?" He pointed out a strip of concrete that branched off from the main path for ten feet or so, then came to an abrupt end in the grass. It was aimed directly at Gates's office. "That's the altar where we go to pray," he continued in apparent jest, raising his arms overhead and executing an elaborate

25

bow. "We just stand there and shout, 'We are not worthy! We are not worthy!' "

The power that Gates exerts over his workers is a function not only of his native abilities but also of the way he runs his company. For all of its rapid growth and immense power, Microsoft is surprisingly small. There is very little in the way of bureaucracy separating Gates from his employees. The *Sendak* design team, for example, which consisted of six full-time Microsoft employees and a fluctuating number of freelance artists, designers, and software developers, was removed from Gates only by one manager, one general manager, and a senior vice president. While each design team reports directly to its manager, each also will, in the course of a given product's development, report directly to Gates. Every team must at some point present a product prototype and its development plan to Gates himself.

This last circumstance strikes most Microsoft workers as proof positive of Gates's superhuman ability to remain a hands-on manager in the face of breakneck company growth. "He still sees every product in this company," says Gammill wonderingly. It also contributes mightily to the drive among employees to work long hours and finish projects on schedule. Accountability to a middle manager is one thing; accountability directly to Gates is quite another.

Having failed to finish *Encarta* on time, the Gandalf team resolved not to repeat the lapse with *Sendak*. Accordingly, Jayleen Ryberg settled on a two-year schedule for the new project, calling for it to begin in March 1993—thereby pretending that the previous six months of planning and work on *Sendak* had never happened—and to be finished in February 1995.

By Microsoft standards, this was an unusually long schedule for a content application (a program used as a source of information or entertainment, as distinguished from productivity applications like Microsoft *Word* or *Excel*), particularly since Ryberg had sketched out the schedule before knowing much of anything about what it would take to develop the product. Virtually everything in *Sendak*, from its reading level to how many software developers would be working on it, had yet to be determined. Faced with the rather daunting task of predicting to the day when a project would be done without knowing what it entailed or how many people she would have available to work on it, Ryberg decided to create a schedule longer than that of any other multimedia project.

For all of the intangibles involved in *Sendak*, Ryberg's schedule was based on experience that few others at Microsoft had. After growing up on a farm near Buffalo Lake, Minnesota, she graduated from Concordia College in 1978, spent three years managing a Singer sewing machine store, then moved to San Francisco. Now, at thirty-four, she had been working in video production for seven years—first at the Bank of America's media department, then for ByVideo, a company that produced interactive touch-screen video programs through which people could make purchases of consumer goods. By the time Microsoft recruited her in 1991, Ryberg was well versed in the practicalities of production, the unreliability of animation and video studios, and the difficulties of rendering moving images on a digital platform.

While agreeing with Ryberg on the need for a longer schedule, Carolyn Bjerke was skeptical about its chances with Gates. "When Bill sees a long development line like that," she said when she saw Ryberg's plan, "you know you're in for a long discussion."

Accordingly, Ryberg began marshaling arguments even before she began husbanding resources. Since Gates already had agreed in principle to the encyclopedia, their presentation to him would be dedicated to convincing him that they would not repeat *Encarta*'s scheduling mistakes. "This product has already been given its go," Ryberg said to me. "The length of time it will take to produce will be the issue with Bill. We'll have to explain to him why it is not as simple as he would like to believe—that *Sendak* pushes more technology issues than anything we've done before."

In settling on a schedule, Ryberg was confronted with three agendas. *Sendak*'s designers and editors would want to pack the encyclopedia with features seen nowhere else, and each new feature would take unpredictable—but certainly long—spans of time to develop. *Sendak*'s developers would want a far less ambitious set of new features and ample time in which to write code for them. Gates would want to be first to the market with a multimedia children's encyclopedia packed with features seen nowhere else. Thus it is with all Microsoft projects: their designers want the best product, no matter how much time it takes; their developers want to finish on time, no matter what features have to be sacrificed in order to do so; and Gates wants both, with none of the sacrifices.

In moving into program management, Ryberg had moved into a position of high pressure and high visibility, as accountability for any given project always falls squarely on its program manager's shoulders. A Microsoft program manager generally serves as the director of his or her product, keeping everyone else on track and on schedule; as the manager who tracks all issues and features, making sure everything is resolved satisfactorily; and as the person to whom upper management comes when something goes wrong. It is the program manager's responsibility to schedule a project, then put the screws to everyone working on it.

This may have accounted in large part for the difference between Ryberg's ambitions for *Sendak* and those of her teammates. Sara Fox saw it as a product that would transform early childhood education and revive children's interest in learning and information. Bjerke saw it as a powerful, engaging children's information tool that could address an array of social problems. Ryberg had fantasies only about "getting it done on time and under budget—something that's never been done here before."

Outwardly, Ryberg is soft-spoken and relatively timid, and she tended to defer to both Fox and Bjerke in matters of *Sendak*'s authorship. While she could be stern with the freelance artists and animators she signed up for Microsoft projects, she often came across—even at twenty-nine— as more grandmotherly than managerial. With short dark hair, large dark eyes, and a habit of sighing and gazing thoughtfully off to one side before speaking, she invariably brought to mind muffins and warm kitchens rather than spreadsheets and production schedules. "There's a natural tendency in the company to think the program manager is in charge," she explained during her early planning for *Sendak*. "But that doesn't go over very well here. Carolyn and Sara have as much command of the product as anybody else, and that probably will continue." This shared authorship was more an experiment than a determined new course of action, and Ryberg, unsure of its prospects, managed only a "We'll see how it works" by way of endorsement.

Craig Bartholomew also had his doubts. "Jayleen," he told me, "is kind of an introspective personality. Carolyn on the other hand is a driving personality. She kind of pushes things forward sometimes when she makes a decision that is not entirely thought out. And Sara is strong-willed as well. With two strong-willed people like that, Jayleen will have to come up with different diplomatic ways of solving things." He was inclined to be patient with Ryberg, as he more or less had forced her into her role. "I had to twist her arm to be program manager," he said.

"As a producer, all she had to do was focus on the process." Should she falter, he was prepared to step in and remove her—a relatively common step at Microsoft, where teams and organizations are constantly being reconstituted or reinvented. "We'll bring her back to producer, where she does an excellent job. She's a very talented person—it's just a question of whether this is a match for her personality, her own expectations."

Bartholomew had been forced to coerce Ryberg into program management by Microsoft's rapid growth, which was causing a severe shortage of managers. As Susan Boeschen, senior vice president of Microsoft's Consumer Division, which included Multimedia Publishing, put it to me one day, "We've reached a stage where many of the products that we're starting up now need experienced management on them, and we just are fresh out of experienced managers."

Everywhere one looked at Microsoft during the days when *Sendak* was getting started, one saw youngsters suddenly being turned into managers and supervisors. Kevin Gammill, at twenty-five, was promoted to development lead for the Gandalf product unit as he was finishing up *Encarta* and preparing to turn his attention to *Sendak*. By the following summer, he would be supervising eight developers working on three projects. The core tools group in Multimedia would be headed by a twenty-five-year-old developer, and all three of Gandalf's new projects—*Sendak*, the Atlas, and *Encarta* 2.0—would be headed by new program managers with no previous managerial experience.

This pellmell promotion of Microsoft employees was just one part of an overall sensation of chaos on the campus. Teams, product units, and divisions were being reorganized so frequently that it had become a running joke. Whenever someone in Multimedia Publishing tried to locate an event in time by referring to it in the context of a reorganization, he or she was immediately asked, "Which one?" Posted in one of the company cafeterias was the following quotation:

We trained hard, but it seemed that every time we were beginning to form up into teams, we would be reorganized. I was to learn later in life that we tend to meet any new situation by reorganizing; and a wonderful method it can be for creating the illusion of progress while producing confusion, inefficiency, and demoralization.

—Petronius Arbiter, 210 B.C.

This tradition was so firmly established that Sara Fox saw it as one of the greatest dangers to *Sendak*. "What I'm afraid of, what would be really awful, and I hope it doesn't happen but I'm afraid it's going to," she said one day, "is we'll have another big *reorganization,* of like our whole department, that would be *awful* if we did that."

Microsoft's volatile corporate culture was not the only impediment to predicting a project's schedule. The state of software development tools also put teams on edge. Multimedia was such a new field that whenever a Microsoft team started work on a new product, it was trying something, however grand or small, that had never been tried before. The group had not only to build the product itself, but also the tools required for it. In scheduling *Sendak*, Ryberg could only guess at the amount of time it would take to build any given feature, as she had no idea what tools her developers and designers would have at their disposal.

Since programming tools were being reinvented and improved at the same breakneck pace as applications and titles, *Sendak*'s team would start out with one set of tools and finish with another. Regarding one such tool, a *Sendak* specifications document read, "Merismus 1.0 will be used until Merismus 2.0 comes out. Since there is a big discrepancy between the two versions of the tool, interim tools will have to be created to allow us to work with 1.0 in an efficient manner until 2.0 is available."

Ryberg's planning was further hampered by the complete inaccessibility of the *Sendak* team to Gammill. Before detailing the schedule and its interim milestones, she needed to assess the feasibility of the features Bjerke and her assistants would be designing into the encyclopedia. And Gammill was the only one who could make that judgment. While designers are mandated to push developers by demanding ever-more-ambitious technical feats, it is up to developers to tell their teammates whether a given feature can be implemented at all and, if it can, how long it will take to do it.

Gammill was unavailable even for casual conversation for another three months because of *Encarta*. Custom at Microsoft dictates that when developers are in the final phase of a project, they are to be left completely alone. People are forbidden even to send them electronic mail. All communication to a developer under deadline is sent to his or her program manager, who decides whether or not to send it on.

Once in a while, the question would be raised, "Do I have permission to talk to Kevin?" The answer, invariably, was "No!" When Gammill was caught outside his office during an infrequent break, he would greet people either with a growl or with the admonition, "Don't talk to me! Don't talk to me!"

Even under relatively normal conditions, it was hard for his teammates to talk to Gammill. An enormous cultural chasm stretched between developers and designers at Microsoft. Often it was impossible for a developer to make a designer understand even the simplest elements of a programming problem. Just as often, designers would work for weeks on some aspect of a product only to be rudely told, when they finally showed it to a developer, that it was impossible to implement.

Although conditions had improved in recent years, the two camps literally spoke different languages and came to the world of computing from opposite intellectual, cultural, psychological, and aesthetic poles. Designers came to Microsoft from the arts; developers from the world of math and science. Developers looked down on designers because their thinking seemed fuzzy and unstructured, their tastes arbitrary. Designers felt that developers were unimaginative, conservative, and given to rejecting their designs out of hand without trying to find a way to make them work. Because programming was inexplicable to designers, they had no way of assessing a developer's insistence that their designs were unprogrammable. "Designers," Tom Corddry liked to say, "are invariably female, are talkative, live in lofts, have vegetarian diets, and wear found objects in their ears. Developers are invariably male, eat fast food, and don't talk except to say, 'Not true.' " He might have added that designers and developers deal with conflict in markedly different ways. When developers, who are given to bursts of mischievous play, begin peppering a designer's door with firings from a Nerf-ball gun, their victim calls the supervisor to complain. A developer would fire back.

A given feature presents both a simple aesthetic problem and a complex mathematical one. The look and feel of a product forces a designer to think about the arrangement of colors and lines on a screen; often, even the most trivial element of that arrangement forces a developer to create an enormously complicated subarrangement of equations, classes, hierarchies, and relationships in the intricate universe of a computer program. During the course of *Encarta*'s design and development, for example, Carolyn Bjerke made a tiny change that grew into a legend. For years after, it was cited as the classic example of how difficult it is for Microsoft designers and developers to communicate.

Bjerke's gaffe began with a small design change in two generic buttons. Microsoft Multimedia products run primarily on computers that use the company's Windows platform. All software designed to run on Windows conforms to certain conventions of appearance and behavior, including the arrangement of buttons, usually labeled with such terms as "Menu," "Find," and "Contents," or with an arrow or other symbol, above or below the screen's windows. A user wanting to find a particular word in *Encarta*, for example, would employ such a button by moving his or her cursor to the Find button and clicking the mouse. A new Find window would open, the user would type in it the word he or she wanted to find, and the computer would immediately display a list of all articles containing the sought-after word.

The buttons are designed to look more or less like the rectangular buttons on amplifiers and tape decks. Shadows and highlights drawn around their edges give them a three-dimensional look. Bjerke, working on *Encarta*'s design, decided she wanted to distinguish the row of buttons along the bottom of *Encarta*'s screen from those along the top by giving the former a slightly different look. She drew a single, nearly imperceptible white line along two sides of each bottom-row button, a corresponding light gray line along the other two sides, and altered the typeface on all of them. "It made a very subtle difference in the look," she said.

Not so subtle was the effect on *Encarta*'s developers. Instead of taking generic Windows code for traditional Windows buttons and plugging it into *Encarta*'s program, they had to write hundreds of lines of new code, over several weeks, to accommodate Bjerke's change. Writing the code for the look of the buttons themselves and for that code's relationship to the rest of the *Encarta* program, to hear a developer tell it, was an operation on the scale of adding a new galaxy to the universe. The code can now be found in Microsoft's code library under the label "sbutton code." The *s* stands for "stupid."

Recalling the episode as she began designing *Sendak*, Bjerke attributed the problem to the traditional underlying hostility between designers and developers. Because her developers had assumed that she cared too much about the look of *Encarta* to make compromises for the sake of the schedule, none of them told her how difficult it would be to encode her subtle change. They believed that she would neither understand nor care enough about a development problem to compromise her artistic vision. While conceding that "there are some designers who are so wrapped up in the visuals that they will never give up something no matter what it costs a project," Bjerke laid the onus in *Encarta*'s case on the developers. "If I'd known what it cost them to make that change," she said, "I never would have done it. They should have explained it to me."

Now Bjerke believed that both sides had learned their lesson and that things would run more smoothly during *Sendak*'s development. "Developers see everything in terms of a power struggle over who has a right to say whether something will be done," she observed. "But the more and more communication gets tightened up, the less prone we will be to disasters."

By now, the *Sendak* team was in the throes of refining a prototype of the encyclopedia for two upcoming presentations: one to Consumer Division senior vice president Susan Boeschen, Tom Corddry, and various other Consumer Division managers, to be held on January 7; and one to Bill Gates, tentatively scheduled for February 8. The first was to be a dress rehearsal for the second, with Boeschen's group serving as a stand-in for Gates, asking the kinds of questions and raising the kinds of objections he would be expected to bring up.

The prototype consisted of a short computer program, composed with a software tool called MacroMedia Director, that contained two scenes, one of the interior of a spaceship and one of a woods inhabited by animals, containing objects children could click on to bring up information. Because Director can only make short animations, and must use large amounts of memory for them, the prototype could contain only a single example of each feature *Sendak*'s designers hoped to include in the final product.

In the course of their preparation, the *Sendak* team had presented the prototype a few weeks before to several groups of seven- to eleven-year-old children and their parents, in a series of "usability" sessions designed to test children's reactions to the encyclopedia. Ryberg and her team had come away from the sessions convinced that the *Sendak* prototype was crude and confusing and that they had done too little thinking about who would be using the encyclopedia, and for what.

The sessions were held in Microsoft's usability laboratory, in a room with videotape equipment and a one-way mirror through which team members could watch the proceedings unobserved. Children and their parents were brought into the room in pairs by Microsoft usability tester Susan Denning. The children were set down in front of a computer while their parents watched from the back of the room. Denning showed off *Sendak*'s features, occasionally directing questions at the parents along the way.

Denning's demonstrations were designed to elicit kids' reactions to the prototype, to get them to tell her how they would use it and what kind of program they thought it was, to see if they could find specific information in it (to this end, the children were given a printed list of questions and asked to find the answers in the encyclopedia), and to determine whether they could figure out how to use its various features without help or explanation. Accordingly, she guided them through *Sendak*, clicking on those items that brought up activities or various media elements, describing features to them and asking them questions. "In a way," she always began, "you're helping us design this program. So if you think something is absolutely stupid, I want to hear you say that." Then as *Sendak*'s opening screen came up, displaying a wall with four doors, she asked them what they thought they should do to advance to the program's next stage, and the demonstration was underway.

Occasionally the kids would neglect the prototype for the more enchanting table at the back of the room, directly under the one-way mirror, sumptuously laden with snacks, cookies, juices, and soft drinks. Walking over to that table, a scant five feet from *Sendak*'s invisible team members, they would stand there completely absorbed in the complexities of snack selection while their elders, facing them from the other side of the mirror, sat expectantly with notebooks and pens in hand, as if ready to write down the significance of every gesture.

Most often, though, the children were so captivated by the encyclopedia that they would forget entirely about the treats behind them. "Oh, God, this is awesome!" exclaimed two eleven-year-old boys at one session. They were watching *Sendak*'s goofy guide move into the control room of his spaceship and open its window shades onto the vista outside. As he was beamed out of the ship and deposited in the nature scene, though, their demeanor changed, for that was when Denning showed the boys how clicking on an animal could bring an explanatory block of text popping up on the screen. "Ah . . . this is some kind of school thing. . . . I don't like school," one of them grumbled.

Once they realized that not all clicks brought up text, however, their excitement returned. Intrigued when a click on a rattlesnake's tail triggered the recording of a rattle, they began moving the mouse pointer around frantically, clicking on nearly every spot on the screen. The two boys were visibly surprised and delighted to get a song rather than text when they clicked on the scene's spider. "Hey, I like that!" one of them exclaimed. "It gives you information in it, too." Moments later, when a click on a hole in a tree trunk triggered a video clip of a bear catching and devouring a salmon, they nearly jumped out of their chairs. Whenever a click brought up printed text, though, they would move on immediately, without bothering to read it—even when they knew the text held the answer to one of the questions on the sheet Denning had given them.

After only a few minutes, in a pattern that would be repeated through all the sessions, the boys began suggesting features they would like to see in the encyclopedia. "Make him get the ladybug!" one of the boys shouted when his partner clicked on the spider. Later, one suggested a section "on aliens. So you could make a different universe, with weird people and stuff." "And a section where you go to a castle," the other chimed in, "get a description of it, who or what is in it, some kind of vampire. Then you have information in there on the vampire, learn what his strengths are, what are his weaknesses, and then you fight him. Then you have to find the weapons, get information on the weapons . . ."

By the time the sessions ended three days later, the *Sendak* team had notebooks full of such suggestions. One child wanted it to be a game, "The Survival Information Kids' Program," where the journey through *Sendak*'s landscapes was fraught with danger and adventure. Another wanted music and sound effects to be conjured up everywhere, when you clicked on anything. As one session was winding down, a nine-year-old boy turned to Denning earnestly and said, "I don't know if you can do this yet, but it would be great if this guide could jump down off the screen and run around on the table, showing you things, explaining things, playing with you . . ."

Sendak was endorsed wholeheartedly by all the children who saw it, and almost as enthusiastically by their parents. The encyclopedia's designers had been particularly heartened by how adept the children were at guessing the purpose of each tool in Troy's backpack. Yet the team saw far more problems and challenges than signs of success. One mother said that her son would grow bored after playing with *Sendak* two or three times, and team members worried that it could never be made replayable enough. When a nine-year-old girl said that it was "both a little too old and a little too young," the designers worried that the true age range of the product would be so narrow, and therefore so unprofitable, that Gates would terminate it. Another girl, asked what she thought might be in Troy's backpack, had said dismissively, "Probably just boys' stuff," touching off fear that the overriding metaphor of exploration via spaceship would alienate girls.

Sitting in the laboratory's observation room after the last usability session, the *Sendak* team was far more anguished than exuberant. Craig Bartholomew worried that the look of *Sendak* was too "young," that it would appeal to too few children above preschool age and that parents would think it was a children's storybook rather than a serious reference product. Everyone but Bryan Ballinger, the illustrator who had done all the art for the prototype and who was to be the lead illustrator for *Sendak*, was worried about the gender issue. Sara Fox was convinced that in order to get kids interested in reading the text, the encyclopedia would have to generate random missions for the user, sending him or her in search of answers that could be found in *Sendak*'s content. It was clear, she believed, that kids would have to be manipulated into reading rather than just playing around. "This is a big issue," she said. "They keep thinking of it as an adventure game kind of thing, and downplaying the information. They're not regarding it as an information source." She was most distressed at one boy who had been asked to find in the encyclopedia information on what porcupines do with their quills. He had clicked on the picture of a porcupine and gotten a small block of text to read. "The kid said, 'Porcupines *shoot* their quills,' " Fox recalled, "even though there was a line of text that said, 'They do not, as is commonly believed, shoot their quills.' They didn't read it! I keep wondering, how can we get their attention enough to read it?"

When the *Sendak* team reconvened two days later, it was to consider a single, complex problem—one that was sure to be posed by Gates: How could they address the issues raised in the usability sessions without throwing out the original vision for the encyclopedia? And for that matter, what *was* their original vision? Gates had certain strategic hopes for *Sendak*, which he called *Encarta Junior*. He wanted it to appeal to children from ages seven to eleven, at which point they would begin using *Encarta*. He wanted it to be the first major multimedia product parents bought for their children. He endorsed Bartholomew's hope of making Microsoft the sole source of a composite "cradle-to-grave encyclopedia." His vision was simple: Gates wanted at least a 50 percent share of the emerging electronic encyclopedia market. *Sendak*, by virtue of its target, was critical to Microsoft's strategy.

The problem, as the usability tests pointed out, was that the more *Sendak* became a reference book, the older and more narrow its target market became. Conversely, if *Sendak* reached down to younger children, the older children would be lost to competitors. To make it more appealing to younger children by lowering the reading level or cutting back on the amount of text would make *Sendak* seem less educational—a move that would amount to commercial suicide, since parents generally judge such large purchases on the grounds of their educational value. "The issue," said Bartholomew, "isn't at what age kids use it, but at what age parents buy it. We want to be fairly business-oriented about this."

Integral to this vision was a children's encyclopedia with a wide enough target market to justify its projected $195 price tag. Parents would not buy both *Sendak* and *Encarta* if the former was neither rich enough in content to be considered a legitimate reference work nor accessible enough to younger children to make it useful for several pre-*Encarta* years.

Until the usability tests, *Sendak*'s creators had seen it primarily as a work of art. Bryan Ballinger had visions of a virtual alternate universe in which every object would animate in some entertaining way when clicked on by a child. In one scene alone, he planned, among other things, to have a hedgehog turning somersaults, an eagle flying around the screen, a television set popping up out of a camel's hinged back to display a video sequence, a camel spitting, cactus flowers blooming to the sound of popcorn popping, a palm tree dropping dates on the ground, a scorpion pinching the hedgehog, and a roadrunner twitching its tail feathers at a snake, whose tail rattles. Should *Sendak* follow Ballinger's designs, it would have videos, cartoons, sound effects, and music popping out constantly, from everywhere. "I just want this whole thing to be as interactive and as fun as it can be," he said. "I want kids to think it's cool."

Fox and Bjerke were also trying to make *Sendak* as engaging to children as possible, and they were attempting to redefine the reference book through the use of multimedia. Except for those times when they would be looking up specific topics through its searching and indexing functions, children using the encyclopedia would set off on a quest through a contrived landscape, and the quest, like those in games, would be full of adventures, surprises, and challenges.

But the usability sessions had sternly reminded everyone that *Sendak* was primarily a consumer product and that it would need an easily understood definition in order to sell. Children had to want it, and parents had to be persuaded of its educational value in order to buy it. Denning pointed out that while parents in usability tests had been quick to pick up on *Sendak*'s educational value, children had not—and when they had, they had been disappointed, as if somehow they had been tricked into enjoying a textbook disguised as a game.

"That's actually a really important positioning concept," said Sonja Gustafson, the woman from Microsoft's marketing department who had been assigned to both *Encarta* and *Sendak*, in a meeting with the team. "Parents are the ones who are buying it, so we need somehow to name it so that kids think it's cool, and parents somehow understand the concept. We need a name that promises the best of both worlds."

Bjerke and Fox felt that the solution lay in making *Sendak* all things to all people. Bjerke proposed making the encyclopedia multilayered, with the layer you experienced being determined by the preference you set when you first logged onto the encyclopedia. Fox, noting that the text in the *Dorling Kindersley Children's Encyclopedia*, the book on which *Sendak*'s printed text was based, tended to revolve around four or five main points, decided to present those points in separate pop-ups, one stacked atop another in a window, with the text edited down substantially. She wanted *Sendak*'s users never to be confronted with large blocks of text, as they were in the current prototype, where text pop-ups took up virtually the whole screen. In Fox's version, no more than three or four sentences at a time would appear on the screen, and each pop-up of text appearing on top of a scene would almost always be accompanied by an additional illustration. Children who wanted to read further about a given topic could advance to the next text window by clicking on a Next icon, and those who did not could close the text window and resume browsing through *Sendak*'s scenes and special effects.

After the meeting broke up, Bjerke and Fox stayed behind to talk about the general purpose of *Sendak*. Bjerke wanted to take advantage of multimedia to reach preschool, learning-disabled, and otherwise disadvantaged children in ways that books could not by increasing the nontextual media elements and by making it as easy to use as possible. And Fox, who was worried that allowing children to replace printed with narrated text would prove a detriment to their learning, wanted *Sendak* to incorporate a story line that somehow would randomly send users into the printed text on quests for information. In order to win the encyclopedia's game, they would have to *read*. "Otherwise," she said, "no one will have the patience to read it. Kids need to be sent on missions." Her team's essential job, she believed, was to come up with a product that had the predictability and navigability of an organized reference book, yet constantly included an element of surprise.

Before designing quests for future users of *Sendak*, the encyclopedia's architects had to complete an arduous quest of their own: selling Bill Gates on the value of their idea. Everyone working on every facet of every emerging Microsoft product, from the look on the screen when it first comes up on a computer to its worldwide marketing plan, constantly tries to anticipate what questions Gates will ask, and what objections he will raise. Product design is undertaken entirely within the context of Gates's expectations, tastes, and track record. More daunting even than a product's deadline is the date of the Bill meeting at which Gates will say yes or no to a product proposal. During the four to six weeks before a product team's audience with Gates comes a series of preparatory meetings: there is always at least one dry run for the Bill meeting, with various surrogates sitting in to raise issues and questions Gates is likely to raise; three or four "Bill strategy sessions"; and a final run-through on the morning of the Bill meeting itself.

First up for the *Sendak* team was the presentation to Susan Boeschen, head of Microsoft's Consumer Division, and to Multimedia Publishing's management group. Preparations for that meeting amounted to three weeks of relative frenzy. When not on the road promoting the forthcoming *Encarta*, Sonja Gustafson worked on a detailed marketing argument for the project, called the *Sendak* product plan. Fox's two assistant editors worked on editing and supplementing Dorling Kindersley's printed text and reformatting it according to Fox's new pop-up designs. Fox herself, cheerfully lamenting her bad timing, left to give birth and commence a three-month maternity leave. Bjerke and her artists and animators continued tinkering with *Sendak*'s design, and Bjerke worked on orchestrating the presentation to Boeschen and her group.

The morning of the January 7 presentation found the *Sendak* team in a panic. Bjerke was quietly and frantically making last-minute changes to the presentation documents. Gustafson was running from one office to the next, firing questions at Ryberg and Bjerke, and gathering up copies of the *Random House Children's Encyclopedia* (the U.S. edition of the Dorling Kindersley book) to distribute at the meeting. The team had begun the day with a dry run for the dry run, and had come away with a list of glitches both in the *Sendak* prototype and in its product plan.

Part of the panic was due to a recent management directive to address the issue of "Microsoft Integration of Like Products." As part of his strategy for Microsoft's new line of consumer products for home rather than office use, Gates wanted all Consumer Division products to be similar enough in look and behavior to set a standard that only Microsoft could meet. For example, owners of *Creative Writer*—a Microsoft word-processing program for children that was a few months away from completion—should be able to pick up *Sendak* a few years hence and immediately know how to use it, its look and feel being familiar. By being first into the market with an array of products that all behaved more or less in the same fashion, Gates hoped to close the market off to competitors.

Sendak needed a blessing from Boeschen and Corddry before the encyclopedia's designers could proceed with preparations for their Bill meeting; support from the two was essential to the project's survival. "This is the biggest presentation I've made since I've been here," said Ryberg. "Our hope is that they will come away saying, 'Yes, they're organized. They've thought through a lot of issues.' So if Bill checks with them on us, that's the kind of thing he will hear." She had been more than a little chagrined when she heard later that morning that Boeschen was home sick and would not be there that afternoon. "She didn't think it was important enough to come in for our little meeting," Ryberg said ruefully.

Multimedia Publishing was among the newest ventures at Microsoft, and because it had shipped almost no products into a market that had yet to prove it would grow enough to merit the company's attention, there was a certain beleaguered camaraderie in the division. Multimedia had to prove to the more established parts of the company—particularly to company president Mike Maples, who viewed Multimedia with considerable skepticism—that it belonged and deserved to be taken seriously as a moneymaker. So whenever a product unit was preparing to go before Gates, those in Multimedia's three other product units tended to band together to help and encourage their fellows, for the sake of advancing the cause of multimedia computing. Any gain before Gates for any one of the product units, the reasoning went, was a gain for all four, for it meant that the company was deepening its commitment to multimedia in general.

Nevertheless, there also was a tremendous amount of competition among the four product units. Each was free to pursue its own vision, and each had sketched out three- or four-year plans that were considerably different from one another's. Each wanted to be the most successful of the four, and prove that its vision was the wisest and most deserving of more money and personnel. "A couple of years from now," Ryberg said, "the four units will be fiercely and closely comparing profit-and-loss statements. Those with the most profit will get the most resources, and the best hearing for new ideas."

These mixed motives, she knew, would only add to the tension in the meeting, since Bartholomew's peers—the heads of the other three product units—would be there. Experience had proven that the fiercest attackers of any new proposal at these dry runs were the managers of the other three units. They were driven to thorough critiques both by the wish to help one of their own succeed and by the desire to find shortcomings in a competing peer's vision.

In this respect, Ryberg was particularly worried about Jabe Blumenthal, manager of the Jurassic product unit, which had taken a strategic course opposite Gandalf's. Gandalf was publishing large reference titles that took years to develop largely because its creators wanted to incorporate as many new features and as much new content as technology and Microsoft budgeting would allow. Jurassic was trying to publish as many small titles—less ambitious both in terms of breadth of subject matter and technical innovations—transferred from books to computers all but unchanged, in as short a time span as possible. "I expect Jabe to say, 'Why should you get to spend two years and all that money on a single project when we're doing more than a book a year?' " Ryberg said. "He doesn't understand that we're trying to push the technology and come up with something more than a retread of a book, ported over to computer."

Blumenthal was particularly feared in Multimedia Publishing because of his stature at Microsoft and because of what many saw as a unique hold he enjoyed over Gates. He had attended Seattle's Lakeside School, an exclusive prep school, five years after Gates had, graduated from Yale with a degree in mathematics, and come to work at Microsoft in 1982. He was the company's first official program manager, overseeing the phenomenally successful *Excel* spreadsheet program, then overseeing a series of projects before moving over to Multimedia Publishing early in 1992.

Tom Corddry and most others believed that Gates regarded Blumenthal as something of a kindred spirit, because of his long tenure at Microsoft, his successes, and his common background with Gates. "They go back ten years," Corddry said. "They're not particularly close personal friends, but they know each other extremely well intellectually."

Blumenthal called attention to his perceived connection with Gates by persistently "playing Bill" at project presentation meetings, peppering the presenters with questions he expected Gates himself to ask, and doing so in a brusque manner that often bordered on Gatesian rudeness.

Bartholomew and his *Sendak* team arrived early at the meeting room, bearing copies of the *Sendak* product plan. A few minutes later, audience members began filing in hurriedly, mumbling greetings to one another. They sat down at the long conference table while Bjerke, wheeling a computer into the room on a cart, struggled with the vehicle's recalcitrant wheels. Corddry was among the last to arrive. He was wearing an over-sized, three-dimensional Goofy wristwatch—an accessory that elicited quick, muttered comments and laconic smiles from all around the room.

Corddry mentioned that Blumenthal was not able to attend, and the *Sendak* team members were visibly relieved. Bartholomew began with some brief remarks introducing everyone from *Sendak* and explaining which areas each person would cover, then said, "Let me just give you an overview of where the product stands, just very briefly, is that the idea of doing a children's encyclopedia as I understand it is approved. This implementation is not, and that's what we're here to show."

Ryberg followed with a plea for criticism. "This is basically a preparation for the meeting with Bill," she said. "Any input you have on the presentation, ways you think we can improve it, holes that you see in it . . . please, let us know." She glanced over at Bjerke, who was supposed to follow her with a description of *Sendak* and a demonstration of the prototype, only to see her dive down under the table to wrestle with one of the cart's wheels. She was still trying to maneuver her computer within range of an outlet. "We want to create an exploration-based, children's encyclopedia title," Ryberg said hastily. "Targeted at children ages five to twelve. We want it to be a fun and engaging information product. And children using it for getting information will then springboard into *Encarta*, to the *Encarta* target market." Seeing that Bjerke had popped up from under the table and turned on her computer, she said, "And now Carolyn will define the project."

"Yeah," said Bjerke, "what we wanted to do when we first started working on the product . . . we wanted this product, when it came on the market, to be the best in its category. In order to do that, we had to come up with a bunch of attributes we thought this product should have. And that's what we called 'defining the bar.' "

As she spoke, her audience read intently through the product plan, occasionally looking up at her and interrupting her with questions. "Can you really serve that broad an age range?" "Can a single style be appealing to that many different kinds of kids?" She identified the two critical challenges to her team as being able to make the encyclopedia multileveled, so that it could be a different product to different kids, and eminently replayable, so that kids would come back to it again and again, finding something new each time. "We want it to be extremely engaging, not only to children but to adults," she said. "As we all know, Disney is very good at appealing to both children and adults, and we want to be able to say that we are the Disney of the computer market." She hoped to combine the high production values of Disney products with the "intriguing interactivity" of Nintendo games, and she hoped to give users "the ability to learn everywhere. We're constantly presenting information to the user."

The whole exercise in detailing her team's ambition and the technical challenges it faced was aimed at justifying *Sendak*'s two-year schedule, which Bjerke and her teammates knew would prove the hardest issue to sell to management. After Bjerke went through a thorough list of anticipated technical problems that would call for months of code-writing and experimentation, it fell to Sonja Gustafson to demonstrate that the long development time and high cost would prove well worth the effort; it was projected that *Sendak* would cost $2.5 million to develop.

"Here's some numbers expressing the opportunity we think is here," Gustafson began. Almost immediately, she floundered, as one of her listeners interrupted with a question that proved, after some confusion, to have been prompted by a typographical error. From then on, she was interrupted almost constantly by questions and discussion among her listeners. She flushed, grew increasingly tense, and found herself apologizing frequently for more and more of her work. "This is a new model we're refining . . . the Mac numbers are weak . . . I shouldn't have left that out . . ."

Eventually, her team's vision of the future marketplace emerged. "The presence of children in the home," she said, "is a super-huge influence in the decision to purchase a PC." Thus children's software sales were going up dramatically year by year as more families bought personal computers for home use. For the first nine months of 1992, $65 million worth of home education software had been purchased in the United States, an increase of 57 percent over the previous year. By 1995, when *Sendak* would hit the market, Gustafson believed that there would be 2.2 million home multimedia personal computers, which would translate into net *Sendak* sales revenues of $8.9 million in that year, rising to $20.6 million in 1997—"assuming a 4 percent penetration rate."

Gustafson was interrupted at that point by Peter Mollman, who, at sixty-two, was one of a handful of elder statesmen at Microsoft. The former president of World Book Encyclopedia, and with a resume that included long stints at Harper and Row, Harper's Magazine Press, and Random House, Mollman had been talked out of retirement by Gates, who wanted someone with experience in the world of print publishing to help Microsoft acquire electronic reproduction rights to books and to guide the company into the publishing world. Since he was part of a tiny inner circle of older men who were believed to hold Gates in thrall, Mollman's pronouncements tended to bring proceedings to a halt, as if they were sent down from the chairman himself.

"You're projecting almost $30 million in net revenues," he said softly.

"I would say at least that much," Gustafson answered.

"Well, Childcraft's print encyclopedias gross $30 million per year," replied Mollman. "That's a helluva target you've set. You're saying you're going to double their sales."

There followed a flurry of skeptical questions from all over the room about Gustafson's assumptions. Finally, Mollman took the floor again. "This is a question that we're going to run into all over the place," he said. "We say we're going to be bigger than the book market, even though only 12 percent of the actual population will own computers. Why do we think that's true?" The consensus around the room was that the market, being so new and undefined, made it impossible to project hard sales figures. "Even pricing is a sensitive area," said one of the listeners. "It's a $195 product when this gets introduced; there's gonna be a lot of changes probably in pricing between now and then. Especially if these things start to become rented."

That observation introduced the dreaded topic of *Sendak*'s long schedule, and Corddry weighed in immediately. Microsoft's strategy, he explained, was predicated on the belief that "sooner or later big publishers are going to be moving into this area. When that happens there will be this sort of ice going out in the spring effect, and as a result the number of products will increase faster than the channel can expand to take them, and that means there'll be price pressure." Although it was unlikely that print publishers would be able to produce electronic titles that would be as good as Microsoft's three years hence, their titles would nevertheless enjoy a number of advantages. "They'll have the publishers' names on them, brand-name authors, brand-name publishers, their profit margins, their panic to get into the market, and it'll be really hard for the customer to decide from looking at the box whether the Microsoft product is better than the Random House product or the Paramount product. They'll end up deciding based on price."

Gustafson, flustered, answered with a vague, "I'll definitely think on that. . . . In two years, who else will be at this price point?" Then she hurriedly handed the meeting back to Bjerke, who began taking the audience through the prototype.

The questions trailed off immediately, as the group fell into a kind of collective enchantment at the demonstration. Occasionally, a question was floated about consistency with other Microsoft products, whether a given effect was technically feasible, or whether the encyclopedia would cover certain content areas. "Oh, that's terrific, that's terrific," Mollman said at one point, "fundamentally right on." Corddry, as he often did when he was favorably impressed with something, veered off into the abstract. "The explorer metaphor," he said of *Sendak*'s explorer-through-the-universe-of-knowledge model, "assumes that over time you get better and better at it; in the real world that's true, you learn that the moss grows on the north side of trees, you learn to read the signs on the freeway, whatever, so it would be interesting to know if an experienced user—this would be very hard to test for—if people who bought this product at first just loved stumbling around. . . . You know, it's like being in the funhouse for awhile. Over time, they'd want to get more efficient, they'd be using it, and you'd need to provide them with shortcuts or else do a really good job of providing meaningfulness. . . . It's a hard problem. . . . How complex a visual language can you expect people to be able to use, when they don't normally use visuals for a language?"

Several seconds of disorientation followed in the wake of Corddry's strange loop, as everyone else in the room tried to get the presentation back on track. Finally, Bjerke turned the discussion to *Sendak*'s technical specifications and the problems posed by many of its features. Since this was integral to her team's argument for a two-year schedule, and since the marketing portion of the program had seriously weakened their case, it was critical that *Sendak* be made to sound as difficult to produce as possible. But whenever questions were referred to Gammill, the lone developer in the room and the sole credible assessor of the project's technical difficulty, he brought Bjerke up short. Sitting bleary-eyed from long night after long night spent finishing *Encarta*, he was the picture of exhaustion and nonchalance. "That shouldn't be too difficult," he said at one point, and then later: "It should be pretty easy . . ." He was in the midst of discussing animation problems when Corddry's Goofy watch interrupted. "Hi, kids!" it shouted, the mouth moving in eerie synchronicity with the words. "The time is . . . I forgot! Yuk! Yuk! Yuk! Yuk! Time to go!" After a moment of collective shock, the group dissolved in a short burst of laughter, then almost immediately composed itself. "You're taking that to your Bill meeting, I hope," said Bartholomew.

Gammill continued without missing a beat. "Basically, what we want is to lay out a bunch of layers of bit maps, and have the possibility of having a sprite like walk behind a tree, give the effect of walking behind a tree." After more technical enumeration, he concluded with, "It should be pretty easy . . . it'll probably be only a quarter of the work of *Encarta*."

Ryberg and Bjerke interrupted with gruesome descriptions of the difficulty and scope of the tasks ahead, but the battle was effectively lost. "I am uneasy with any product that takes two years," Corddry said, "just because Microsoft hasn't done very many of them, and most of them slipped badly." Referring to Gates, Microsoft Vice President Mike Maples, and to Susan Boeschen, he continued, "The rule of thumb here is that you should never take a job that takes more than twelve months at Microsoft, because if you don't ship something, Bill will run out of patience. Bill and Mike Maples and Susan will always be reacting to that schedule, and you'll be constantly justifying it; it's going to really be a headache."

Bartholomew and Bjerke raised objection after objection, but their arguments fell on deaf ears. "Devil's advocate position that you will have to deal with," said Corddry, "because it comes not from me but from Bill. He will say, 'Give me a comparison, call this Plan A and Plan B, begin with a date, say we have to ship *Sendak* on September 1, 1994, what kind of children's encyclopedia can you do for that? What kind of a price can you get for what you can do? And why can't you do that, then two years later, or a year and a half later, come out with a Version 2 gangbuster?' The idea is to put a preview product out there early, and potentially become established as the owner of the category."

The value of being first rather than best, Corddry reminded his troops, was too much a part of Microsoft's culture ever to be questioned. "One of the things that's a real hot button around here is how expensive it is to come from behind even if you're better," he said. "Someone told me once that it was costing *Excel* [one of Microsoft's all-time leading moneymakers] $25 million per share point to close the gap on *Lotus 1,2,3*. *Excel* has been better than 1,2,3 for eight years now, and it's still clawing its way up. And it's taking everything, and it costs a fortune. So it's in the culture here, this knowledge that it's really hard to come from behind. And I think there's real fear here on Bill's part that we'll get into some of these juicy categories late."

To the chagrin of Bjerke and Ryberg, Bartholomew finally conceded. "I agree, I think we need to bring the schedule in. It just seems like politically this isn't going to get by Bill and Mike with the current schedule. We can defend our longer schedule rationally, but we're trying to refute an irrational argument."

After the meeting was over, Bartholomew stayed behind to commiserate with Ryberg and Bjerke. The three agreed that things would have been much worse had Blumenthal been there. Then Bartholomew said, "I can tell you right now that this product is going to ship in September of 1994." Although agreeing with his troops that Gates's reasoning in comparing the multimedia market with the spreadsheet applications market was faulty, he wasted no words in telling them that he now expected them to succeed within the confines of a shorter schedule. "I don't think the encyclopedia has to be scaled back to make it, either, to tell you the truth. I think you guys have a lot of padding in your schedule. You guys should spend a lot of time just organizing stuff, how we can organize with the utmost efficiency. The optimum way of doing it is just not going to happen."

"I'd rather not fight management on this schedule issue," said Bjerke, "and put the energy instead into being smart about trying to make this thing." While Ryberg stared in glum silence down at the table, Bjerke and Bartholomew continued talking over her head. "What on earth was Kevin *talking about?*" Bjerke wondered. Bartholomew laughed. "I just don't think he's had time to think about all these issues—that's why he said it would be so easy."

I spent the days after the pivotal meeting dropping in at various offices to assess the group's mood. Corddry was alternately amused, dismayed, discouraged, and encouraged by what he had seen and heard. "I looked at that two-year schedule," he said, "and I thought, 'God, that's amazing—why does that take so long?' I think that they faked the schedule because they were afraid of repeating the mistake they made in promising too tight a schedule for *Encarta*. I also think they were trying to take advantage of that disaster, saying, 'Oh, we learned our lesson from *Encarta*, we're going to take a *really long time* for this one!' " He laughed. "That wasn't the lesson I wanted them to learn."

Corddry believed that *Sendak* was shaping up to be a classic multimedia project: many of its features had never been done before; it was pivotal to Microsoft's overall strategy; and it was a product of potentially far-reaching social importance. Consequently, its creators tended toward defensive enthusiasm. "They get kind of in love with their concept," he said, "and they feel threatened by questions about the schedule. They think you want them to eliminate features. This has all the earmarks of a product around which a team would kind of get messianic. It's new, it's a breakthrough, it's artistic. . . . So I can see them really circling the wagons on it."

He wanted the *Sendak* team to understand that their mission was to beat Microsoft's competition rather than change the world without considering the commercial consequences of their work. Overzealous product teams tended to lose the ability to tell useful features from gratuitous ones. "The essence of success in this business," Corddry said, "is the trade-off between schedule, budget, and features. I mean, that's the core core core nature of the business—spending your money on the right features means you're creating more opportunity for return per dollar you spend." By forcing the *Sendak* team to adhere to a short schedule, he was simply trying to provoke more rigor and discipline in their designs. "To add a lot to the schedule to implement features that don't add much to the product . . . you do that enough times, you're out of business."

Ryberg and Bjerke, who had conferred by telephone with Fox, felt that they were agreeing to an impossible schedule, given that there were so many technical and editorial unknowns in the production. "We're facing an incredible number of black holes," Bjerke said. The longer schedule had been planned to allow time to figure out how they could implement unprecedented features. Now, they would have to try inventing features as they went along and hope they encountered no setbacks.

Peter Mollman had seen the presentation as one more example of the need for discipline among Multimedia Publishing's product planners. "It's always easy to think, 'Let's do more, let's add this, let's add this,'" he said. "Somebody really needs to draw the line. Craig is starting to understand that a little bit. I was looking at *Sendak*, they wanted to do a two-year thing, I was saying, 'For God's sake, first of all, a children's encyclopedia is an oxymoron!' So you're gonna put in stuff that's fun. And stuff that gives you enough knowledge so it's gonna be fun. It *can't* be complete. So draw the line—get it out. And see what happens."

While noting the disappointment of his subordinates, Bartholomew considered the meeting a success. "By and large, I think it went well," he said. "We have a tendency sometimes to get so involved in our products, it's like a fortress mentality—we're gonna defend this against all costs. And there are certain times where you have to know what to defend and what to concede. I think Sonja has the most to learn in that regard. That was a pretty confusing document she wrote. There were times when we were getting into numbers, we were questioning things, and she would kind of cut people off rather than just say, 'Sure, we'll look into that' or 'I'll get back to you on this.'"

Gustafson, for her part, felt more misunderstood than mistaken, and questioned the blind faith everyone else had in Mollman. She felt less undone by her own shortcomings than by a corporate power play. "I think some of his advice is really bad," she said of Mollman. "But Peter's got incredible clout with Bill. Bill knows that he was a former president at World Book, and he's a very persuasive salesman, if you will, with that personality. I don't know what his role is, or why there's this sort of love affair between those two, but he's managed to really seduce Bill into his thinking."

However convinced Gustafson was that Gates's thinking was misguided, Bartholomew wasted no time in making it clear that Gates's thinking was all that mattered. Two days later, an e-mail copy of Gustafson's product plan arrived, with Bartholomew's comments inserted. It was a devastating critique, a line-by-line dissection of her argument. Gammill, joining Gustafson later that day at a *Sendak* "Bill meeting strategy session," laughed sympathetically when he saw her carrying the edited document. "I feel sorry for you," he said, "because I can *smoke him*. But he used to be in marketing, so you can't."

The others in the room laughed, then stopped abruptly when Bartholomew entered. They discussed preparations for their presentation to Gates for an hour before Bartholomew concluded the meeting with what apparently was intended as a pep talk. Looking self-consciously down at the table, he said, "My role now . . . I feel like I have to be hard on you at times, challenge you. It's like there's a contract between you and me. I have to come down on you, be skeptical at times. It's better for me to be that way than for Bill. You lose no face with me. I'm going to have to be brusque or rude at times, because I won't have time to be diplomatic." He paused, then said, "I think we're at a stage right now where the intensity level needs to be turned up. Everyone but Kevin's been off of *Encarta* for a couple of months now." There was resigned laughter all around as the meeting broke up.

Digitizing the Soul

There was no end to the troubling technical problems confronting *Sendak*'s designers.

For all of its apparently miraculous powers, the personal computer is little more than a mathematical jukebox, a Wurlitzer of digits. It repeatedly fetches sets of the same two numbers, one and zero, from where they are stored in the computer's memory, and moves them onto a microprocessor chip—a rectangular piece of silicon as small as a postage stamp on some computers, slightly less than an inch square on others—where they are used to turn the chip's tiny switches, or transistors, on and off. These switches, which are linked on a chip by intricate pathways ¹⁄₁₀₀th the width of a human hair, are turned off, or closed, if the number assigned to them is zero, and are turned on, or opened, if the number assigned to them is one. Electrical signals flow through the microprocessor along routes shaped by the pattern of open and closed switches. The resulting pattern of signals eventually translates into words, decimal numbers, colors, and sounds.

The computer, then, is a high-speed simpleton. It inhabits an unambiguous world, where everything it considers is either one or zero, yes or no, on or off. It is a retriever and deliverer of binary digits, or bits, whose arrangement can represent anything from a decimal number (the number 13, for example, written in binary form, is 1101) to an animated drawing, on the screen, of a duck swimming across a pond.

The story of the personal computer revolution is the story of humankind's success in coping with the computer's shortcomings. Since all a computer can do is store and retrieve, it can be made more adept at computing only by being made to store and retrieve bits in larger batches and at faster speeds. The more transistors you can pack on a chip, the faster it can work. Microprocessor chip designers, led by those at the Intel Corporation, have been able to double the processing power in computer chips roughly every eighteen months by steadily increasing the number of transistors on a chip and making the paths between them shorter. In 1978, Intel's first microprocessor, the 4004, had 2,300 transistors. Intel's 80486 microprocessor chip, the industry standard in 1993, contained 1.2 million. The next generation of microprocessor, the Pentium, which first appeared in 1993, contained 3 million. By the end of the century, scientists at Intel predict, a single microprocessor chip will contain 100 million transistors.

With each leap forward in chip technology has come a corresponding leap in software capability. The ability of personal computers to have color rather than black-and-white screens, to display information in an endless variety of type sizes, typefaces, colors, and formats, to play sound, and to display video images and animation is a direct result of the steady increase in the number of switches on a microprocessor and the resulting increase in a computer's power and speed. Since people have been able to record music, sound, color, light, and movement in digital form—that is, as binary digits—and since such memory-storage devices as the compact disc have been widely available for some time, the only thing keeping personal computers from displaying digitally stored photography, sound, animation, and video has been their inability to store and retrieve bits in large enough chunks and at fast enough speeds to render realistic images and sounds on screens and in speakers. But by 1993, chip technology had advanced to the point where a personal computer—by virtue of its microprocessor's ability to process 20 million instructions per second and the development of supplementary cards (circuit boards) designed solely to play back sound and video images—was close enough to television in terms of picture and sound quality to make it a viable alternative to TV.

Even so, the multimedia computer was still performing the same simple task its forebears did—fetching and storing binary digits.

The degree of labor a computer puts into the delivery of an image can be seen in the makeup of its screen: an extremely fine grid composed of thousands of tiny squares, or pixels. In 1993, screens in *Sendak*'s target market ranged in size from 196,608 pixels to 786,432. Computers render images by firing electrons at the computer screen at a given bit-per-pixel rate, ranging from one bit per pixel to twenty-four, depending upon the sophistication of the machine in question. Where a computer's user sees a set of black words on a white background or a complicated color image, the computer itself sees a bit map—a set of ones and zeroes directing the flow of electrons to the screen. Every time the user changes the image on his or her screen, the computer instantaneously assembles a new bit map and displays a new bit-mapped image.

This is a complicated proposition when the screen is displaying a color image, for then each pixel is assigned an RGB (red-green-blue) value. Pixels are flooded with a mix of red, green, and blue light, the mix determined by the values stored in a given bit map. A pixel that looks turquoise to the viewer, to cite one example, has an R value of 64, a G value of 224, and a B value of 208. Multiply that set of numbers by 196,608 or more pixels on a screen, and you begin to appreciate what masses of numbers are required for a computer to process a single image. When it comes to displaying video images or playing sounds, these mixes reach almost unlimited proportions. To play an eight-second video sequence, for example, on a two-inch-square section of screen, requires 1.2 megabytes of storage in memory—as much as it takes to store four hundred pages of text.

Developing a multimedia software product for a personal computer, then, is a little like trying to show a movie on a calculator. No matter how much you improve the PC, it is still a machine built to crunch numbers rather than broadcast moving pictures.

What would have been relatively simple production problems on television turned into all-but-insoluble problems for *Sendak*'s designers. The computer, for example, sees the world as two-dimensional, with everything placed on an x/y axis. It therefore required prodigious feats of mathematics and imagination to make a "sprite"—an animation that moves about on the screen—appear to move in front of and behind other objects on a two-dimensional computer screen the way it would in a three-dimensional world. The best the *Sendak* team could manage in the prototype stages of product design was to treat separate segments of an animated character as separate characters entirely. A computer displaying a picture of a bear walking behind a tree, for example, would have to consider the front half of the bear, the tree, and the back half of the bear as three different members of the animation's cast. Should the bear reach around the tree, its limb would not be a part of the bear but yet another separately identified character.

All of this, of course, only added drastically to the amount of data that had to be entered into the computer in order to display an animation. *Sendak*'s designers soon found that as few as four short animations scripted in this manner exhausted the random-access memory capacity of their computers. (Random-access memory, or RAM, is that part of the PC's memory that is stored on chips rather than on disc. When a computer is working, it temporarily retrieves the information it needs from where it is stored on a disc and moves it to its RAM, where it can be moved and manipulated far more quickly and efficiently.) Since *Sendak* was to be largely an animated product, it would be impossible to develop unless its team could devise a more efficient means of displaying animation.

The problem of rendering colors properly was similarly complicated. Because of the way colors are indexed in a computer, it would take special, largely undefined measures to prevent flashing whenever the scene on *Sendak*'s screen would change. Flashing confronts the user with an unwanted psychedelic spectacle—purple skies, red-and-green eagles, violet grass, and so on—before the colors in the new scene are properly indexed and displayed. Sometimes a *Sendak* scene's color data would get scrambled in the transition from another scene, with the result that the screen might display anything from a scene in which all colors were comically wrong to one where they were just slightly off, or where some colors were speckled, or where the whole scene was rendered in shades of gray.

Added to these were hundreds of other, smaller production problems, and on the horizon beyond them lay problems of speed and performance. Because *Sendak* would have so much video, animation, sound, and color, and because the product would be expected to have so many functions, its creators would have to invent ways to speed up its retrieval-and-display procedures. *Sendak* designers feared that a child trying to trigger an animation or a transition in *Sendak* might have to wait six or seven seconds—an intolerably long wait to computer users—for the PC to find the appropriate information on the compact disc, load it into RAM, compose new bit maps, activate the appropriate engines, and get the new data up on the screen.

But these were problems more or less within the *Sendak* team's control.

More troubling were the challenges posed by the array of personal computers on the marketplace. In order to succeed commercially, *Sendak* had to run smoothly on as many different kinds of computers as possible. Since many computers are made up of parts from different companies—a given system might have its processor, monitor, CD-ROM drive, keyboard, mouse, video card, sound card, and so on all made by different manufacturers—the *Sendak* team would have to ensure that their product could work on every conceivable combination of components. Testers of *Encarta*, by the time that project was finished, had had to test the encyclopedia on more than three hundred different equipment configurations. Given the constant rapid rate of change in personal computing, *Sendak* likely would have to run on even more.

Sendak was also being developed for what Microsoft called a "moving platform." Computer hardware and software change constantly, and with every change comes changes in the capability of the personal computer and in the expectations of its users. The *Sendak* team was planning a product for a marketplace nearly two years distant, when there certainly would be profound changes in the quality and character of personal computing. *Sendak*'s designers would have to anticipate with some degree of accuracy exactly what those changes would bring about. In many respects, they were designing a product for computers that did not yet exist.

These were relatively tangible problems, scientific in nature—the sort of problems Microsoft prided itself on solving. Not so simple was the intangible problem posed by the titanic clash between Apple's Macintosh personal computers and those known as IBM-compatible machines, nearly all of which ran Microsoft's Windows platform on Microsoft's MS-DOS operating system. While a complicated technical challenge for the *Sendak* team, it was less a technological matter than a combined philosophical, psychological, political, and cultural one. Mac and IBM-compatible PCs had defined the parallel-and-opposed paths along which personal-computer technology had been moving since 1981, when the monolithic IBM first joined upstart Apple Computer and assorted other small companies in the PC marketplace. The differences between IBM and Apple cut to the heart not only of the fight for dominance over the PC world but also of the means by which products are developed at Microsoft.

Two decisions had directed the fates of Microsoft and Apple from 1981 on. In Microsoft's case, the opportunity in its early days to ally itself with

IBM and the world of corporate computing put it on the road to industry domination. In Apple's case, the decision to direct its efforts toward the home and school market ultimately would help consign it, by comparison, to a small niche in the PC market. By 1993, Microsoft's operating system, MS-DOS—which more than ten years before had been licensed by IBM to competing hardware manufacturers, thus giving rise to the huge IBM-compatible industry—ruled the PC world, while Apple's share of the personal computer market was only 10 percent.

By 1993 the domination of the machine that ran MS-DOS was reflected dramatically in the vocabulary of the computer marketplace: the generic term "personal computer," or PC, had come to mean an MS-DOS machine, while a Macintosh was known not as a PC but as a Mac. The computing world was divided not into realms ruled by manufacturers of two types of personal computer but into the PC side and the Mac side. On the PC side stood Microsoft and the hundreds of hardware makers who manufactured MS-DOS–based machines and their components. On the Mac side stood Apple, alone.

This difference in fortunes was only partly due to IBM's having allowed competitors to build MS-DOS machines while Apple refused to license its operating system to other manufacturers. It also was due to Apple's early determination to design a computer so easy to use that someone could buy it, set it up, and start using it without having to read any manuals. Makers of IBM-compatibles, meanwhile, were more intent on building faster and more powerful computers to be used in corporate workplaces—IBM's traditional territory—as corporations figured to be early buyers of computers in large volumes. To corporate PC purchasers, ease of use was of less importance than number- and word-crunching. While Apple busied itself making computers that were painless and pleasurable, makers of MS-DOS machines focused on making workers more productive.

The sheer numbers of manufacturers and early high-volume sales on the IBM-compatible side made the DOS-based design the immediate world standard. Since all IBM compatibles ran Microsoft's operating system, the company, in spite of the fact that it made the first applications software to run on Apple's Macintosh and continued to be the world's leading manufacturer of Mac applications, was forever identified with the corporate world of IBM-compatible machines.

The stark differences between IBM and Apple in corporate strategy and identity were highlighted with Apple's introduction of the Macintosh in 1983. The Mac was a revolution within a revolution, in that it introduced graphical user interface to the PC marketplace. The Mac became the machine of choice for schools and colleges, writers, desktop publishers, and graphic artists, while DOS machines remained the computer of choice for the corporate and technical worlds.

Ultimately, differences between Microsoft and Apple came down to a difference in vision so stark that the purchase of a personal computer became a declaration of personal and political values. Microsoft's vision was of bringing the power of mainframe computers to the desktop machine, and of putting a personal computer on every desk, running Microsoft software. Apple took a purportedly more idealistic tack, expressed not only in the pleasure-quotient of its machines but in its advertising. By buying a Macintosh, the company trumpeted constantly, you were unleashing your creative potential and rejecting the values of Corporate America in the bargain. Theirs was a vision of putting a politically correct computer on every desk.

A computing cult of devoted and righteous followers, who brought to the personal-computer world the values of 1960s counterculture, sprang up around the Macintosh. Macintosh User Groups, or MUGs, formed in cities all over America, swapping shareware, trading computing tips, and bashing Microsoft. The Mac became not so much a computer as a cause, the conventional wisdom among devotees being that all real innovation came from Apple, then was stolen and turned into profits by Microsoft.

By 1993, cultural stereotypes of both Mac people and DOS people were firmly entrenched. The two types were as opposite and nearly incompatible as cat people and dog people. Mac people were free thinkers with artistic temperaments, given to reacting emotionally to issues and only occasionally following up with more or less rational arguments. DOS people, in their own view, were purely analytical thinkers whose approach to computing problems was scientific, rational, and unclouded by emotion. Each claimed to see profound shortcomings and failings in the other, and the two groups disagreed on virtually everything. Developers on the Mac side constantly upbraided their counterparts from the DOS world for making computers too hard to use and for failing to incorporate features in them that had long been a part of the Mac machine. For their part, DOS developers treated Mac people with condescension and contempt. The favorite insult among developers at Microsoft was "Mac user"—an opprobrious term that effectively shut off all argument and defined the person in question as someone hopelessly benighted and uneducable.

The Mac-DOS war presented the *Sendak* team with a difficult technical challenge. Because the two types of machine used different chip architectures—MS-DOS machines were based on the Intel Corporation's x86-series microprocessor chips, and Macs on Motorola's 680 series— and because they used different operating systems, any application written for one could not be used on the other. Like their users, the two types of machine could not talk to one another.

In the past, Microsoft had first put out an application for the MS-DOS world, then followed with a Mac version months later. But *Sendak*, in a break with company tradition, was to "simultaneously ship" on both DOS and Mac machines. For *Sendak* team members, this mandate was one more potential obstacle threatening a deadline already in peril. Under the old DOS-first, Mac-second system, according to Carolyn Bjerke, dealing with incompatibility problems between the two architectures accounted for fully 30 percent of a design team's time. Under the simultaneous ship mandate, she feared that percentage would skyrocket.

More immediately nightmarish was Microsoft's need for talented graphic artists who did their work on personal computers, for these were exclusively Mac people. Throughout the Multimedia division, Mac people and their machines moved in to design the division's titles, which then were to be rendered on the PC by Microsoft's developers. Needless to say, this brought a certain level of tension and mistrust to Multimedia's product teams, the customary cultural gap between designers and developers being all the more heightened by their technical allegiances: at Microsoft, developers were DOS people, designers Mac people.

There was some grudging acknowledgment on the part of traditional Microsoft types of the need for Mac-using artists. Without their aesthetic senses and skills, a company that "processes" its words and expresses all of its dreams and aspirations in spreadsheet form would be helpless when it came to creating engaging products for the consumer market. But even so, Microsoft's Mac people were reminded daily that they were immigrants to an alien and hostile culture.

The *Sendak* team included an archetypal representative from each camp: Kevin Gammill and Bryan Ballinger, *Sendak*'s lead illustrator. Although the two had little directly to do with one another, much of the process of *Sendak*'s design was an unspoken argument between them.

Ballinger, who grew up in Vermont, graduated from the Columbus

College of Art and Design in 1990, and moved back home to find that there was nothing other than occasional T-shirt work for artists to do there. After moving to Rochester, New York, where he found very little more in the way of work, he bought a Macintosh, taught himself to draw and paint on it, then drove to Seattle because, as he put it, "it was sufficiently far from Vermont."

Once the Mac was in his hands, Ballinger was hooked. It was a far more powerful artist's tool than anything he had ever used before. He noticed early on that most art done on computers looked rather self-consciously like "computer art," and he resolved to take a different tack, using the computer as a tool in the service of art rather than using his artistic training as a means of paying homage to the computer. He saw the machine as a medium, like oil or watercolor, rather than an end in itself. "When you do *serious* art with a computer," he says, "it becomes more reflective of the person doing it rather than of the fact that it was done on a computer."

Ballinger found freelance work easy to come by in Seattle, as artists facile on computers were hard to find. He immediately started freelancing for Nintendo of America, located near Microsoft in Redmond, and for an area T-shirt manufacturer. Within a few months, he was a contractor doing work for Microsoft on *Encarta*. When production on that project began winding down, Bjerke lobbied hard to have him hired full time. In her view, he was a tremendous asset to the company not only because of the quality of his work and his willingness to put in long hours, but because his technical knowledge of the inner workings of the Macintosh was far beyond that of any other artist she knew.

Ballinger was fascinated with Macintosh technology, knew the strengths and weaknesses of each of the more than one hundred Mac art applications on the market, and knew exactly what he could get out of every available piece of Mac hardware. He read Mac literature voraciously, attended Mac conferences, and spent virtually all of his waking hours in front of his machine. In a company where software developers tended to look down on editors and artists because they spent relatively little time at work, Ballinger's focus on work was so obsessive that even developers worried about him. Gammill was constantly admonishing Ballinger to get a life outside Microsoft.

There was something addictive about Ballinger's attachment to his Mac. He spent so much time in front of his machine that frequently he took all three of his daily meals at his desk. He kept a pillow in his office because there were often nights when he crawled under his desk and slept there. He seldom shaved or combed his hair, and he was extremely pale and gaunt. A short, slight young man with rounded shoulders and a chronically dreamy expression on his face, he looked like an anthropomorphized puppy—a character in a children's book.

This impression was heightened by Ballinger's shyness. He seldom spoke at all and when he did it was only to utter short sentences in a barely audible voice. His office was a cluttered cave few felt entitled to enter. It was dark and packed with junk: posters of children's art, little clay figures, miniature cereal boxes, art supplies, books, diskettes, a Bible, and—sitting atop his computer—a large stuffed orangutan wearing a gas mask and a Mousketeer's hat.

At twenty-four, Ballinger was filled with idealism and artistic ambition. An avid student of art for children, he dreamed of being a children's book illustrator who would be taken seriously as an artist. He disdained commercial considerations and composed art solely with the aim of pleasing the children in his audience. His appointment as lead illustrator on *Sendak* presented him with the opportunity of a lifetime, one seldom afforded artists so young and inexperienced: the chance to oversee the creation of art for a massive book, packed with his own work and defined by his own aesthetic. He was to be, in effect, master of his own atelier —a high-tech Leonardo, teaching and directing legions of apprentices.

The only thing standing in Ballinger's way was his crippling shyness. Creation of titles in Multimedia Publishing was very much a collaborative process, particularly for those who worked under Bjerke. Meetings led by her were brainstorming sessions in which people's worth was measured by the degree to which they pitched in with ideas, however good or bad. Under her demanding tutelage, it had taken Ballinger more than a year to open up, even tentatively. Should anyone else be in a conference room with the two, he would say very little, if anything at all.

Bjerke saw this as a serious detriment to Ballinger's advancement both as an artist and as a Microsoft employee. She also worried about his disdain for commercialism. "He's got a lot of raw talent," she said one day, "but you have to mold him for this environment. He is by nature the loner artist, and we can't afford to have loner artists on staff. We pay them a lot of money to have broad skills and be leaders and all that." She also wanted him to learn to take direction—to draw to order for marketing and management—and to think of his work more as a commercial product than as pure art.

In drawing the nature scene for the first prototype, Ballinger had drawn animals with comically bulging eyes—something of a signature device in his art—in the cartoonish style of books for very young children. The creatures were aggressively endearing, like dolls or stuffed animals. Tentative suggestions from Bjerke, Bartholomew, and Corddry that he might want to make the animals slightly more realistic, as befits an encyclopedia, were ignored.

Bjerke was gently trying to make Ballinger understand that he was not *Sendak*'s sole designer. "We had a fairly painful discussion about this," she said, "where I had to make it very clear to him that this is not fine art. You have to please all these people. So he's extremely talented—it's just that he draws to an emotional level and he needs to be more conceptual."

At the beginning of the project, that meant that Ballinger was to help Bjerke come up with a wish list of *Sendak* features and a rough model of its overall design. In a series of meetings that included two other artists—Lindsey Smith, a contractor who had been a production artist on *Encarta* and now was slated to be the production lead on *Sendak*, and Shelly Becker, the Loretta Lynn lookalike who specialized in scripting animation on the Macintosh—Bjerke would stand at a whiteboard, Ballinger would sit at a table, and they would go over *Sendak* from top to bottom, beginning to end. They tried to determine such things as how many scenes would be in each of the four units—Nature, Civilization, Geography, and History. Would twelve to fifteen each be enough to cover all of the encyclopedia's topics? They tried sketching out the scenes in the Nature unit, and came up with twelve: an evergreen forest, a deciduous forest, a desert, a grasslands, a wetlands, a lake, a beach, a shallows, a reef, ocean depths, mountains, and outer space. They tried to imagine how the user would picture these units. Would the user's mental map of a given unit have the scenes laid out in a line, or connected by paths, or clustered like states in a map of the United States? What was the logical order of scenes? How would you navigate from one to the other?

They discussed having users extract from the guide's backpack, by means of a mouse-click, a remote-control device with which they would summon a helicopter or some other vehicle to take them back to the spaceship, on which they then would travel to whatever other scene they desired. They discussed having directional signs in each scene, so that a sign in the forest might direct the user to the adjacent scene, which might be the desert or the wetlands. They considered giving the user two or more options: not only would there be directional signs and the ability to navigate by spaceship, but one might also be able to go, say, from the forest to the mountains by clicking on the mountains in the background of the forest scene. But giving the user this option might lead to confusion, for he or she might click on the mountains expecting to see text pop up and instead find the entire scene changing.

A similar problem was posed by Fox, who—her maternity leave notwithstanding—found ample time to brood about *Sendak* and send e-mail about it. In mulling over how children would explore in *Sendak*, Fox realized that they would get inconsistent responses to their mouse-clicks. Sometimes they would get printed text, but other times they would simply enter a building or a cave. "I've been thinking about the Civilization 'unit' more," she wrote to Bjerke, "and remembered that it differs from Nature in that there are buildings that you need to go inside of to get information. For example, we put lots of topics in a hospital, many in a theatre. . . . In these cases, although the hospital would be in the city, if you click on it we don't need information to come up about the hospital, we need some way for you to get inside."

Meeting after meeting was devoted to deciding what tools to put in the guide's backpack and what they should look like. Bjerke and Ballinger wanted *Sendak* to include the searching, indexing, cataloging, and navigational functions of a standard encyclopedia, along with a set of more gamelike functions. They wanted users to be able to type and save notes on their travels through *Sendak*; to draw, color, and paint creatures and scenes; to copy and print pictures and text from the encyclopedia; to play sounds, videos, and animation; to find hidden things in scenes; to keep track of topics visited so they could return to them at any point during a session; to browse, reading about things randomly and at leisure; and to go on information-gathering missions, generated by *Sendak*, in search of answers to questions.

For each of these activities, they wanted a tool, stored in the guide's backpack, whose appearance immediately would signal its function to the user. Bjerke wanted the overall model for the tool set to be verbs-to-nouns—in other words, the tool would be a verb and the user would point it at or drag it over the noun to be acted upon. To play a video sequence, for example, users would click on a pocket of the backpack and a remote control device would pop up. They would click on the device and it would be transferred to the guide's hand, pointing at a video monitor. Then users would click on one of the remote control's buttons: Play, Rewind, Stop, Pause. For copying pictures or sections of text, Bjerke and Ballinger considered including a "dust buster" in the backpack. After clicking on the appropriate pocket, users would drag the dust buster over the text or picture to be copied and vacuum it up. Later, they could take the tool to a word-processing program and spit out the dust buster's contents, including the copied material in a report they were writing. "The trouble with that," Ballinger said one day, "is that 'vacuum' is a metaphor for 'erase.' The tool should be a camera—'camera' is a metaphor for 'copy.' "

Discussions of the guide's tool set went on for months. What should the word processing tool look like? Should it be incorporated in the draw-and-paint tool? Should there be a flashlight in the backpack, and if so, what would it do? How about a magnifying glass? Would binoculars be understood as the lookup tool with which you could search directly for topics in the text rather than having to navigate through the scenes to get to particular pieces of information? Ballinger protested at one point that the number of tools was so great that the backpack would dwarf the guide. At another meeting, he and Bjerke decided to include not only a backpack, but a belt around the guide's waist, from which would hang even more tools. A few days later, they jettisoned the belt. A few days after that, they reinstated it, only to eliminate it once and for all at a subsequent meeting.

In addition to designing their product, Bjerke and Ballinger spent much of their time designing procedures. Gates preferred that Multimedia's titles be composed, or authored, either in Viewer or in another program called Visual Basic, both of which ran on Windows. Multimedia's artists were adamant that all their work be done on Macintoshes, then ported over to the Windows world, as many of the effects they wanted were either unattainable on the PC or would be executed less effectively there than on the Mac. Having been designed with fun rather than corporate productivity in mind, the Macintosh had a far more extensive and appealing color palette than did the PC; moreover, there was an infinite array of artists' software that ran on the Macintosh but was unavailable for the PC.

After weeks of lobbying by Ballinger, who argued that the project could never be kept on schedule if artists were forced into the cumbersome procedures necessitated by the PC's authoring programs, Bjerke agreed that the artwork should be done on the Mac and that the early prototypes should be built on it. The decision made her uneasy. She believed that

Gates hated being told that certain tasks were better done on Macintoshes than on PCs. It was bad enough that she would have to relay that news to him; worse, when it came time for her team's Bill meeting, she would have to demonstrate *Sendak* on a Mac.

Ballinger also insisted, and Bjerke concurred, that *Sendak*'s artists work on 24-bit-resolution machines. Such Macs allowed them to work with a seventeen-million-color palette that allowed for the creation of breathtaking images. Most PCs in the consumer market, though, were equipped with monitors and video cards that would display the images at 8-bit resolution levels, with 256-color palettes. Rather than have his artists work at those lower levels creating relatively nondescript art, Ballinger wanted them to create 24-bit images, which then would be "dithered down" for display on lower-end machines.

Dithering is a process by which a computer analyzes an image's colors and renders as close an equivalent as possible with a smaller palette. It does this by juxtaposing different colors on adjacent pixels in order to create the illusion of a third color. A rich medium blue, for example, available at the click of a mouse button on a high-end Macintosh, can be dithered down on an 8-bit machine by programming it to alternate dark blue and light blue pixels on the screen. Similarly, a certain subtle shade of green can be faked on a low-end machine by making every fifth pixel on the screen yellow. It would be up to Microsoft's developers to come up with a dithering algorithm that would render, on 8-bit computers, Ballinger's artists' 24-bit images in a way that did not seriously compromise their quality.

Among other effects on Bjerke's and Ballinger's wish list was the ability of sprites to move across the screen independent of their backgrounds. On the PC, all objects—images and hot spots—were, in the eyes of the computer, squares or rectangles. If a butterfly were to fly across the screen, it would do so as part of a square, meaning either that it would be moving across the screen in a square white window or that it would take along with it, wherever it went, the square of background behind its original position on the screen. Ballinger and Bjerke wanted the PC to be able, as the Macintosh was, to make one of the colors on the machine's palette transparent. By assigning the transparent palette value to those parts of the sprite's square that were not the sprite itself, the scene on the screen behind the traveling sprite would show through properly as the sprite moved across the screen.

Sendak presented a similar problem with hot spots. Because *Sendak*'s scenes were to be packed densely with clickable creatures and objects, Ballinger wanted its developers to allow for irregularly shaped hot spots rather than the PC's customary rectangular ones. In order to get enough into a scene to allow users access by mouse-click to all of the encyclopedia's information, objects with square hotspots would have to overlap, leading to hopeless confusion. A user trying to click on a small desert animal might end up inadvertently popping up text for the date palm under which the animal was resting. *Sendak* needed polygonal hot spots—something available on the Mac, but never before featured on the PC—that could conform exactly to the outlines of the object they represented.

Similarly intricate and complex issues appeared everywhere. Bjerke and Ballinger had only the dimmest notions of whether or not a given wish could be implemented. Some of the things they wanted to do might take only a few hours of a developer's time. Others might prove to be impossible. They also had no idea which of their features would be assigned to Kevin Gammill and which, if any, to Phil Spencer's core tools group. This division of labor was of critical importance. Gammill, they knew, would stop at nothing to get his *Sendak* work done on time. But the tools group, doing work for several product teams, could not be counted on to put *Sendak*'s features at the top of their priorities list.

As they tried to predict Gammill's reaction to their desires, Bjerke and Ballinger found themselves unable to settle on how much or how little certain of these effects would matter. One minute Bjerke would say, "Get all this down. Get a time with Kevin and Phil. We need their signature in blood. If there's no decision, we'll just have to go through and figure out how we're going to do everything." The next, she would be saying, "If we don't get this tool, it won't kill us." Still later, still trying to define exactly what they wanted from Gammill and Spencer, she said, "I'm sick of this issue, I want to get it over with, write out a specification for it once and for all."

The problem, of course, was that she and Ballinger were working almost completely in the dark. Had Gammill been sitting in the room with them, he might have saved them hours of dreaming and analyzing. In his cloistered office down the hall, where he occasionally heard rumblings of what Bjerke and Ballinger were up to, he would look up from his work on *Encarta* and mutter, "That palette thing they want—there's no way," or "You can't show a video in an irregularly shaped hole like that," or "You can't show a video inside a sprite." Mostly, he would remind himself sternly of the reason he was behind schedule and working around the clock on *Encarta*: he and his fellow developer, Jay Gibson, had promised too much to the encyclopedia's designers. There might be some mistakes from his past that he was doomed to repeat, Gammill admitted, but promising the impossible to designers would never be one of them.

The Big Picture

While the *Sendak* team was maneuvering in the foreground, grander moves and stratagems were being effected in the corporate background. The *Sendak* initiative was just a small part of Microsoft's response to its explosive growth, which brought with it an overabundance of danger. Depending upon Microsoft's ability to prepare for them, coming changes in the personal computer industry would prove to be either enriching or fatal.

The most immediate challenge for Microsoft was to devise a way to force dramatically faster growth in the PC industry, in order to forestall an inevitable slowdown in the company's own growth. Microsoft had been growing faster than the industry in general for nearly ten years, and simple logic—to say nothing of federal regulatory agencies—dictated that Microsoft's expansion eventually would have to slow, if not stop altogether.

Microsoft, then, was trapped by its own phenomenal success. Should growth slow, and should stock performance fall, say, to a level only twice that of the best Fortune 500 companies, Wall Street would exact a heavy penalty. Stock prices would plunge. Traditionally, Microsoft had offered low salaries combined with stock options rather than salaries comparable to those offered by its strongest competitors, and having less valuable stock to offer would make it harder for Microsoft to compete with other software companies for the best new developers coming out of college. As long as the price of its stock kept rising, Microsoft could continue to hire the ablest in its industry while keeping its payroll relatively low.

In an effort to stave off the inevitable, Microsoft was trying to help move the personal computer beyond the office and into the home, car, and wallet. The company hoped to enter new markets by creating more new uses for the PC, thereby creating more opportunities for the company to sell software. Gates, who had long recognized that the corporate market for productivity applications would someday be glutted, had declared that Microsoft's future lay in the Consumer Division, which included Multimedia Publishing.

Computers were constantly becoming faster, more powerful, and more portable. With those attributes came more versatility, as more and more functions migrated onto the PC. Formerly, people had required separate tools or services for virtually everything: they did spreadsheets with pen and paper, typed on typewriters, sent facsimiles by fax machine, listened to music on stereo systems, kept track of their finances in checkbooks, corresponded and received magazines by mail, and used dedicated machines for telephone messages. All of those things could now be done on a single machine—the personal computer—and the advent of CD-ROM and fiber-optic technology would soon make it possible for the PC to take over many of the functions of the telephone, the television set, the mail-order catalog, the library, and the video-rental store.

The more activities migrated to the personal computer, the greater the need for software, as the migration essentially was a replacement of hardware by software. This transformation of the personal computer into an all-purpose multimedia machine suddenly threw companies from previously disparate industries into competition with one another, and all were now maneuvering for advantage in the emerging multimedia computing market. By 1993, virtually every hardware, software, consumer electronics, cable television, publishing, and entertainment company in the world, including Microsoft, either had entered into multimedia computing partnerships of one kind or another or was negotiating to do so. Microsoft, in concert with General Instruments and Intel, was designing a new cable television box that would send and receive digital interactive television signals over fiber-optic cable. When that relationship foundered, Microsoft commenced a similar arrangement with John Malone's TCI, the largest cable television company in the country. The company hoped to repeat its MS-DOS coup by being the operating system supplier to whatever hybrid machine—most likely a computing television set or a personal computer that could send and receive content in all media—

ended up being the home's entryway to the superhyped information superhighway.

Microsoft also was discussing a possible partnership with Disney Studios to publish multimedia titles on CD-ROM, and already had a multimedia publishing agreement with Dorling Kindersley. The previous year had seen so many television- and film-industry executives visiting the Microsoft campus that Gates was moved to quip, "We're not in the software business anymore—we're in the lunch business." As Tom Corddry put it, "Everybody in Hollywood, everybody in the book business, in the computer business, is sort of circling one another nervously right now, trying to figure this thing out."

Corddry's assigned contribution to this effort was twofold: on the one hand, he was to get multimedia titles out of the laboratory and into the marketplace; on the other, he was to divine where multimedia publishing was heading and to ensure, by means of his prescience, that Microsoft would dominate the industry.

This mixed mandate of managing the present and envisioning the future had been causing Corddry no end of vexation. He had been putting off strategic vision for months, for the sake of starting more projects and garnering more resources for Multimedia Publishing. "We've had so little time with Bill for the last six months," he told me during preparations for his division's February 8 meeting with Gates, "that we've used the time we've had to ask for resources that we need and that we know we can get from him."

For years, Gates had supported multimedia wholeheartedly, against the wishes of his executive staff and nearly all of his board. "Every so often," Corddry said of Gates, "he gets one of these visions—and boy, is he tenacious." Corddry found that in order to get more money from Gates, he had only to show him the prototype for a new product, along with a budget and schedule, and make a reasonable market argument for producing it. Gates invariably would give him the go-ahead with very little questioning. "If we can show that we're not too dumb about how to pick products," Corddry said, "that there are no blocking issues, and that we're not totally incompetent, he likely will say, okay. Basically, we have to show that we're competent, that it's the right time, and that we have the right plan. As long as we've been doing that, he's been saying yes. But what's been missing is the bigger plan."

Corddry had been dropping "the bigger plan" from his Bill meeting agendas for the last six months, as he was never allotted enough time both to argue for product-specific resources and to "do a hand-waving vision thing." While recognizing that the lack of strategy was "a building problem" in Microsoft's executive suites, he knew that as long as "we were shipping products, selling products, and want to build more products, each one of which Bill thinks is okay, then it's not a crisis for him."

It was, however, a crisis for company president Mike Maples, a former IBM executive whom Gates had recruited to bring corporate expertise and experience to Microsoft, where Gates and all of his managers were in their late twenties and early thirties. Maples brought with him a lifetime of computer-industry experience, an ability to manage large organizations, and a reflexive prudence when it came to vision. Much of what others at Microsoft regarded as vision, he regarded as fantasy, and he was determined to keep purported visionaries, Gates included, from luring the company outside the bounds of fiscal responsibility.

When Corddry first was put in charge of Multimedia, Maples advised him to keep the division small and to grow no faster than Multimedia's profits would allow. Make and market a product, he said, wait for it to make money, invest the profits in the next product, and so on, growing only in the black. Gates, however, preferred to invest early in an effort to be in a dominant position when multimedia grew into a big and profitable market. "Bill has been growing in the red for a long time here," Corddry said, "spending money faster. The faster you try to grow, the more difficult it is to make money, because you're spending the small amount of money you made from being a small business yesterday to build the products to be a huge business tomorrow. Essentially, how much we lose is a measure of how hard the foot is down on the accelerator."

In Maples's view, this was folly, and in his eagerness to apply the brakes, he had been finding it increasingly difficult not to object to Gates's recklessness. Things had come to a head the previous December, when Jabe Blumenthal presented plans for several new products to Gates and Maples. While Maples sat watching in silence, Gates took in Blumenthal's presentation, then, Corddry recalled, "said yes to a baseball encyclopedia, said probably yes to a science encyclopedia, said yes to five more smaller titles, and said, 'Let me think about language, a whole language learning series, but I might say yes to that, too. Give me some more time.' "

Maples was furious after the meeting, drawing Susan Boeschen aside to vent his frustration. He told Boeschen that Corddry and Blumenthal had manipulated Gates into giving them more resources and that under no circumstances would he, Maples, have given them anything. "He was feeling end-runned," said Corddry. "And I would have been pissed off, too. You have a job to do and people who work for you are not in your plan, and they have direct access to the chairman. Bill's always managed down quite a few levels that way, and Multimedia's always been one of his pets, so managing Multimedia is a dangerous job in terms of dealing with the hierarchy."

An electronic maelstrom followed, with e-mail flying all over the Microsoft campus. Maples sent mail to Gates, copied to Corddry, Blumenthal, and Boeschen, saying that the newly approved titles should be canceled, and that Multimedia Publishing should not be allowed to continue growing at all. Since this was his first public declaration of his position, he was raising the stakes for Gates by forcing him either to scale back Multimedia's growth or to disagree with his company president in full view of their subordinates. Gates mailed Boeschen, Blumenthal, and Corddry with the news that he was thinking over what Maples had said and that he would have to talk things over with him. He also copied the mail to Maples—thus, as Corddry saw it, warning Microsoft's president that "he might not say no."

Blumenthal, reading between the lines and drawing on his ties with Gates, mailed a personal message to him, reminding him that Maples was objecting not to the specific titles in question, but to all of Multimedia. If you don't draw the line and disagree with him now, Blumenthal wrote, you will have to do so sooner or later. Gates did not respond.

Finally, Corddry sent mail to all concerned, suggesting that he and Maples were operating from wildly different business models and that the coming February 8 meeting should be devoted entirely to strategy. Gates responded immediately with a yes. Corddry sent word to the *Sendak* team that they were being dropped from the February 8 agenda—an announcement the team greeted with undisguised joy. Corddry then set to work articulating a strategic vision.

Microsoft's core business had always been corporate software. Selling MS-DOS and applications software to large corporations had made the company fabulously rich. Maples felt that the way to cope with Microsoft's inescapable day of reckoning in the stock market was to concentrate on that core business, which still was in its relative infancy, and keep company costs in other areas low while continuing to computerize the business world. By staying lean elsewhere in the company and by maximizing profit margins in its traditional business, Maples reasoned, the company could extend its period of economic growth and be in sound financial condition when growth began to slow down, thereby reducing the consequences in the stock market.

Corddry felt that Maples's plan was flawed because it was based on the IBM business model, in which you sell a single product or set of products to the same small group of customers for decades. In the corporate market, a software vendor generally deals with customers who buy in huge volumes, purchasing whole systems for big companies. A single sale can be worth hundreds of thousands of dollars. In that marketplace, a company does best by securing an advantage, then keeping it by devoting all of its energies and resources constantly to improving the same product.

But Corddry felt that that market was reaching the limits of its growth. If Microsoft were to continue to prosper, it would have to develop and dominate new consumer markets. By moving away from the corporate arena and into consumer electronics, it was moving into a world where, Corddry said, "Everything is different: totally different price points, different margins, different organizational models, different kind of people . . . the works."

More important, there was a totally different level of competition. When Microsoft entered personal computing, there were no competitors at all, and the company leveraged the huge revenues it enjoyed from MS-DOS sales into an applications market where there was virtually no serious competition. But by moving into multimedia, it was risking battles with such gigantic companies as Time Warner, Random House, Paramount, Disney, Sony, Rupert Murdoch's News Corporation, and others.

Maples was constantly asking Corddry how he could expect to compete with such companies—particularly those who already had content in their inventories—while Microsoft had to acquire previously published print material for its multimedia content, such companies as Time Warner and Random House had warehouses of content just waiting to be converted to an electronic format. They also had experience in publishing and marketing for the consumer market—crucial experience that Microsoft lacked.

But Corddry believed that Microsoft was entering the multimedia market with so much more working capital and technological expertise than its competitors that those advantages alone made his company all but indomitable in the early going. Nearly all of Microsoft's putative competitors knew nothing about software and were heavily leveraged, their revenues being funneled into heavy debt service. "It's a great time to be Microsoft," he said. "Technology is a tremendous gating factor. The tools are lousy, and we do a lot of custom code-writing." None of their potential competitors had software developers of skill or numbers equal to Microsoft's. "They know nothing about software," Corddry continued. "And if they were to hire somebody, they'd have no idea whether they hired a good one or a bad one for years."

Corddry also believed that his company would be the sole competitor with money to burn. "These content companies," he said of Microsoft's most threatening competitors, "are all leveraged to the hilt. Time Warner is hosed for years. News Corporation, with $8 billion in revenues, has no money. And in the publishing business, the margins are very thin. They sell books by an old creaky system and there's no money left. So a company as big as us in sales might only be an eighth as big as us in profit, and that profit goes away to pay debt service. So when we say it costs $1 million or $1.5 million to do a title right now—which is way more than it should—we just wince because it's inefficient. But we could build a thousand of them. Random House couldn't build one. They couldn't spend that much money right now."

For weeks now, Corddry had been sitting in his office staring thoughtfully at a whiteboard on which he continually refined notes for his Bill meeting. He saw three stages coming in the multimedia marketplace, with the market just then entering stage one, during which Microsoft would enjoy its biggest advantage. There would be very few competitors, and most titles produced would be of relatively poor quality. Everyone would be learning as they went along. Microsoft's strategy would be to publish the best title in whatever categories it chose to enter. "They won't necessarily be the ultimate title," Corddry said, "because we're not smart enough to do ultimate. We're going to learn a lot from our customers. But anything we pick, we want to do the best one." The list of competing titles would be small—somewhere between ten and one hundred—and the distribution channel would be narrow, consisting solely of software outlets.

If Corddry had his way, Microsoft's strategy during that period would be to establish itself as the world's best publisher of multimedia titles by making the most of its two temporary advantages. The key was to have more titles published than anyone else, and to own as many categories of title as possible. To that end, Multimedia Publishing needed "to go like hell. As fast as we can. You give us twice as much money, we say thank you and spend it and say, 'Can we have some more?' "

The more Microsoft invested in this stage, and the more titles it produced, the more prepared it would be for multimedia's second stage, when "the market eventually gets big enough to attract content companies. The technology barriers are going to inch down, if for no other reason than that there will be better tools. About a year from now, people who are not programmers will be able to do credible titles." Corddry expected then to see a rush of titles, as had happened in the music industry in 1990 when compact discs completely displaced long-playing records. For years previous to that, the CD had been a fringe product, until enough people finally bought CD players for the machines to reach what Corddry called critical mass. Suddenly, every record company in the world began converting all of its record content to CD format. "In the music business," Corddry said, "they called it 'software overhang.' This huge backlist came roaring in. It all happened at once—one day everything came over to CD. There was a time two years ago when the best-selling charts were totally dominated by old material. The Beatles were number one again one day, you know, *Abbey Road* was number one." The same thing, he said, happened with video rentals. "For awhile, *Casablanca* was the best-seller again, because everybody wanted to see it."

That phase would be critical for Microsoft, because by then it would have lost the technological advantage it currently enjoyed and would be at a new disadvantage. "The market will go from five hundred titles to five thousand," Corddry said, "with a lot of them being sort of middling, ported over from other formats according to formulas and templates. That will be a tough time for us, because we don't own content—we won't be able to compete on volume of titles." While the company would have to do enough titles to ensure that it was a big enough player in multimedia to compete for retail shelf space, it also would have to compete on quality rather than quantity. Corddry wanted his division to build "a highway across the flood" of titles—to select a few categories and concentrate on being the best in each one.

This phase in multimedia would be short-lived, as it had been in music and video. After that would come Microsoft's greatest challenge. "Phase three will be dominated by new creative work," Corddry said. "It'll be like books and movies and music, where you get that hit-and-star system in place. The revenue will come from the top of the charts—new material from major artists." For Microsoft, that would mean converting to a business like that of the current movie and book businesses: one that is "very relationship-driven, very talent- and agent-driven. And so we look down the road there and say, 'Gee, one of these days we're going to have to be a lot better than we are now in dealing with a lot of people who don't necessarily have IQs of 160, who haven't been incredibly analytical their whole lives, and we're going to have to have them working here, internally on products. And we're going to have to have special relationships with them as independent people. We're going to have to deal with monstrously successful people on the outside.' "

As things stood now, Microsoft dealt exclusively from a position of overwhelming strength. The dominant company in its industry, it more or less had had everything its own way from the beginning. But now it would be entering unfamiliar territory, dealing with unfamiliar people who played by unfamiliar, if not indecipherable, rules. "The money will be in products done by people who are the equivalent in this medium at that time of say a Paul Simon or Steven Spielberg," said Corddry. "It can't be a major cultural issue when they have dinner with an executive from Microsoft. It's going to take a cultural shift here, an internal appreciation of what the value of it is. That means Microsoft's current culture has some work to do. We have to change the value structure of this company."

Under Microsoft's present value structure, the sole measure of a person's worth was his or her ability to think analytically. A worthwhile person at Microsoft was analytical or technical. A person of little worth, a person not to be taken seriously, was "random." To be anything other than analytical—to be instinctive, emotional, or what is generally called "creative"—was to be random.

Corddry, who had come up through the recording, alternative-radio, and advertising industries on his way to Microsoft, was a creative person caught in an analytical culture. "There are days when I come in here," he says, "and go, 'God, what am I doing?' " Coworkers and employees viewed him as a weird and unpredictable figure, as apt to come up with things at meetings that made no sense as he was to give a straightforward answer to a subordinate's question. On more than one occasion, he had been known to jut out his jaw and say defiantly to a critic, "I think 'random' is good sometimes!"

Everything about Corddry seemed to set him apart at Microsoft. At forty-five, he was one of the oldest people in the company. With a bald pate, he wore a corona of hair and a full beard, the whole looking like a sculpture balanced precariously on his ears. Surrounded by young, earnest, aggressively analytical people who walked around all day long with grim and purposeful expressions on their faces, he stood out not only because of his age but because of his demeanor. Try as he might to look serious, Corddry could never quite eradicate the mischievous glint in his eye—a glint magnified by his Professor Peabody-ish spectacles—or the impression that he was about to burst out laughing. He also had an irrepressible urge to utter wisecracks, which he indulged even at the most serious meetings. In a company where analysis and reason were the only acceptable modes of discourse, his mode was laughter.

Thus it was that the documents, or slides, that he prepared for his Bill meeting were full of odd details, long on vision and short on data. The set began with the caption, "A strategy for World Domination"—the lower-case *s* an apparently accidental note of self-deprecation—and a picture of a man's hands holding a globe atop which sat a pot of gold coins. Intended to accompany his verbal presentation to Gates, these slides laid out graphically Corddry's envisioned three stages of multimedia market development. Throughout, the analytical material was decorated with just enough illustration and odd vocabulary to make the reader think it was a sly parody of the generic corporate presentation. One chart was decorated with the silhouette of a ballet dancer; others tracked the relative progress of "shovelware," "silverware," and "flatware" through the coming phases of multimedia marketing; yet another, on "platform categories," listed four: "very engaging," "very mobile," "very productive," and "very connected." With each came an illustration: a teddy bear, a paper airplane, a cement truck, and two sumo wrestlers.

Corddry was putting his finishing touches on the slides when e-mail from Gates came down, passing judgment on the presentation to him of a planned title called "Play It by Ear." "This project sure seems random to me," Gates's mail began. "It doesn't seem to be something that we can do uniquely or that we will have a long term asset in doing." Gates went on to reiterate the importance of the economic issues he wanted addressed in order to persuade him that there was definable dollar value in getting seriously into multimedia. Then he closed with, "A game product like this just reinforces my belief that there isn't enough business thinking. I know this is the focus of our upcoming meeting but I wanted to share my concern a little bit more in advance. I want to invest but I want to invest where we will win in the long run—not just to create a market or to do cool things."

Corddry, taking the letter to heart, threw out his slides and started over.

Addressing the Chair

On the morning of February 8, Corddry and his juniors convened at 7:00 A.M. to go over their presentation to Gates. Two hours later, they emerged, each scurrying away to make final adjustments in his or her part of the program. Corddry, who was to do most of the talking, disappeared into his office, closed his door, and set to work.

A few minutes before ten, Multimedia managers began walking over to Building 8, and through the maze there to Gates's office-and-boardroom suite. On the way, Craig Bartholomew, noting that "seating is crucial," explained the importance of choosing one's chair at the boardroom table according to how much of Gates's attention you wanted either to attract or avoid. Those hoping for invisibility always sit immediately to the right of the center chair on the side of the table nearest the door. Gates generally takes that center chair, then directs his attention leftward throughout the meeting. So those hoping to hold the bulk of his attention sit either directly opposite Gates's chair or in the closest possible seats to the right of the chair opposite—across from Gates and to his left.

When he first started attending Bill meetings, Bartholomew made the mistake once of sitting in what turned out to be the seat directly to the right of Gates, while everyone else sat to the chairman's left. Afterward, he recalled, "Everyone's perception was that Bill was giving me the cold shoulder."

Bartholomew's story trailed off at this point, as he discovered that he had taken a wrong turn somewhere and was lost. Microsoft buildings are built according to an interlocking diamond design in order to provide as many people as possible with offices that have windows to the outdoors, and people constantly are getting lost in the hallways as a result. Even so, Bartholomew got back on track soon enough to be first to arrive at the boardroom, where he immediately took the choice chair. The chairs to his right were the next to be taken as others filed into the room, conferring in hushed tones before sitting down. Next were the seats opposite Bartholomew, on what was expected to be Gates's left. There followed a great deal of whispering, nervous laughter, soft-spoken wisecracks, and questions about where Corddry could possibly be.

One wall of the boardroom is made mostly of glass that affords a view of the hall leading to Gates's office. Just as people began to relax a little and allow themselves to speak at normal volume, Gates appeared in the window, walking quickly toward the boardroom door, his head slightly bowed. Instantly, the room fell silent. Then the chairman walked in and sat in the chair at the head of the table, throwing everyone into momentary panic.

The disorientation brought on by Gates's choice of a different seat immediately gave way to confusion over Corddry's unexplained absence. Since he had scripted the meeting, would be leading the presentation, and was bringing the slides, the meeting could not begin without him. And since this presentation was more or less a life-or-death proposition for his division, he might be expected to arrive on time. "When he was last seen, where was he?" someone whispered. Susan Boeschen, in a voice apparently intended to be audible to everyone but Gates, asked, "Does anyone know his number?"

Boeschen, who has long been one of Gates's most ardent defenders against charges of callousness and cruelty, and who describes him as "really a sensitive person, and a pleasure to work with," looked completely undone by Corddry's transgression. She fidgeted in her seat, looking now anxiously toward Gates, now around the room for someone who might find a way to get the meeting started. She got up and walked quietly over to a telephone in the corner and called Corddry's office. There was no answer. "He's not there," she said softly, to no one in particular. She went back to her chair and timidly suggested that perhaps there were some matters they could cover before Corddry's arrival. Gates, who was reading, looked up and said that he'd rather wait.

Although I had attended meetings before at which Gates exploded in anger, I was mystified now at the palpable nervousness in the room. Gates's guests were terrified. Yet his tantrums had always struck me as a kind of act, a contrivance. His is an odd sort of rage that explodes and subsides instantly, as if it were turned on and off by a toggle switch. When not expostulating, Gates sits stock-still in his chair, his gaze directed at the edge of the table in front of him, his mind wholly concentrated on what he is being told. His displays of wrath always seem more Socratic than Hitlerian, designed not to intimidate or insult, but to elicit more thorough thought. It is not uncommon, toward the end of a scream-punctuated meeting, for him to say calmly, "Okay . . . go ahead," as if his tantrum had never taken place.

It is no less uncommon for him to walk away from such a meeting filled with admiration for his victims. "Those were smart guys," he told me once after a meeting that had consisted largely of his shouting. "I really questioned the approach they were taking, but actually, it turns out that there were some good ideas in that thing, and some problems I had with it that they had actually thought through." He had been hard on them, he said, "because it's super important—I mean, we're going to make a big decision there. And they were trying to take a shortcut, basically, and were a little vague."

Gates's histrionics, however nerve-racking, provoke more admiration than fear in his employees, who constantly profess amazement at the depth of his technical knowledge and the breadth of his vision. "He has this laserlike ability to hone in on the absolute right question to ask," says Brad Silverberg, vice president of Microsoft's Personal Systems Group. "You may think you have everything totally prepared, and the one area you weren't quite sure about, somehow he just finds it right away, and asks you the one right question. He'll know some intricate low-level detail about a program, and you wonder, 'How does he know that? He has no reason ever to get to that level!' Some piece of code, or some other technology that Microsoft isn't even involved in. You just shake your head."

Technically adept as he is reputed to be, Gates is no less adept at keeping his eye on the bottom line, and those appearing before him must make irrefutable business cases for their projects. "How much of a mission should we be on with this thing?" he asked a subordinate one day. "Do we view this as an industry initiative? How is it helpful for Microsoft to have done this? Is it gonna help Windows sell better than something? Is it just good for the use of computers? It's one of these projects like so many now where I think our business thinking on why it's helpful to do the thing is actually kind of weak."

Gates's ability to leap agilely from the technical details of any given project to its business case and back again is most often cited as the attribute setting him apart from everyone else in his industry. His intelligence and drive have led people to compare him with John D. Rockefeller, Henry Ford, Thomas Edison, David, Goliath, Hitler, Darth Vader, Warren Buffett, and, as one ecstatic Microsoft worker puts it, "General Groves and Oppenheimer in the same person!"

Gates's competitors described him constantly to journalists and federal investigators as a titan determined to drive them all out of business. Rivals depicted him as a monomaniacal figure fixated solely on gaining more power and wealth at their expense. His most outspoken and oft-quoted opponent, Phillipe Kahn of Borland International, frequently referred to him as "Citizen Gates," and accused him of wanting to take over "not just the software industry, but the whole world."

At thirty-seven, Gates still looks vaguely boyish, like an aging Dennis the Menace. He is freckled, with wide, lively eyes and thickish lips that contort themselves into impossible shapes whenever he grows animated. He wears large glasses that persistently slide down his nose. When not moving forward, he is in constant nervous motion; when walking, he moves with an almost aristocratic leisure and grace. The middle-aged dignity imparted by the softening and thickening of the flesh on his neck and under his chin clash constantly with his youthful face, the high-schoolish costume (slacks, long-sleeved shirts, sweaters or sweatshirts) that he wears everywhere, every day, and with his incessant slang: "scary," "cool," "superneat," "hardcore," "jeez."

Gates has a maddening habit of rocking constantly. When confined to a chair, he sits leaning forward, elbows on thighs, arms crossed, rocking back and forth insistently and with unvarying rhythm, his feet beating out an exacting, metronomic Tap! . . . Tap! . . . Tap! . . . Occasionally, certain questions or topics so engage him that he will stop suddenly and sit perfectly still, his head turned slightly to one side, listening with feral alertness. In his boardroom, sitting in a high-backed chair that rocked, Gates and his rocking chair would keep working their way wackily out of synch, and he would have to stop from time to time to get realigned. Stop him while he is walking somewhere and he will stand, arms crossed, one foot in front of the other, rocking like someone trying patiently and with minimal effort to get his trailing foot unstuck.

Even so, he is not the nerd he is reputed to be. He often has a relaxed and friendly air, and habitually breaks into smiles or soft laughter.

Friends and associates describe him as a decent athlete. He is an avid water-skier and swimmer, and an occasional basketball player. He speaks deliberately rather than in the rapid-fire computerspeak of many of his employees, and his conversations cover an astonishing range of topics, bouncing from the fiction of John Knowles to Japanese business practices to the ups and downs of the American tire industry. Trying one day to find an apt comparison between writing computer programs and other forms of intellectual and business activity, he drew and partially rejected analogies with engineering, architecture, pharmaceutical research, theoretical science, and art. "And so there's so many thousands of judgments a person's applying," he concluded, "and they have an aesthetic about how much they care about their program being good. So there's this element of art. But there is in the end a test of 'Does it work, is it fast, is it small, does it get it done?' And so, like scientific theories, even the most elegant one is not too exciting if what it predicts is not real. . . . A good scientist, a theoretical scientist, you know, you sit there for years and make no progress, and so you have to be driven in a certain way, it's a little bit like art with your own confidence maybe, that you'll do something worthwhile."

By dint first of his drive, then of his growing power, and now of those things combined with his immense wealth, Gates had arrived at what Tom Corddry liked to call "the center of one of the information centers of the universe. It just flows into him at a tremendous rate, from all directions. If information were some kind of tribute, he'd be Kubla Khan." This is due not only to his powerful position as chairman of the world's leading software company, but also to a less measurable but no less noticeable personal power. People are drawn to Gates, who is blessed with a certain quirky charm. "For a guy who's allegedly a brainy nerd," Corddry said one day, "Bill is extremely charismatic. He can really make you want to please him. That's one of the reasons the company works. And when he's not happy, it usually seems like disappointment, like he thought that maybe you understood along with him a direction towards a vision, a grand architecture of some kind, then you came back to him with something flawed."

Apparently unconcerned with Corddry's tardiness, Gates began talking with those at his end of the table about recent talks with Disney. The entertainment conglomerate had approached Microsoft about doing joint multimedia projects, and Microsoft outlined an ambitious plan, involving every conceivable platform, in which the software company would invest some $10 million. Disney, apparently unnerved by the scope of Microsoft's proposal, backed off to concentrate on licensing its content and characters for video-game development and to consider developing other software on its own. "People were saying to them," Gates was saying now, " 'Microsoft! Oh, my God! You're working with the Devil!' " Those listening to him laughed heartily, and Gates continued: "People were saying, 'They're always doing deals that totally favor them and just screw the other guys. You just should think twice before you give all that stuff away.' So now they think it's their mandate to just do it in-house."

After Susan Boeschen and Peter Mollman weighed in with their impressions, Gates said, a little more heatedly, "One thing that pisses me off a little bit is the notion that there is this understanding that we are just PC people, and these other platforms are separate." In all of its dealings with multimedia partners—particularly content companies—Microsoft had aggressively gone after publishing rights not only for personal-computer products but for all other electronic platforms, even those not yet invented. Some companies, Disney among them, had reacted less than enthusiastically to the gambit. "But *we* introduced this notion," Gates was saying, "this . . . come on, nobody . . . the word PC doesn't mean anything! Other platforms are vague, the notion that you duplicate all your work"—here he was referring to doing titles twice, once for the PC and once for the Macintosh—"you know, one group doing PC stuff, somebody else doing that other stuff, that's completely absurd! So from the beginning we wanted to go after anything that moves, basically." His listeners burst out laughing again.

Conversation drifted for a few more minutes on the vagaries of the publishing business and the kinds of risks Microsoft was undertaking in entering it. Worrying out loud, Gates went over some questions he had been posing to Corddry for the past several months. He was leery of short-term contracts with publishers, as he was convinced they would find a way to keep future long-term multimedia profits to themselves once they learned from Microsoft how to produce CD-ROM titles. Dorling Kindersley, Gates noted, was so determined to learn how to publish on electronic platforms that already it was as much a competitor as a partner. DK had software developers of its own and was developing the capacity to digitize its content even as Microsoft was publishing DK books on CD-ROM, and Gates worried constantly that his partners were playing Microsoft for a sucker. He wanted to lock up rights to the digital-format reproduction of a given publisher's printed content for as long as possible so as to keep content partners from learning how to do software, jettisoning Microsoft, and turning into competitors. "If you do deals where the content guy owns you," he said, "I just don't see where you can make money. The content guy always gets to do whatever he wants in the long run."

Gates also worried that the personal computer was simply a primitive forerunner of some future, as yet undiscovered, mass-multimedia platform where the real publishing money was waiting to be made. The last thing he wanted was to lose money proving the viability of multimedia on the personal computer only to have someone else rake in the profit on a future, more popular machine. "If you do deals where you just do the content on a finite number of platforms," he said, "you'll really . . . for the content guy, it's a windfall. If you prove out the title and the concept on a few platforms, and you don't get to do the big platforms, then you're just totally creating a windfall for the guy who owns that content. We could find ourselves in that position on a lot of these things."

Suddenly Corddry came charging into the room, out of breath, and began distributing his slides and accompanying financial projections. His attempt at an apology, lost amid his gasps and wheezes, brought a tiny grin to Gates's face. Once the material was distributed, Corddry sat down in the chair to Gates's right. "I don't know if I got all the questions that are around on this issue," he began. "Hopefully we got most of them down. What we want to try to do is argue that this is a business we should be in for a long time. Looking at it, we tried to measure the long-term revenue margin potential, strategy . . . The main vulnerability is that we don't own a lot of content, but we think that's a manageable problem, and we have a strategy for how to deal with it."

Corddry saw the multimedia market as one that would grow from 2.6 million households in 1994 to 22.1 million in 1999. By 1998, he predicted, all personal computers shipped to homes would be multimedia-capable, and virtually all software would be multimedia software. The multimedia machine with a CD-ROM drive would be so common that there no longer would be any need to distinguish one set of Microsoft products as "multimedia." According to his plans for dominating that market, Microsoft, which then had two multimedia titles (*Bookshelf*, *Cinemania*) on the market, would have 42 by 1995 and 141 by 1999. It would be the biggest and best multimedia publisher in the world, having been first into the arena with a broad selection of titles. Corddry expected

Microsoft to reach $200 million or more in sales by 1998. "If we can't do that," he said to Gates, "you should question whether we should be in this business."

Gates interrupted. "This $200 million," he said, "if that's really a rosy scenario, people in the company at large shouldn't think of this as the engine of growth." He laughed. "We'll need something else. To be the engine of growth for the company, it has to be more in the $500 million range."

There followed a discussion of publishing companies that had managed revenues in the $200 million range or above, with 15 to 20 percent after-tax profits—the profit level Microsoft regarded as minimal. Peter Mollman, taking the baton from Corddry, listed three: Random House Juvenile, "which," he said, "really carries the whole Random House line"; Rodale Press, a "major force in the health world now," a "$400 million company" that did nearly all of its business by direct mail; and Prentice-Hall College, a textbook publisher with a solid 20 percent to 25 percent share of its market. Gates interrupted constantly with questions: "Do they pay royalties?" "What kind of share do you think they have?" "Who's the next biggest?" "Does something ever die, or do you keep it on the backlist?"

Mollman's intent was to argue that Microsoft could duplicate these feats in multimedia by imitating these publishers' methods in "staying close to their market" and assiduously cultivating relationships either directly with customers, as Rodale did, or with retailers, as did Random House, which tended to outmaneuver its competition in the battle for more—and more visible—shelf space.

But Gates felt that these companies, whatever their merits, had an advantage Microsoft could never have. "Random House," he interrupted at one point, "what's their sustained competitive advantage? What's their advantage? It isn't because people who buy kids' books look on that spine and say, 'Ooooh, it's a *Random House!*' They own titles!"

From there, the meeting fell into a pattern, with Corddry, Mollman, and Jabe Blumenthal alternately advancing arguments in crisp, high-speed monotone and Gates interrupting with questions either about their thinking, about the conventions of publishing, or about details of their current contracts with print publishers. Each interruption brought an instant tightening of nerves in the room, as if the sound of Gates's voice brought with it the expectation that he was about to start shouting. But each time, his interlocutors had a ready answer—or, at least, the promise that an answer was coming later in the presentation—and Gates was quieted.

Mollman described the present as a rapidly closing window of opportunity for Microsoft. Content companies were interested in multimedia but incapable of producing it themselves, so they were pursuing partnerships with Microsoft, which was widely perceived as the only company currently capable of producing decent multimedia content in a timely fashion. He told Gates that Microsoft was being approached by nearly everyone in the print world. "The keenness and awareness and heatedupness toward getting into this business has just shot up," he said. "People know that the multimedia publishing world is really going to be it. They do not want to be left out. And we have done an awesome job of showing what really can be done. We have knocked people's socks off. We get five or six calls a week from people who want to talk."

Mollman insisted that Microsoft had no choice but to exploit this early advantage. "We need to make key moves now," he said, "or we could be affected by shutting off our blood supply three or four years down the road. That's the big danger—the inability to have that content, that blood flowing through us three or four or five years down the line." By signing up as many publishers as possible now, for as long as possible, the company could both eliminate its sole current disadvantage vis-à-vis media companies and gain an advantage over potential future competition from companies with more software expertise than content.

Microsoft could pull off this latter feat, Mollman believed, by packing new titles with effects and user-interface features that would be so expensive and difficult for others to equal that they would be discouraged from getting into the market at all. It was simply a matter of making high-quality, high-performing titles at the outset. "The stuff that we're doing," he said, "the quality of it, the technical superiority, that fact that it's already out there, gives us a phenomenal advantage."

"You know," Gates interjected, "you basically have to convince the other guys not to spend enough money to compete with us, to just keep making it harder and harder, move the terms up, budgeting, promotion, and quality, we just keep raising"—here he burst out laughing—"the bar, and eventually maybe one of them will try to do stuff with us. But a lot of them will just say, 'Forget it.'"

The more titles Microsoft did earlier, Mollman resumed, the more likely Microsoft was to produce better work than competitors who already owned content. And by being positioned early as the best publisher of multimedia materials, the company would be all the more attractive when multimedia reached its third stage—when Microsoft would have to begin dealing directly with creative talent. "Eventually," he concluded, "we'll be able to deal directly with creators and their agents."

That notion appealed to Gates. "The least greed is down at that author level," he said. "Whatever amount of money is involved, he's going to be more reasonable than publishers."

"That's why Michael Ovitz is worth talking to now," Corddry interjected, referring to Hollywood's most powerful agent, "even though he's driving up the food budget."

Before buying off on their strategy, Gates grilled Mollman and Corddry on the kinds of platforms they were reserving for Microsoft's exclusive use. When Mollman suggested that it was best to concentrate on the personal computer first, then gradually broach the idea that Microsoft wanted all future digital electronic platforms, Gates reacted as if Mollman were negotiating on behalf of an unscrupulous adversary. "It's just completely unfair to have somebody say you have limited platforms!" he shouted. "That is *just not fair!* Because you can clearly create the image of what the product can be and come up with the design and popularize it and it's totally a windfall for them to be able to go tuck in on those other platforms! The only way we should share platforms is if we fail to exploit our platform, they should be able to go on and give it to someone else. But we . . . the default position is that it should be broad platforms! But if we can't get that, screw 'em! I mean, it's just *not fair!*"

After Corddry and Mollman eased his concerns, Gates began ruminating aloud on his fears of dealing with publishers. Although Microsoft had made its fortune largely by dint of extremely advantageous contracts with some of the computing industry's most powerful and experienced companies, Gates was fearful of his potential new partners. "I just don't think we know this territory very well," he lamented. "I do worry that we don't put enough IQ time into really thinking about these business relationships. I just worry that we're like babes in the woods."

He was primarily concerned that Microsoft not inadvertently give away technical secrets to publishing companies like Dorling Kindersley, who then could turn around and drive Microsoft out of the business. In order to prolong his company's advantage past the days when multimedia publishing tools would become widely available, he wanted Corddry and his division to be particularly protective of technical achievements and user-interface designs. "Let's say we're making a lot of money at this," he said. "And we've already proven that what we need to make to stay in this market publishers *will* define as *a lot of money*." He was interrupted by laughter. "If their print business is starting to suffer because of us, then we're putting them in an awkward position." Gates was terrified that Microsoft would invest heavily in early conceptual work in multimedia, only to see content licensors turn around and clone it just when it came time for Microsoft to reap the profits of its innovations. "If they start doing electronic versions of their own titles," he concluded, "we would be extreme bastards about them doing anything that looked like our user interface."

As Corddry outlined his vision of multimedia's future, Gates interrupted less often, and then generally to register approval. He endorsed virtually every type of title Corddry and Mollman brought up for consideration, saying, "I'll entertain some pretty wild things," as long as the contract details were favorable enough. He gave particularly strong endorsement to "*Encarta*-type titles," which he regarded as having the greatest immediate revenue potential and the greatest potential for establishing Microsoft as the preeminent publisher of multimedia.

The meeting now was well into its second hour, and Gates's petitioners were beginning to relax. There was a dawning sense in the room that they were scoring a remarkable triumph. But then Gates's mood changed abruptly. "Before we get to headcount," he said, his voice rising, "one thing I'm disappointed in not seeing in here is the leverage of user interface and common content elements across the entire product line." It was as if he had suddenly sucked the air out of the room. "I mean, I swear, I want the way you navigate maps, the way you navigate time lines, the way you get the definition of a word in a dictionary—if we stick the dictionary in all our titles—you're just way way way weaker on leveraging UI common elements in here than I expected you to be! And you know, it really makes me wonder about your organizational structure, whether you're ever going to do those things right!"

There followed a flurry of soft-spoken objection, with Bartholomew saying that they were working on those things, trying to improve them title by title, and Susan Boeschen saying that they were reserving their presentation on that topic for a February 23 meeting at which they would be presenting specific titles to him. Gates answered that this was of critical importance in helping fend off future competition. If all Microsoft multimedia titles—particularly reference titles—had similar design and behavior, then the Microsoft look and feel would come to define the norm in the industry. It would be one more part of the package helping beat competition. "We have common UI," Gates said, "it puts other people at a substantial competitive disadvantage. And so far, you are only paying lip service to it."

The meeting wound down. Gates approved Corddry's request for increased headcount and endorsed Corddry's strategic vision. "But understand," he said by way of closure, "there is no way I would agree to anything like this if we hadn't had this business framework discussion. We have to be businessmen *every day*. And you said the right things on all that stuff, which makes me pretty interested in being aggressive." Then, in a surprising break with his own tradition, he said, "You don't have to have a meeting with me on every title. If the model is right, you can just e-mail me. Eighty percent of that you don't need to meet with me on." Lest his audience lapse into complacency, though, he finished with a warning: "But if our performance is like it was on *Encarta*, then we'll have to rethink whether we'll even be in this business."

Bartholomew, who looked both sick and stoic, answered in a barely audible voice, "It won't—it won't happen again."

After that, the meeting broke up with Gates saying, on his way out, "Yeah—it was good." He left in his wake an elated group. For all of the questions he had raised, he had been, by his standards, indulgent. None of his concerns had gone unaddressed, and he had given virtually a blanket endorsement to Corddry and his vision. Moreover, Mike Maples had sat silently through the meeting, not once raising an objection. The group had done better than anyone expected. "I'll go into a meeting with him," said an ecstatic Boeschen afterwards, "thinking, 'I can't do this any more,' then I'll come out an hour later saying, 'Yeah! That's it!' It's real motivational."

The sole glum face on the way out of the meeting belonged to Bartholomew, who was smarting from Gates's parting shot at *Encarta*. Corddry, by way of both consoling and warning Bartholomew, took him aside and said, "Bill is very, very happy with the quality of work you've done on *Encarta*. He's just worried that when this business gets very competitive, competitors will get a jump on us because of our slipped schedules." Bartholomew conceded the point, but walked away muttering to me, "I guarantee you that I'll hear about this from Jabe later. He has a tendency to bring this kind of thing up in a passing shot, in meetings when Tom and Susan are there."

Less than an hour later, Susan Boeschen's postmortem came through to group members on e-mail. "CONGRATULATIONS!!!!" she wrote. "That was an amazing meeting. . . . That is one of the clearest endorsements of strategy I've ever seen coming from Bill. . . . Wow! We have a ton of work to deliver on that strategy but for now we can bask in today's success."

While regarding Gates's endorsement as a victory, Corddry was more philosophical than triumphant. "Bill had been counting on Multimedia Publications to be a growth engine," he said, "an accelerator. So that $200 million figure for 1996 was kind of a disappointment." Sales for Microsoft *Word* alone, he noted, had been $750 million in 1992. "So in light of Bill's expectations, ours was kind of a low number."

It was particularly low in light of Corddry's ambitions for Microsoft. "The PC industry now is a $10 billion business—about the size of the movie industry's ticket sales and video rentals," he said. "That's only one-tenth of the print information business, a $100-billion industry. Microsoft needs to move into that bigger pond."

While gratified that Maples had backed off in his attacks on Multimedia, Corddry did not regard it as a personal victory. "The value of Maples to Bill is to come in here, cap off his career, get immensely wealthy, and pass on his ability to manage large organizations to Bill's boys," he said. "And I need to go to him now and say, 'Now that we're going to do this, can I get some bandwidth with you, some process with you, and talk about how we can go about doing this right?' We want to run this like a business, keep our margins up—and he can help us do that."

Out from Under
the Shadow of February 23

Late one worknight, Carolyn Bjerke was driving home from a Microsoft league volleyball game when *Sendak* began to unravel in her mind. The more she measured the scale of the project against the tight schedule forced upon her team, the more she feared it was impossible.

She could see already on *Sendak* the beginnings of what she had been through on *Encarta*. She and Bryan Ballinger were designing according to their wishes and tastes alone, without proper regard for the constraints of schedule and technology. They had fallen into the dreamy habit of relying on Kevin Gammill's exceptional skills to find a way to implement whatever they wanted.

Yet Bjerke knew that the means for delivering many of the features planned for *Sendak* were not yet developed. Just as the *Encarta* team had been disappointed in Viewer 1.0, which was being developed as they worked, the *Sendak* team was setting itself up for disappointment in the new multimedia tools group. Realistically, Bjerke admitted to herself, she could hardly expect the new tools team to do any better than the Viewer team had. Yet here she and her teammates were again, pretending there were no limitations. It was as if they had learned nothing from the *Encarta* experience.

Bjerke had no choice but to look for ways to simplify *Sendak*'s production. In her panic to be practical, she decided to try to replace its navigation-by-spaceship metaphor with something less difficult to produce.

At Microsoft, demanding issues or expensive elements often are called hits. A design idea that entails heavy editorial work is an editorial hit, an idea difficult for developers to implement is a development hit, something that takes up huge amounts of disc space is a disc space hit, an expensive feature is a budget hit, and so on. To Bjerke, the spaceship metaphor was a huge "production hit." This visual metaphor for exploration would tax artists, designers, and developers far out of proportion to its thematic benefit. It would require the drawing of a base outside the ship (a sort of dock or launching pad where the user would pick his or her guide from among a group of representatives from various races and both genders); the drawing of a ship's interior, with a window out onto *Sendak*'s four-unit universe; and the production of a whole set of large sprites—animations of the guide leaving the ship for a given scene and of the ship coming back to retrieve the guide and take him or her to a new scene. Bjerke decided to replace the spaceship and its station with some sort of home base, like a kid's bedroom. Then there could be a magical means of moving from one scene to another. Not being visible, the way the ship-to-scene transitions were, the magic mode would save her artists months of work.

This was not a particularly easy decision to make. The spaceship was among Ballinger's most treasured *Sendak* features. So it was with some trepidation that Bjerke went into the next morning's design meeting with Ballinger and Lindsey Smith, the contractor who was to be in charge of *Sendak*'s art production. Bjerke waited twenty minutes before she abruptly cut short a discussion on backpack tools and said, haltingly, "Here's a conceptual question"—she interrupted herself with a brief, guilty giggle—"now, don't have a cow, Bryan . . . but what if there was no ship? What exactly is the ship buying us?"

Whatever the circumstances surrounding him, Ballinger's face was devoid of expression. At most meetings, he would sit slumped down deep in his chair, with his feet wedged against the edge of a table. His lower lip jutting out, apparently oblivious to everyone else in the room, he would draw complicated patterns on his sneakers with a black pen. Now, when Bjerke mentioned abandoning *Sendak*'s ship, a glimmer of shock flashed across his face. But he said nothing, and his drawing—an intricate spider web pattern, already extending from the toe of one shoe to its throat—kept up its steady pace.

"The schedule and the amount of artwork is what prompted me to ask this question," Bjerke said. "There have to be less cumbersome alternatives to the ship. We settled on the ship early, but we need to ponder it more." Drawing on the whiteboard as she spoke, she suggested that a bedroom might be better, with pictures on a wall to represent the four units, and dolls on a shelf to represent the various guides. Clicking on any doll would bring it to life as a full-sized guide and clicking on the picture of a nature scene on the wall would instantly change the screen from the bedroom to a picture of the chosen guide standing in a forest. "The question now is, 'What can give us what the ship gives us without the cost?' " Bjerke said.

Had Bjerke not preceded her question with such a detailed answer, she might have been inundated with a brainstorm of proposed answers from Ballinger and Smith. But she had a habit of thinking grand designs through in solitude, then presenting all-but-finished ideas to her cohorts. On *Encarta*, where she had more or less been a lone designer working among marketers, developers, and editors, such an approach had been necessary. But with *Sendak*, Ballinger—largely because of Bjerke's encouragement—expected to be a collaborator rather than a subordinate. Now, he was too overwhelmed by Bjerke's apparent answer to her own question to posit any answers of his own.

He was less upset by Bjerke's new design than by her having formulated it without consulting him at all. He felt betrayed. He had struggled for nearly a year against his own shyness, finally reaching a point where he trusted Bjerke enough to brainstorm uninhibitedly with her. Now she appeared to have jettisoned an idea to which he was deeply attached without even asking for his opinion. Although neither of them realized it at the time, she had just committed a managerial transgression that would exact a heavy tax over the life of the project.

As if the issue were decided, Bjerke moved on to the next design problem: the look and behavior of the lookup tool—an alternative means of navigating through *Sendak* by searching for topics, particular words, or places previously visited. For the most part, Ballinger was silent while Bjerke and Smith talked almost constantly, throwing out idea after idea in the kind of exuberant free-form session Bjerke loved.

When the meeting ended, Ballinger darted off to his office without saying a word. Lingering behind to explain her decision, Bjerke said, "I started thinking about this because of our schedule problem. But I figure if an idea even gets into my brain, then there's a reason to finish exploring it. So if this ship-room thing snuck in somehow, there really is probably a reason why maybe it's not what I think it is." She argued that girls had not cared for the ship in usability testing, and that Craig Bartholomew wanted to jettison it for that reason alone. And although she thought, for some reason, that she had presented her question to Ballinger as if her mind were not yet made up, she suspected that her decision already was made. "I don't know what the answer to this question is," she said, "but I have sort of an emotional feeling that I'm ready—that the ship is history."

I was surprised at how little Bjerke seemed to care about Ballinger's reaction, or the possibility that he might grow so disenchanted with her that his work would slide. But she seemed to have no patience for wounded egos or artistic temperaments. She had dreaded bringing her decision up to him, as he generally resisted all suggestions from managers and supervisors for changes in his designs. "He tends to arrive at solutions that are attuned to what he loves to create," Bjerke said. "He brushes off information that runs counter to what he wants to do by saying that it's just another design opinion."

Sitting in his office, thumbing through a dog-eared copy of Vladimir Nabokov's novel *The Defense*, Ballinger complained less about the possibility of getting rid of his spaceship than about Bjerke having decided the issue without consulting him. He thought the two were codesigners of *Sendak* rather than that she was its designer and he a production artist working for her, as had been the case on *Encarta*. "This kind of shocked me a little," he said. "I had never heard that it was even being considered. It's probably a good idea to explore other ways to do this, but I mean, I should have been in on it from the beginning."

This was the first setback for Ballinger in what had been something of a meteoric rise. Only a few months before, he had been one among hundreds of young freelance artists cranking out pieces to order for Microsoft. It was rare for the company to hire artists as full-time employees rather than assign work to them as contractors. Lindsey Smith, for example, who was only a year younger than Ballinger and had been doing work for Microsoft for nearly as long as he had, worked as a contractor rather than an employee. So when Ballinger had been hired into Gandalf the previous May, it was like being promoted from an assembly line to a boardroom. He took to creation and coauthorship wholeheartedly, and expected to be treated by Bjerke and other employees as an equal. Now, in having a decision handed down to him, he felt arbitrarily demoted.

In the days that followed, Ballinger reacted childishly to Bjerke's treatment, thereby deepening their estrangement. His behavior at meetings changed noticeably. His habitual silence took on a sullen, almost aggressive air. Where before he would sit silently for long stretches, then burst out with an enthusiastic answer when asked for an opinion, he now refused to offer anything useful. He chose instead to sit glumly by while Smith began emerging as Bjerke's collaborator. On rare occasions when Ballinger spoke, he tended to utter gruesome jokes rather than proffer serious ideas: "The guide can descend into the ocean in a bathysphere, and it can explode when he goes down too deep"; "He can have a sling-shot tool, and shoot birds with it"; "We can have him pull the wings off flies, pour salt on slugs"; "You can use the magnifying glass to train sunlight on ants in the forest scene, then watch them catch fire." This line of humor was relieved only occasionally by sarcasm, as when he responded to Bjerke's idea that the guide comment on things in the scenes by suggesting that it offer "context-sensitive irrelevant factoids." More and more often, Bjerke would try drawing him out, asking him point-blank what he thought about an issue she and Smith had been discussing. Each time, he would say, "I don't know" and stare dully ahead.

Finally, after a meeting a few days later, Bjerke hauled Ballinger into her office and asked him what was wrong. "I had to do something," she said later, "because he was just so uptight about everything." Hesitantly, Ballinger told her that she was treating him unfairly by making decisions without his input, then pretending that issues were still open when in fact she had already made up her mind. "Once I go down a path trying to figure something out," she said, "he thinks it's already written in stone. I tried to straighten him out on that, make him understand that in order to sort of finish your train of logic out, you have to sort of follow a premise for awhile, make sure you flush out everything you can think of, then get to the right conclusion." In her mind, the problem was not that she was unfair to Ballinger, but that he grew too emotionally attached to his ideas and regarded any questioning of them as a personal attack.

Previously, Bjerke felt compelled to coddle Ballinger because his talents as an artist more than made up for his organizational failings. "Bryan is a little bit of a burden," she said, "but I've always wanted to support the notion that he's valuable, and that we do need people like him around." Lately, though, she had been less inclined to nurture and more inclined to goad. "He's a cranky guy. I have to keep an eye on him, rein him in every once in awhile. This was a pretty painful discussion. I had to make it very clear to him that he wasn't an equal with me in this product. He's *not* the designer. And I can't give final approval on his work because he hasn't shown good judgment yet on what is appropriate for everybody."

Bjerke felt the *Sendak* project beginning to slip through her fingers, to the point where she could no longer afford the luxury of indulging Ballinger. The more he sulked and resisted, she feared, the greater the danger that *Sendak* would miss its deadline. Missing *Encarta*'s deadline had cast such bad political light on the Gandalf product unit that it was impermissible even to acknowledge the possibility of *Sendak* slipping. In meetings, the deadline was referred to as "the only invariable number" in the *Sendak* product plan.

Bjerke felt just as imperiled by Kevin Gammill. Still tied up with *Encarta*, he either could not or would not provide answers to her questions about the feasibility of features she was designing. Instead, he consistently opted to answer in one of four ways: "I probably can't do it," "I have to think about it," "Save it for Version Two," or "No." Bjerke had yet to hear an unqualified yes from Gammill to any of her requests, and she was growing more and more skeptical about him. "Kevin's main drive right now is just to say no," she said. "He's very bruised from *Encarta*." While sympathetic, she also felt that Gammill was "going to an extreme. He's not willing enough to push the barriers. There are some things that he just can't say no to—he's got to find a solution." She was desperate for him to devote all of his attention to *Sendak*, as she could not complete her designs without definitive answers from him. "Anything he says now I don't consider as an answer until he's had time to think about it, which means when *Encarta* is out the door."

For his part, Gammill tended to roll his eyes and growl when confronted with a question. His responses constantly were framed by expressions of disgust and skepticism about the ability of designers to think realistically about development issues. "How many pop-ups are you planning to have?" he asked at one of the rare meetings he found time to attend. "Five thousand," came the answer. He snorted. "I'll write down ten thousand." Another time, he snapped, "We will not be able to support that!" Asked why, he paused, as if to underscore his conviction that designers are incapable of understanding the complexities of development. "Let's see," he said, his voice trailing off in showy despair, "how can I explain that to you?"

"He's just got this attitude," Bjerke said with resignation, "that designers are kind of wacky, and they're always coming up with things that just aren't doable, and it's the developer's job to say no to the designer.

And he is practicing that religion at the moment." She was prepared, if necessary, to enlist Bartholomew in an effort to bring Gammill into line. "We'll probably have to push him hard to get him to be a team player —that'll be up to Craig, I guess."

Gammill's assessment of his relationship with the rest of the team was more succinct. "I think once I have time to sit down with the prototype for about an hour and really put some thought into it," he said, "they'll be in for a shock."

Bjerke felt no less abandoned on the editorial front. In losing Sara Fox to maternity leave, she had lost her most important collaborator. Fox's coauthorship now was reduced to occasional panicky e-mail messages to Bjerke. Rather than being a help, the missives were a hindrance. Bjerke felt either that they were based on some misunderstanding on Fox's part or that they were overreactions caused by her belief that *Sendak* would die without her hands-on supervision. In either case, Bjerke had to waste time reading and responding to them. "She's brooding all the time," she said, "about how we might be doing something different from what she envisioned because she's not here."

For Fox's sake, Bjerke was trying to put off as many decisions as possible until her return at the end of March. But Bartholomew was pressuring her to move forward, and the more Fox heard about that, the more panicked she grew. For the next two months, Bjerke saw her job primarily as an exercise in keeping Bartholomew both from driving Fox crazy and from self-destructing. "Craig thinks we should have the pressure-cooker on all the time," she lamented. "I'm like, 'We should go home at five and have a life.' I think he'll snap, unfortunately. I tried to talk about this once with his wife, but all she said was, 'I have to live with him.' "

Fox, meanwhile, spent her days caring for her new baby, Henry, and restlessly pacing back and forth from the kitchen to the living room in her home across Lake Washington. "Craig, his whole thing is to get started, get started," she said one day. "I just think, let's do it right! So I don't think we can rush ahead. We should make a rough draft. I mean, Bryan's made final drafts of the Nature scene, he's so invested now in how it looks, and they want to make all the scenes that way. . . . We can't do it that way. . . . It's completely phenomenal. . . . They say we're doing things one way, but we don't. . . . I feel like we're going to make the *Encarta* mistake again, fixing things on the fly all the time." She was trying in particular to resist Bartholomew's orders to Bjerke to start hiring freelance writers and editors before Fox had finished designing the tone and style of *Sendak*'s writing. "You can't hire these people in advance," she said. "You have to know what you're asking for." She fretted about decisions Bjerke was making on her own. "My God!" she shouted one day, reading e-mail from Bjerke about a new design feature. "I can't believe this! I'm embarrassed to see this in a document . . . this is editorial . . . it's appalling, way too complicated. It's humiliating! The scary thing is that someone might think I had something to do with this!" Where she had hoped before that editorial decisions could be put off until her return, now she felt forced "to do my whole job while I'm on leave."

The more the team began to drift, the less it seemed that anyone capable of getting the project on a straight and narrow course was about to grab its controls. Most troublesome to Bjerke was *Sendak* program manager Jayleen Ryberg's approach to management. Ryberg had settled into a facilitating role, meshing the rest of the team members' schedules and keeping track of issues without offering opinions of her own. She had been careful to keep silent during the ongoing ship-versus-room discussion, rather than enforce a solution as Bjerke felt she should. Bjerke believed that Ryberg should be driving the team, holding it to deadlines, and forcing decisions by essentially rendering a verdict when members were at an impasse. "She should be telling me that I should be doing this, that, and the other thing," Bjerke said. "I ask her if she wants me to have something ready by a given meeting, and she'll say, 'That would be nice . . . if you could.' She should be saying, 'Yes! Do it!' "

Ryberg, though, reluctant by temperament to confront or drive people, may have been particularly reluctant to disagree with Bjerke, who had nearly four years' seniority over her and who had worked with their manager, Bartholomew, all four of those years. Moreover, Bjerke often unwittingly signaled tremendous anger when questioned. She began a meeting one day by describing a plan for having somewhere between two and seven levels of experience in *Sendak*. She hoped to broaden the encyclopedia's audience by programming *Sendak* to respond differently to users of different ages and reading levels. In particular, she wanted *Sendak* to reach down to reading-disabled kids by allowing users or their teachers or parents to set their *Sendak* machines to display information at varying degrees of complexity. At its highest level, *Sendak* would give users complicated clues, the solutions to which could be found by tracking down information in the printed text. At its lowest level—for pre-readers—nothing more would happen when a child clicked on a hot spot than for the creature in question to animate, and its name to appear on the screen while the computer said the name out loud. Click on the eagle, for example, and the eagle would fly in a circle while the word *Eagle* popped up and the computer said, "eagle."

"That's all that would happen?" a dubious Ryberg asked.

"Yes," Bjerke snapped. "*Eagle* would pop up, and it would say, 'eagle.' " Then she blushed flamboyantly, from her neck upwards.

Everyone else's reaction was immediate. It was as if Bjerke had started screaming at them. While Bjerke stared at Ryberg, the others at the meeting looked around in alarm. Ryberg stared fixedly at something hovering just above the table in the middle distance. A moment of fearful silence passed before the color in Bjerke's face began to fade. Then she moved on to the next item on the agenda and the meeting resumed—almost as if nothing had happened.

The variety and degree of pressures on Bjerke were considerable. In addition to being lead designer on *Sendak*, she was designing a new interface for *Encarta 2*, as Microsoft had not yet been able to find a suitable graphic designer to fill that position. She was also the designer for a new multimedia database, called Merismus, that was to be a massive, powerful, and ambitious catalog of all multimedia elements included in all Microsoft multimedia publications; she had taken on that assignment because Gandalf desperately needed Merismus and because she was the only designer at Microsoft who understood the complexities of the database and its uses.

Bartholomew particularly prized Bjerke because of what he called her "conceptual" abilities, and he generally put her in charge of design efforts involving cross-product features. So Bjerke was helping direct an effort throughout Microsoft's Consumer Division to make the company's products more accessible to the handicapped, and she was head of a committee that was trying to formulate identical set-up and installation screen design rules for all Microsoft children's products, so that they all would appear to be part of a "kids' family" of products, similar to one another and different from those manufactured elsewhere.

Each day, Bjerke started by consulting a To Do list, kept either on paper or on the whiteboard in her office, that typically contained anywhere from twenty-five to forty items like these: "Merismus meeting—

could create VFW [Video for Windows] list for scenes"; "Get Encarta tech spec (Cinemania from Kevin)"; "New code (class) list for Sendak."

Bjerke also felt burdened by the weight of Microsoft's historical record. No new product in company history had ever shipped on time, and *Sendak* was loaded with features never before attempted. Virtually everyone Bjerke knew from outside her product unit was betting on it to miss its deadline. The rest of the company looked upon Multimedia Publishing as a combination toy department and research-and-development laboratory, and its people were considered misfits. Suggestions that Multimedia's teams could begin shipping products reliably were usually greeted with laughter.

These pressures would wear anyone down; they were made all the worse for Bjerke by what Tom Corddry called the "motivational chips" on her shoulder. She was out to prove that Multimedia's designers and artists could cut it on traditional Microsoft terms. As a designer, she was acutely aware that Microsoft was a developer's culture, and she was determined to think as analytically, plan as carefully, and manage as intelligently as developers could. "Every time I meet with a developer from outside this group," she said one day, "they treat me just like they would treat any graphic designer off the street who doesn't have anything technical. It's one of those battles you fight one by one. You have to constantly prove that you're worth having here."

Bjerke was prone, then, to see danger lurking at every turn. But even without this predisposition to worry, there was one particularly maddening circumstance about which she could do nothing. The most important work on *Sendak* was being undertaken by developers outside of her group— one by the new core tools group, the other by a renegade Microsoft developer named Richard Hobbs. Since they were writing code for *Sendak*'s most important and most challenging work—the composition and display of its animations and the arrangement and display of its text—she was trying to design and schedule a product without knowing when, or even if, its most vital code would be written.

The years-long attempt at Microsoft to develop a core set of software engines and authoring tools for use in all manner of multimedia titles amounted to a quest for the Holy Grail. Gates had first put developers onto multimedia tools development in the mid-1980s, before the company formed its Multimedia division. Two sets of developers—one in the Windows development group, the other in the CD-ROM division—worked separately on this effort for several years before Microsoft formed Multimedia Publishing and Multimedia Systems, moving the tools developers from Windows and CD-ROM in together at Multimedia Systems. The designers and editors left behind in Multimedia Publishing forever resented Rob Glaser, the head of Systems, for taking these developers out of their group. Glaser, in turn, resented those in the publishing group for their attempts to keep developers for themselves, then for attempting to get his developers to work on tools for their titles specifically rather than on more ambitious and complex tools for all multimedia publishers.

Meanwhile, the merged tools development groups from Windows and CD-ROM feuded constantly among themselves. Each group felt that it already had come up with the best development approach, and the groups maneuvered against each other to win management's approval of their vision. Tensions between the two were heightened by Gates's increasing frustration with his company's inability to come up with anything workable. Rather than settle on a single common approach, as Gates had hoped, the developers split into two groups again, each working on its own vision. Finally Gates was forced to choose one over the other. Those in the losing group either left Microsoft or drifted off to work in other divisions.

With Gates's blessing, those continuing the tools effort began adding full-text search features to a set of code called WinHelp, which had originally been built to display—in a small window that could be opened atop a program's main window whenever users wanted—explanatory text that helped them learn how to use their software.

Calling the tool-in-the-making WinBook at first, then WinDoc, and finally Viewer, its developers started with a simple mission: take the basic text-display engine from WinHelp and add a few features to it so that it could be used to build multimedia titles. They intended simply to add the kinds of searching and indexing features that can be found in most word-processing programs to WinHelp's ability to display text in a window surrounded by other elements on the screen.

Almost immediately, though, the project lost its focus. Between 1989, when Viewer work began, and 1991, when the first version of Viewer was finished, feature after feature was added to it and more and more members were added to the Viewer team. So many people with so many ideas were working on it that the original, relatively attainable goals for Viewer were lost. Then, as part of yet another Microsoft reorganization, the Viewer developers were merged with another Windows development team. In the months that followed that merger, a number of frustrated people left Microsoft, in the words of one ex-Viewer developer, "to go listen to music in Indonesia and stuff like that." After the shake-out, many of the people who best understood Viewer's original core code were gone.

They left behind an impossible and conflicting set of tasks. Viewer 1.0, already completed, needed substantial improvement. As work began on Viewer 2.0, Multimedia Publishing, now hard at work on *Encarta*, lobbied the Viewer team for a text-display engine that they could graft onto their encyclopedia's interface. Rob Glaser directed the team to develop a full authoring and display tool, complete with its own interface, for use on every conceivable kind of title. Richard Hobbs, in an attempt to answer both mandates, decided to ship Viewer 2.0 in two phases— the first one to meet the *Encarta* team's needs, the second fulfilling Glaser's vision. By the time "Viewer 2.0, Phase One," as Hobbs called it, was finished, there was a mass defection from the Viewer team. In the months that followed, Glaser retired, the Viewer team broke up completely, and the plans to develop further versions of Viewer were abandoned.

By Hobbs's reckoning, nearly seven years of development had left Microsoft with no viable multimedia tools. He moved over to Multimedia Publishing, set himself up in an office, and decided once and for all to build a multimedia text-display engine that would allow MM Pubs finally to show text among pictures, video, and animation without having to write a new text-display engine every time. Hobbs called his project MediaView—a tool for displaying text in one among many "windowpanes," which would allow print to sit in the same window with other forms of media. "I've been at Microsoft for coming on seven years," he said one day, "and I think the thing I've learned is that the best way to get things done is to just start doing them when you know that it's the thing to do, and then try to convince people around you that it is the thing to do."

Hobbs studied Viewer's code in detail, comparing it to the original WinHelp code upon which Viewer had been built. The years of effort by disparate groups, Hobbs decided, had added up to extremely confusing and bulky code. Accordingly, he spent months separating the original WinHelp engine from the mess it had been buried under, and began building MediaView from it. In essence, he was going back to the original multimedia tools-development foundation and starting over. No sooner had he set to work than he was given a developer to help him, and

Multimedia product designers—Bjerke among them—declared themselves eager to use MediaView once it was finished.

Bjerke doubted that Hobbs could deliver MediaView in time to help *Sendak*, however, and was even more doubtful about Phil Spencer's tools group, to which she was forced to turn for her sprite authoring-and-display engine. Spencer's group would be developing something far more complex than MediaView, and far more important to *Sendak*. While there existed less robust text-display alternatives to MediaView, there was nothing to fall back on should Spencer's group fail to deliver on time.

Bjerke was not the only one with doubts about Spencer. When Spencer sent out e-mail early in February outlining his preliminary thoughts on the mission of his tools group, Hobbs replied immediately with a long, emotional e-missive. "We could use these new resources in MUCH more meaningful ways than to try YET AGAIN to create YET ANOTHER AUTHORING TOOL FOR MULTIMEDIA TITLES," he wrote. He was particularly skeptical about Spencer's ultimate goal. Spencer had written, "If a designer designs a product that has no new functionality, just new content with new treatment ideas, that designer should be able to create the title without a developer." Hobbs mailed back, "A worthy goal, but this is literally the tenth time I've heard someone say this at Microsoft over the last 6 ½ years!" His sentiments were shared by a solid majority of the developers in the MM Pubs division.

Kevin Gammill was most skeptical of all. He believed that even under the best of circumstances, Spencer's group could not have a workable sprite-authoring tool ready for his team to create animations in time to meet *Sendak*'s deadline. Moreover, although he and Spencer were close friends—the two had attended the University of Washington together, known each other since their freshman year there, and had come to Microsoft within months of each other—he was convinced that Spencer did not understand the complexities of the sprite engine *Sendak* needed. Time and again Gammill would say, "Phil just doesn't realize how complicated this is. He's never worked on anything this difficult."

An affable young man who loves nothing more than to talk at length about software code, Spencer laughed when told of Gammill's doubts. "Kevin never can take me seriously," he said, recalling one of his more memorable college drinking bouts, "because the first time we met, I was standing in our dorm shower with all my clothes on, covered with puke."

Spencer saw the history of tools development at Microsoft in much the same way as Hobbs did. Rob Glaser, he believed, had wanted to create multimedia authoring tools for use by software companies other than Microsoft because he wanted to evangelize for the Windows platform. The more ways there were to build Windows applications, the more such applications there would be, and the greater would grow the demand for Windows. But in trying to make Viewer have that broad an appeal, Multimedia Systems had burdened it with features that got in the way of Multimedia Publishing's developers. By concentrating solely on MM Pubs's needs, Spencer reasoned, and by developing a tool exclusively for Microsoft, he could turn Multimedia Publishing into a division that cranked out titles quickly and consistently on schedule. "The Microsoft mentality," he said, "has always been, if you can't find it somewhere, just write it yourself. That's how our group came around. And we're not interested in supporting other people. We only want to answer to people inside Multimedia Publishing. We don't want to be doing global multimedia Windows authoring systems. We just want to put out titles."

Much of Gammill's and Bjerke's skepticism about Spencer had to do with internecine politics. Spencer was in Jabe Blumenthal's Jurassic group; he reported directly to Blumenthal. Gammill and his teammates believed that Spencer would tailor his group's work to Jurassic-type titles rather than those from the other product units. The Gandalf product unit considered itself more ambitious than Jurassic, and more willing to push the technology. If Spencer concentrated on Jurassic's titles, Gammill feared, he would never get around to doing the complex sprite-engine work that *Sendak* needed. Gandalf members believed that the Jurassic group was simply porting Dorling Kindersley books over to the computer while Gandalf was trying to do titles in a completely new format, packed with far grander multimedia effects.

"I know what this looks like," Spencer said. "I need to fight the stereotype that this is just more developers for Jabe's group. But I think the only way to effectively fight that is just to start doing stuff. I mean, I can say all I want, but it's just talk until we actually help another product unit develop and ship a product on time using technology that came from this group."

Alas, before he could begin the journey toward that goal, he had to finish up his work on Jurassic's *Dinosaurs*. And *Dinosaurs* was slipping. As its deadline came and went, Spencer dove into the same round-the-clock regimen Gammill was suffering under on *Encarta*, and there was no predicting when he could turn his full attention to the formation of the core tools group and the formulation of its mission. So, before work on core tools had even begun, the project had slipped behind schedule.

The news from Hobbs was little better. After looking over Hobbs's plans for which features would come first in MediaView, Gammill sent e-mail to Bjerke warning her that *Sendak* might not be able to include full-text searching—the ability to have the computer scroll through text and find all instances of a given word in it. Bjerke had been working on a backpack tool that would allow kids to type in any word included in *Sendak*'s contents or text, and have the tool list every topic in which the typed words could be found. Without full-text searching, the feature would be impossible. "I am assuming this will cause quite a stir . . . so feel free to ask any question you want," Gammill wrote. "I just don't think it is possible under the current timeframe." Since no one at Microsoft ever takes no for an answer without calling a meeting, Bjerke's answer was terse and reflexive: "Sounds like a meeting is in order on this one!"

Bjerke did receive one piece of good news, at least, that February. "We can now focus our sites on the March 8 usability sessions," Jayleen Ryberg wrote in e-mail, "because we are off of the agenda for the BillG meeting. . . . Don't know whether to be relieved or disappointed!" Bjerke was thrilled. "Yes!" she shouted when she got the news, thrusting her fist in the air. "It would have been a complete waste of time to do that presentation. We would have been derailed all this week when we could have been doing stuff for the usability prototype. God! We would have had three or four meetings this week just to revise our document for that thing. We would have been scrambling all week just to get a decent prototype working." Now they could concentrate on features they wanted to test in the next usability session, nearly a month away, rather than on features hastily thrown together just to show to Gates. "All riiiiiight!" Bjerke shrieked.

Turning her attention back to designing *Sendak* and getting it on a schedule, though, was a little like getting on some bizarre carnival ride, half treadmill, half rollercoaster. For every brainstorming high, where Bjerke felt she was dispensing forever with some heretofore difficult design problem, there was an immediate corresponding low in the form of a new design issue or a struggle of one kind or another with one of her teammates. While Bjerke felt that her team was moving, she did not feel that it was moving forward. Decisions made at one meeting would somehow emerge at a future meeting as problems. It was as if they were thinking and planning in place while their deadline rushed ever closer.

"This is great! This is fun!" Bjerke, on a high, said at the end of one characteristically feverish design meeting. Looking at the whiteboard, which was covered with colored writing, she continued, "I hardly know where to start copying. . . . We have so many ideas up here. . . . Too cool. . . . I love solving problems!" Then she went back to her office to find, in the e-mail stacked up in her computer, a new low in the form of a long debate on the relative merits of the ship and room navigation models.

While Bjerke found the sheer volume and confusion of the mail frustrating, it fell to Jayleen Ryberg to move her to outright anger. "The more I hear you explain the 'place' idea," Ryberg wrote, "the more it sounds like you have decided to rule out the 'ship' idea without testing it. I really think we need to put these two ideas side by side in front of many kids —presumably in the upcoming usability session. . . . I know you are frustrated with Bryan's apparent close-mindedness but we still need to thoroughly explore both areas." Bjerke read into that an accusation that she was too biased in favor of her room notion to consider evidence in favor of the ship. "I believe that the team and many other adults that we have talked to believe the magical room is more engaging and appropriate," she wrote back, the inconclusiveness of her teammates' opinions notwithstanding. "I do want to find out if the kids generally agree but I have a feeling that they may not have a strong enough reaction to one or the other to help us decide and it will still be in our court. I truly believe this issue is one of authorship and that there are certain parts of our products that we can go beyond what kids can presently imagine and give them something magical that may take them time to truly explore."

Privately, she was more exasperated with Ryberg. "We really could have used some guidance from her on this issue," she said one day, objecting to the way Ryberg let the debate go on and on, instead of forcing a decision. Ryberg had decided to have Smith and Ballinger do artwork for both a ship and a room, and have kids try both out at the March 8 usability sessions, to see if they preferred one strongly over the other. Beyond that, she seemed unwilling to push the matter toward resolution.

One day shortly after their e-mail exchange, Bjerke stormed back into her office after a meeting with Ryberg, shut her door, slammed her notebooks down on her desk, and shouted, "We can't keep going on like this! She's not holding us accountable for anything, pushing us on any deadlines! She's got to be harder on us!" With pop-up production supposed to start in three months, the final design of pop-ups was still unresolved, no production artists had been lined up, and there was no production plan in place. Further, the team's ambitions for *Sendak*'s guide characters were growing out of control. The plan now was to give the user some twelve guides to choose from, the characters representing children of both genders, every imaginable race, and disabled children as well. Ryberg's sole move toward finding artists to create these characters was to send out mail to her teammates asking if anyone knew of artists or agencies she could contact. After three months of work on *Sendak*, nothing concrete had been done, and nothing much was on the horizon. "She needs to be pushing us on things!" Bjerke exclaimed.

With that, she walked off to Bartholomew's office and vented her frustration. Bartholomew, who also was beginning to worry about *Sendak*'s slow start, responded by asking Bjerke to become program manager.

The request caught Bjerke completely by surprise. Back in her office, she turned it over and over again in her mind. She was both hesitant and intrigued. It would mean, she said, giving up design, the work dearest to her heart. But it was a step into a position of respect and prestige and was also a way out of the designer track at Microsoft. Program managers at Microsoft came almost exclusively from the marketing and software-development ranks. By becoming a program manager, Bjerke would be proving to the rest of the company that designers could be just as analytical, organized, and reliable as developers. She saw such a promotion as a major coup, a symbolic advance for designers throughout the company.

Still, she fretted—particularly about Ryberg's potential reaction. "If I were Jayleen," she said, "I would be furious about this." She was somewhat relieved to hear that Bartholomew planned to present the move to Ryberg not as Bjerke moving into program management, but of Ryberg moving back to producer, where she could coordinate art production for all Gandalf products. Bartholomew would argue to Ryberg that she was sorely needed there and that Bjerke would take over management of *Sendak* not because of Ryberg's failings, but because schedule and other constraints kept Microsoft from looking outside the company for a new manager. By telling Ryberg that she was indispensable as a producer rather than a failure as a program manager, Bartholomew hoped to eliminate the possibility of future bad blood between her and Bjerke.

Bjerke also hesitated because her ambitions and those of her family were pulling her in yet another direction. She had long dreamed of leaving Microsoft and setting up her own business, with two of her brothers and her husband, making a compact-disc multimedia guide to the Pacific Northwest trail system for hikers. On days—and there were many of them—when she felt particularly guilty or uncomfortable about working for a large, powerful corporation driven by a need to make ever-larger profits, she dreamed of owning a small business, doing products she loved, with friends and siblings who were dedicated to an ideal rather than market domination. She was the primary driving force behind *Sendak*'s more idealistic features—its planned multiethnic array of guide characters, features making it easier for the handicapped to use, and its various levels of complexity—and she grew increasingly frustrated with the company's insistence that such features could be included only if a solid business case could be made for them. In a smaller, less profit-driven company, she believed, she could align her work more closely with her principles.

Bjerke was passionate about *Sendak*, though, and about succeeding at Microsoft. Two days after Bartholomew's offer, she accepted it. "I'm cautiously excited about it," she e-mailed me later. "It should be a good show to watch and see if I can do it, after I've gone on and on about program management in general." She and Bartholomew agreed not to announce the change until a product unit meeting scheduled ten days later—the day after the other units presented their proposed new titles to Gates.

In the interim, *Sendak* continued to founder. Sara Fox was finding it all but impossible to make its History and Geography units conform to its overall design. She could not find a way to devise a sensible access to epochs and historical events by way of clickable scenes on the screen. She originally had wanted users to enter the Geography unit through a view of a spinning globe, then by clicking on specific countries they wanted to visit. But then she realized that that would mean there would only be one Geography "scene"—the globe—while each of the other units would have fifteen or more scenes. Now, she was trying to divide the world into fifteen regions—analogous to scenes in the other units—that could be sensibly portrayed on the screen. The effort was not going well. The world did not lend itself to logical scene divisions, and the sizes and shapes of certain countries—Italy, to cite one example, and Chile, to cite another—did not fit very well on a square screen. Nor was it feasible to have a separate scene for each continent.

Bjerke had been hoping that as Gammill had more time to spend with the rest of the team, he could help Fox think through History and Geography, and help answer more of her own design questions. But at a core team meeting where she presented her five most pressing design issues to him, Gammill gave her no answers at all. After staring at her list for several minutes, growling incomprehensibly, he finally looked up at her and said, "Can we go offsite?"

"Yes," Bjerke answered.

"Cool."

Although she had gotten no real answers from Gammill, Bjerke was somewhat heartened by the exchange, for in calling for an "offsite"—a meeting of the team away from the Microsoft campus—Gammill finally was declaring his faith in *Sendak* and its team. He was invoking a company ritual regarded by employees with an awe bordering on superstition. Generally held in area hotel conference rooms, or at the nearby Salish Lodge in the Cascade Mountains, offsites were catered brainstorming sessions at which participants expected to resolve every manner of difficult issue. It was believed that the journey off-campus, away from the corporate habits of mind and heart, restored the imaginations of company pilgrims and brought them renewed and refreshed to the battles at hand.

Gammill fixed on the offsite as the event at which *Sendak* would miraculously be restored to health. For days afterward, in answer to everyone's questions, he would ask, "When's the offsite?" The word seemed to energize the whole team, which began looking forward to the date, a few weeks distant, as the time when *Sendak* finally would start moving briskly forward.

The lone exception was Ballinger, whose depression deepened day by day, meeting by meeting. Now working long hours readying pictures of both a ship and a room for the next usability test, and putting in what little time he could spare from that effort sitting silently through design meetings, he grew increasingly withdrawn and glum. Alone in his office, with the blinds drawn and the lights turned off, he sat for hours at a time staring at the images on his screen, one hand on his keyboard, the other moving a stylus over the electronic graphics tablet he kept in his lap. As he drew with his stylus, the image of a paintbrush moved over the screen, drawing and painting the interior either of Bjerke's cherished magic room or of Ballinger's cherished spaceship.

More and more, design meetings consisted of Bjerke and Smith wantonly generating ideas, and Bjerke ending the meeting with instructions to Ballinger on what to do for the next meeting. Often, a conversation between Bjerke and Smith would end with Bjerke saying, "Play with that, Bryan," and getting no response. Relations between the two hit a bottom of sorts when a meeting ended with Bjerke turning to Ballinger and saying, "What do you think?"

Ballinger stared straight ahead, silent.

"Anything else?" Bjerke asked.

Finally, she sent e-mail to Bartholomew, asking for help. "I am really struggling with getting Bryan to be unemotional about the work in *Sendak* and contributing freely and openly on any issue," she wrote. After praising Smith and asking that Bartholomew hire her full time as *Sendak*'s designer, she suggested that Bryan go from being lead illustrator on *Sendak* to being a production artist for all Gandalf titles. "I will keep trying to work with him on this issue but I must say that I have found Lindsey to be infinitely more valuable as a team player than Bryan," Bjerke concluded. "I know I fought pretty hard to hire him and he definitely has value but at this moment in time he is doing me, and the product a disservice rather than being a positive asset. Sigh. . . ."

Bartholomew decided to move Bjerke into program management, Smith into the lead design position—while keeping her for the time being as a contractor—and to move Ballinger into the general production-art position Bjerke suggested, under Ryberg. Ryberg, as Bartholomew had hoped, was delighted to be moving back into production. But Ballinger was shocked at what he saw as yet another demotion. "I've been extremely involved in the design of this from the beginning," he e-mailed to me, crestfallen. "Now I've got to let it go." He understood that the move was a form of punishment, and he took it hard. "I guess I just need to learn to distance myself emotionally from what is going on," he wrote, "and to stop *living* here. In other words, get a life."

His gloom stood out in an increasingly celebratory air at MM Pubs, particularly after several in the division went before Gates on February 23. Three Gandalf members—Whit Alexander, Sonja Gustafson, and Bartholomew—presented their plan for a digitized atlas of the world, and representatives from the Variety product unit presented plans for a series of children's fiction titles—most notably the Dr. Seuss series, ported over to compact disc and made interactive. As is customary at Microsoft, the meeting was preceded by tremendous tension on the part of the petitioners. But Gates, in spite of the grumbling he had done in advance about children's fiction titles, and in spite of his avowed skepticism about Alexander's plan for implementation of the atlas, proved a relatively soft sell. He devoted the meeting alternately to raising objections to everything put before him and wondering aloud at why competitors from the print publishing world were not moving faster into multimedia, where he was convinced the opportunities to make millions were both obvious and vast. "What are they sitting there *thinking?*" he asked at one point.

"Well, they're privately held companies," someone answered, "uptight about doing development." Gates, suddenly reassured, interrupted, "So they have finite greed."

During the presentation on the Seuss titles, Gates complained almost constantly. Pronouncing Seuss's name "Zeuss" every time he uttered it, drawing out the *z,* he moaned about the risks throughout the meeting: "I'm skeptical about this . . . so *educate* me . . . Random House [Seuss's print publisher] shouldn't be doing this deal. . . . They should try and do it themselves. . . . They could have a very profitable business with these titles. . . . I don't have a sense of how the experience of using this product is different than just turning the pages of this book. . . . These books are for very young kids. . . . Adding things in the computer, you extend the age, but you don't want to lose the original audience. . . . I'm not understanding how we add value to the story. . . . All this other stuff gets in the way of the *story!*"

As I sat there listening to Gates, it seemed to me that he was hitting on the essential question about multimedia. The simple fact that computer technology made it possible to blend text with animation and video did not make such a blend inherently better than any of these media by themselves. Yet the assumption among design team members seemed to be that the multimedia whole was by definition better than the sum of its individual media parts. Gates himself may not have been aware of what he wanted, but he essentially was asking his designers to be more creative. He wanted them not so much simply to render old stories from old media on a new multimedia platform, but to come up with something creative and compelling enough to make a consumer prefer the digitized multimedia version over its predecessors.

Gates ended his long litany of objections with a protracted silence, during which he sat staring down at the table. Finally Tom Corddry said, haltingly, "At this point, do you feel like these are reasonable titles, and that we should go ahead with them?" Without hesitation, Gates answered nonchalantly, "Yeah . . . I guess you should . . . because I understand the value added, and partly because the potential even if the PCs aren't the dominant platform, it's a hell of an asset to have done these things well, and to be out in front. We may have competitors for these products, loosely defined, who don't even think of the PC as their target, who will just go after those other platforms. So even nine months from now it will be interesting to see who will start up doing these things. We won't be a high percentage of the children's books done, but we could be a high percentage of the dollars."

His listeners escaped as quickly as they could, as if they were afraid Gates might change his mind. Back in their own building, they gathered in the hall outside their offices and began shouting, shaking hands, and high-fiving all around. "Five wins!" someone shouted, "Five wins!"—one for each title Gates had authorized. Whit Alexander, having noticed that I tape-recorded the meeting, asked to borrow the tape. "I want to play this for my family," he said, his eyes misting.

A few yards away, around a corner, Ballinger sat in his office, laid low by melancholy. His graphics tablet in his lap, he sat slumped over, his head lying face-down on his keyboard. The only light in the room came from his computer screen. It imparted a faintly noticeable, depressing, bluish tinge to the back of his head.

Hacking

There was a celebratory glitter in Kevin Gammill's eyes as he ran down the hallway toward Bjerke's office. He paused outside her door and thrust his head in, shouting, "I'm at zero bugs on *Encarta*!" Then he ran on.

A grand moment of liberation for a Microsoft developer, "zero bugs" is the end of months during which it seems that a project is doomed to remain forever on the verge of completion. After a product is built and run through tests, problems in performance—bugs—are entered in a file called "Raid" and assigned to specific developers to fix. Bug-fixing can be extremely tedious work—a whole day can be devoted to fixing one or two—and *Encarta*, with its 2,100 bugs, took Gammill and his cohort, Jay Gibson, months to clean up. Each bug required a search through *Encarta*'s code, looking for the offending line, and either the writing of additional code, the deletion of an error, or the rearrangement of existing code. Occasionally, newly written or newly arranged code would introduce new bugs, requiring yet another round of repair.

Now, with Gammill at zero bugs and Gibson only a few away, the March 8 ship date for *Encarta*, only a week off, looked secure, and Gammill could look ahead for the first time in years at a long stretch of relative relaxation. Before he could begin work on *Sendak*, its design would have to be complete—a circumstance that was two or three months away, to judge from the behavior of his teammates. The closest anyone had come to involving him in *Sendak* work was occasionally to ask him whether a given feature could be implemented.

It was not only *Encarta* that had kept Gammill from closer involvement in *Sendak*'s planning. Gammill had no patience for the often directionless path that product design took, with groups of people randomly wandering all over the conceptual map. He preferred being given specific features to evaluate, thinking about them on his own, then coming back to designers with either a yes, a no, or an assessment of how long it would take him to implement their design. He detested trying to explain development problems to nondevelopers.

In the early weeks of my stay at Microsoft, Gammill's distaste for making development understandable to the ignorant posed a serious problem for me. Gammill's answers to my questions were always deliberately vague and incomplete. Finally, I complained. "You know you can explain these things to me," I said. "I'm capable of understanding them."

His answer was a little grandiose, "You think it's that simple? Explain the Theory of Relativity!"

When he attended design meetings, Gammill generally displayed so much impatience and contempt for his teammates' meanderings that before long they were as unhappy with his presence as he was with wasting his time there.

Gammill always begins development projects by writing down what designers want, then thinking about ways to grant their wishes. He calls this the digestion phase of a project, during which, he wrote me in e-mail, "I try to think about the important things they say, then digest it at a later time. During 'digestion,' I think about possible ways of implementing what they want, of problems that may come up, other variables that come into the whole picture, and other possible solutions in case a particular thing isn't feasible with our current schedule and headcount." His *Sendak* notes from February, scribbled in a notebook and on documents given him by Bjerke and Ryberg, tended more toward indigestion: "Buttons on pop-ups How?"; "3 kinds of pop-ups—Please define!!"; "Drag & drop—do they know what this looks like?" "How many pop-ups? . . . ~2000 (main) . . . ~10,000 secondary . . . say—20,000 reality"; "No visits!!!"; "?????????"; "No"; "No schedule before spec!"

This last was particularly important to Gammill, for whom work on anything is impossible until every conceivable detail, however small, is nailed down. The "spec," or specification, in Gammill's notes was actually two documents, each more than one hundred pages long. The first, to be written by Bjerke, would be the design specification, which was to describe *Sendak* in exacting detail. The document would include a picture of every *Sendak* screen, would describe the behavior of every feature, and would list exactly how much of all media was to be included. Gammill expected, for example, that if a given screen included a "Copy" button, the design spec would describe what the button would do when the user clicked on it, whether or not it would remain in its working, or pressed down, state while the machine was doing its copying, and when and how it would return to its ready state.

Nearly every time Gammill was asked a question by a designer, he answered with a flurry of new questions, his voice tinged with contempt. It was a habit that wore his teammates down. "Does the pronunciation button stay down until the file is played?" he asked at a design meeting with Bjerke and Smith, when Bjerke described for him a button that users could click on to hear the pronunciation of a topic title. "Does the cursor change over it?" There was no answer. "How about the 'Narration' button?" (Bjerke wanted the encyclopedia to read the text to young users when they clicked the appropriate button.) "Does it flex? Does it stay down until the file is played? And if it does, can they click on it while it's playing?" Bjerke and Smith, chastened, quietly wrote down his questions and promised to follow up via e-mail.

Developers, who cannot tolerate carelessness or inexactitude in even the most trivial of conversations, can drive nondevelopers mad with their fixations. Gammill's friend Phil Spencer, asking Bjerke, who lived in his neighborhood, to feed his pet bird while he was away on a trip, explained one day that the bird flew freely throughout his house. "How do you clean up after it?" she asked.

"Our dog eats its shit," said Spencer, smiling.

"An ecosystem!" I interjected.

Spencer corrected me. "Well, no," he answered earnestly. "It would only be an ecosystem if the bird ate the dog's shit, too."

Once Bjerke's design spec was completed, Gammill would write his technical specification, a far more detailed description of how his program was to be constructed, and how he would go about making the designs in Bjerke's document workable. Only when that was finished could he begin to schedule his work. His "No schedule without spec!" was an expression of dismay at his team's apparent plan to schedule the project before defining it. To his way of thinking, it was impossible to write a schedule before knowing exactly what the work would entail.

Gammill, like all developers, detests ambiguity and disarray. This is most apparent in his helplessness with the English language, where every rule has a number of exceptions and where the systematic mind is forced to despair of ever understanding the reason underlying the rhyme. Both Gammill's speech and his e-mail are peppered with malapropisms, grammatical errors, and mispronunciations and misspellings—these last, often unintentional puns or editorial comments that, when committed in writing, elude his mail system's spellchecker. He pronounces *faux pas, foo pas; Laotian* is *Loatian.* He writes *vary* when he means *very, through* when he means *throw.* A sprite engine, in his e-mail, is a "spit engine" one time, a "spite engine" the next. An increase in a program's speed is a "speed increasement." One routine, he wrote one day, "was implemented in Viewer in a straightforward manor." Of a concert by Blue Oyster Cult, at which he found himself to be among the oldest in attendance, he e-mailed me, "But I defiantly enjoyed myself." When I asked him about it, it turned out that he meant *definitely.*

Gammill confesses to this failing with more pride than embarrassment. The fact that he cannot learn the arbitrary and inconsistent rules of English is, in his mind, proof of his worth as a developer. He believes that no one who can think consistently and analytically, as a developer must, could ever learn to think in English. "In programming, there's this finite set of rules," he says, "where English is all evolved over the years and all fucked up."

This is a common attitude among developers. Like Gammill, Spencer feels that English is clumsy, vague, incoherent, and inefficient. Coming back from a weekend spent rock-climbing in the mountains east of Seattle, he told Gammill and me about a conversation with his climbing instructor, who asked what Spencer did for a living. "I work at Microsoft," Spencer answered.

"What do you do there?"

"I'm a programmer."

"You're a programmer?! You know how to do that stuff? How do you know how to tell a computer what to do?"

"I told him," Spencer said, "that it's a lot easier than English. It's easier to tell a machine what to do than to describe what it's doing. Like, instead of saying, 'Okay, I'm going to iterate over this array of numbers until this happens,' I just say, 'for *i* equals one to ten.' "

The few meetings Gammill attended during the previous weeks persuaded him that *Sendak's* designers were nowhere near ready to talk in concrete terms about what he would do for them. So he decided to turn his attention for a few days to other matters—particularly a partial reorganization in Gandalf that called for him to supervise all eight of the product unit's software developers. The reorganization had immediately put him at loggerheads with the new program manager on Version 2.0 of *Encarta*, Jay Gibson. Gammill had insisted that if Gibson wanted a given feature in *Encarta*, and Gammill and the encyclopedia's developer, Amy Raby, agreed that the feature could not be included because of schedule constraints, then Gibson would have to take their no for an answer. Gibson preferred to have the last word himself. Gammill had taken the matter to Bartholomew, who took his side. "Jay wouldn't take that answer from me," Gammill said. "But when Craig says it, he's very agreeable. Craig's real good at making things sound better even though you're getting screwed." He laughed. "He's real good at *personal communication.*"

Gammill also decided to take a vacation, his first in two years, on March 13. "I'm taking five days off!" he said to everyone he encountered. It was a measure, perhaps, of how severely his perspective had been distorted by *Encarta* that two of the days he was "taking off" from work were Saturday and Sunday.

He was clearing stuff off of his desk as he discussed his plans, piling *Encarta* work and infant's toys into boxes. The array of Diet Sprite cans, computer terminals, compact discs, and mutilated dolls on the desk and floor remained untouched. With the Seattle grunge band Nirvana droning nihilistically in the foreground, Gammill ecstatically considered his vacation. "I'm going *home* for vacation," he said. He lived nearby, in Kirkland, a Seattle suburb, with his wife and daughter. "I'm gonna do yard work! I'm gonna mow my lawn, fertilize it . . . I'm thinking about painting our deck again, staining our outside deck . . . going to do some laundry. . . . I used to hate mowing the lawn. I used to come home from college, my dad would say, 'Mow the lawn!' . . . I hated it. And now it's my lawn, it's different. . . . I don't know what it is. . . . I have a push mower, I go out there and push along."

Microsoft's success was built on the brains of Gammill and others like him—young, energetic software developers who came to the company directly from college. If there are four fundamental characteristics that all successful Microsoft developers can be said to share, they are these: they can solve complicated mathematical and computing problems quickly; they thrive under pressure; they love their work more than other people love theirs; and they believe themselves to be by far the best in their profession.

To these can be added a fifth—they are extremely young. This can make for odd-looking job histories. Were Gammill to put together his resume, it would list the following work experience: counterman at Kentucky Fried Chicken; a meteoric rise during his high-school years from delivery driver to night manager at a Pietro's Pizza outlet; package handler for one summer at United Parcel Service; student assistant in the University of Washington computer lab; and software development engineer at the Microsoft Corporation.

Now twenty-five, Gammill was nearing completion of his fourth year as a full-time employee at Microsoft. He had begun working there as a contractor in 1988 when he was a computer science student at the University of Washington. One of his classmates was the son of the CD-ROM division's then-general manager, Min Yee, and he told Gammill and Phil Spencer that his father was looking for software developers. Microsoft's demand for developers in those days was insatiable and so many were hired through informal networks that Richard Hobbs, the developer working on the MediaView text-display engine, liked to joke that he was the only one to have found a job at Microsoft by sending in a resume. Gammill and Spencer drove across the lake one day, liked what they saw, signed on as contractors, and began working on the first version of Microsoft's *Bookshelf*.

For Gammill, it was a heady and exhausting time. While still attending college and carrying a full academic load, he was working full-time in an exciting new field—multimedia computing—for the world's fastest-growing and most powerful software company. Since he was a contractor rather than a salaried employee, he was paid for every hour he worked, earning time-and-a-half wages for all hours in excess of forty per week. And since 120-hour weeks were not uncommon in those days, this often translated into biweekly paychecks that totaled $4,000 after taxes. "It was crazy," he says now. He vividly remembers getting a W-2 form that listed his previous year's wages as $50,000. "I was twenty-one years old and making $50,000 a year! I bought all kinds of junk—everything I wanted . . . I had this big-screen TV that I kept in this crummy little student apartment."

After more than a year of doing contract work, Gammill became a full-time Microsoft employee in the wake of an IRS crackdown on the company's use of contractors. In 1991, he married another Microsoft employee, Nicole Mitskog, and the two bought their home in Kirkland. Within a year, their daughter, Cassidy, was born.

With a wife, daughter, suburban home, and a job in America's most successful corporation, Gammill comes across in some ways as the consummate 1990s organization man. He is on an established career track at Microsoft, earning generous raises and bonuses every six months and moving up the salary ladder as quickly as company custom allows. His manager, Craig Bartholomew, regards him as a superb team player and one of the brightest and ablest developers at Microsoft.

In manner, appearance, experience, and tastes, though, Gammill is a brash and irreverent kid. His hardest habit to break after getting married was sleeping with the radio turned up loud all night long. "My wife didn't care much for that," he says. Once a month or more, he walks from his home down to a nearby video arcade, called Quarters, and plays games for hours at a time, his favorite being Total Carnage. He drinks beer with the fervor and bravado of a college sophomore. He is an avid sports fan and an even more avid fan of rock music. He faithfully attends as many concerts as he can, whether they are held in outdoor arenas on the other side of Washington state or in downtown Seattle bars. The schedule kept on his computer at Microsoft might have recorded, on any given day, a business matter, two or three meetings, and a concert: "9:00 Mail stock to broker! 10:30 New palette meeting. 2:00 Technology update. 5:00 BOC and Bathtub Jin," this last appointment being in a downtown Seattle tavern. His musical tastes run to grunge, enraged post-punk, and heavy metal—turned up loud, all day long, in his office. Among his favorite groups are Nirvana, Alice in Chains, Soundgarden, Mudhoney—all Seattle grunge bands who regularly played in local clubs during Gammill's college days, then went on to national and international stardom; Rage Against the Machine, a black rap 'n' roll band whose primary musical characteristic is immeasurable rage; Primus, a post-punk industrial hate-rock band; and Tool and Megadeth, two bands known mostly for being gratuitously gross.

For all of his zest for upward mobility—a philosophical stance that is essentially optimistic—Gammill is a devotee of depression. He loves an album by Alice in Chains, called *Facelift*, because, he says, "It's so *dark*." His office, particularly during the fall and winter months, is nearly pitch-dark, the blinds kept closed around the clock. In discussing with his wife the home they planned to build someday, he insisted that his office be deep inside the house, surrounded by other rooms, and windowless. Visiting my home for the first time, he noted with approval that my office was in the basement. "It's dark," he rhapsodized, "it's cold, it's damp . . . it's perfect!"

Gammill constantly displays the division in his soul between the earnest young corporate achiever and the adolescent rebel. A conversation with him about his new managerial responsibilities, which he takes very seriously, was conducted one day in a near-shout, over the voice of Zack de la Rocha, lead singer of Rage Against the Machine, screaming an obscenity-filled refusal to knuckle under to any authority, anywhere.

Asked about his favorite memories from youth and childhood, Gammill comes up with three: attending a Rolling Stones concert with his father, an electrical engineer, when he was thirteen; beating his father for the first time at arm wrestling; and, most satisfying, beating his father for the first time at chess. Gammill was seventeen. "He was after me constantly after that," he recalls with a laugh, "to play again. 'Come on,' he'd beg me, 'let's play! Let's play!' And I'd just say, 'Naaaah, I'm busy.' "

A fourth memory comes from his early days at Microsoft. Gammill's favorite radio station, KISW ("Solid Rock. No useless talk"), was broadcasting one day from Microsoft, whose workforce makes up a large share of its audience. The station brought male heavy-metal rock legend Alice Cooper to the Microsoft campus, and the singer was given a tour. Gammill and a brace of similarly starstruck developers followed Cooper on his way out the door. The star turned around as he was leaving and asked, in mock bewilderment, "Wouldn't you rather be called . . . *Macro-Hard?*" "I thought about that for a long time," Gammill says, laughing heartily. "Man, is that funny."

With the exception of Douglas Hofstader's *Godel, Escher, Bach*, Gammill's literary tastes run to the popular and the occult. He loves the work of Tom Clancy—"The only author who I've read all of his books"— Steven King, Robert Heinlein, and J. R. R. Tolkien. He has particularly happy memories of reading L. Ron Hubbard's *Battlefield Earth*, King's *Pet Sematery*, Tolkien's *The Two Towers*, and Jean Auel's *Clan of the Cave Bear*. The book he was most taken with in high school—Homer's *Iliad*—is as highbrow as his reason for liking it is lowbrow: "I couldn't believe how graphic that book was when I read it!" he says excitedly. "They should make a movie out of it."

Indeed, Gammill is an unembarrassed aficionado of action and horror films. He lists as his favorite movies *Alien* and *Aliens*, *The Thing*, *Escape from New York*, *Die Hard* ("Although," he adds, "you have to be in the right mindset"), *Evil Dead*, and *Evil Dead 2. Silverado* and *Stand by Me* are also favorites, the best scene in the latter, according to Gammill, being the "barforama." "I don't see what people say is so great about

Citizen Kane," he says. "That is a *long* movie." His favorite actor is Clint
Eastwood.

When he moved into his Kirkland neighborhood, Gammill was the talk
of the block as his new neighbors, all of them as old, if not older, than
his parents, tried to figure out what sort of person had moved in next
door. After word finally got around that he was a Microsoft developer,
Gammill's next-door neighbor, a middle-aged airline pilot, came over to
introduce himself. "I always wondered how a punk like you could have
so much money," the neighbor said, "until I found out you work at
Microsoft."

Gammill soon found that he had more in common with the neighbor's
seventeen-year-old daughter than he did with her parents. Before long,
she was enlisting his complicity in concealing her high-risk driving habits
and evidence of parties held in her parents' absence. "Please don't tell
my parents about this!" she would plead with him. "Don't worry about
it," Gammill invariably answered. "I did stuff like that all the time."
Talking about her later, he said with undisguised admiration, "Man, she
has got them *so* snowed."

On March 7, the day before *Encarta* was to ship, Gammill had been
home on a Sunday night for the first time in months, looking out the
window at his teenaged neighbor, when the telephone rang. His wife
answered. "It's Craig," she said, handing him the phone.

"Oh, fuck!" Gammill muttered. *Encarta* was supposed to be done and
ready to ship first thing next morning. Bartholomew was particularly anxious that it be sent out then, and no later, because he needed to get it
to Sony's Terre Haute, Indiana, disc pressing plant before the arrival of
Windows NT, a new operating system that would keep the plant busy for
weeks. Should NT arrive first, *Encarta* would slip again. If Bartholomew
was calling now, Gammill knew, it could only be because something had
happened that put *Encarta*'s ship date in jeopardy.

Bartholomew, Gammill told me later, "was more pissed than I've ever
seen him in my life." He told Gammill that a final pass at proofing various
features in the encyclopedia had uncovered, in its Contents wordwheel,
the entry "Slayer sucks like a vacuum"—Slayer being a heavy metal
band, and "Sucks like a vacuum" a critical appraisal. One of *Encarta*'s
contract developers had sneaked it in, as a prank, or hack. Could Gammill come in immediately and figure out how to remove it?

Encarta's Contents window is a high-speed, scrolling table of contents.

When a user clicks the Contents button, a two-part window appears. In the upper, narrow part, the user types the name of the topic for which he or she is searching. As the name is typed, the alphabetic list of titles and topics in the lower window scrolls upward. If you are typing *Wisconsin*, for example, the list jumps instantly to the section of words beginning with *w* as you type that letter. When *i* is typed, the list jumps to words beginning *wi*, and so on. Names of people are listed in various forms. What would be "Washington, George" in a book is listed in the Contents window both in that form and as "George Washington," with the former version being part of a list of "normalized names" linked to the latter version.

While Bartholomew fumed, Gammill drove into Microsoft, called *Encarta* up on his machine, typed "Slayer sucks like a vacuum" in the Contents window, watched it scroll up, clicked on it, and watched the encyclopedia entry on the Lollards, a medieval French religious group, appear. He knew then that "Slayer sucks like a vacuum" had been entered as a normalized name for Lollards. He also knew that removing it, and thus keeping it from showing up in the Contents list, would require the rebuilding of the entire encyclopedia—a procedure that would take three days. So he came up with the only solution he could that would conceal the "Slayer sucks" line and still send *Encarta* out the door on time. He typed:

```
if ( lPrefix = = SLAYER__SUCKS )
    + +lPrefix;
```

It was, as developers say, a hack—an inelegant solution. (As is typical of English-language words in software development, the meaning of the word *hack* changes depending upon its context.) It caused the wordwheel to skip "Slayer sucks" in the hidden list of normalized names and display in the Contents window "sled," the entry after "Slayer sucks like a vacuum," twice—once in place of "Slayer," and once in its own place. The problem would be properly fixed for Version 2.0 of *Encarta*.

It took Gammill only half an hour to solve the Slayer problem, and it took Bartholomew scarcely more time than that to find the offending developer, a contractor named Mike Nelson, and tell him that he would never work for Microsoft again. A heavy-metal reference had been found in Nelson's code months before, and Bartholomew had asked him then to remove any others he inserted. Nelson forgot about his "Slayer" entry.

Since his work in other respects had been good, however, Bartholomew promised to give Nelson a favorable recommendation when future prospective employers contacted him.

Bartholomew's muted reaction was driven somewhat by resignation. Such pranks and their detection are common in computer programming everywhere, and Microsoft managers accept as part of their job ferreting them out in time. Pranksters are motivated both by innate mischief, a trait shared by all developers, and, at Microsoft, at least, by malice. Many developers contract for a given project with Microsoft in the hope that it will lead to a full-time job there, and when it doesn't, they leave a malicious calling card by way of revenge.

In any event, with "Slayer sucks like a vacuum" properly concealed, *Encarta* was sent off to Terre Haute on schedule Monday morning, March 8. It was regarded in MM Pubs as an event of historic proportions, the legitimization of a dream. Bartholomew, with a characteristically stiff upper lip, sent out a laconic announcement on e-mail, thanking the "135 full-time employees and freelancers" who had worked on the encyclopedia. Tom Corddry adopted a more effusive tone, appending to Bartholomew's mail a long accolade. "Yes!!!" it began, and went on, after recapping *Encarta*'s history, to proclaim:

> The story has been one of incredibly hard work and a tremendous learning curve for all of us. . . . As Craig doesn't say, his personal contribution was particularly immense, and, among the many who have done so much, he deserves a moment of personal recognition for pushing, pulling, and holding this project together to the finish line. It should also be read into the record that *Encarta* undoubtedly sets and will always hold the record for "Encyclopedia whose team had the most babies while the product was being built," and it's nice to think that *Encarta* will be waiting for them when they begin to boot up over the next few years. And last, at the risk of pandering, it should be noted that Bill is a man of considerable faith and patience, who supported and defended this project for years before there was a single customer who would be able to buy it and use it. I believe *Encarta* rewards that faith, and I'm incredibly proud of all who made it so.

With *Encarta* gone and *Sendak* nowhere near ready for him to begin work on it, Gammill, having nothing better to do, decided to help interview prospective new software developers.

Those applying to be Microsoft developers are subjected to a grueling immersion in the company's ethos and culture. Applicants who pass an initial screening on their college campuses are brought to the Microsoft campus for a day. There, they are taken to a series of developers, each of whom spends an hour with them. A typical interview series begins at 9:15 A.M. and ends, five conversations later, at 2:30 in the afternoon. After a break, the guest is given a tour of the campus and treated to dinner that evening. Sometimes applicants are tendered a job offer at the end of their interview day; sometimes the offer comes after they return home. Most often, no offer is made. During the previous twelve months, Microsoft had received 120,000 resumes from people seeking work there. The company invited 9,000 on campus for interviews, and eventually offered positions to 2,000.

The developers conducting interviews follow a standard procedure. Having seen the applicant's resume in advance, they ask a few perfunctory questions about his or her education, work, and approach to programming. Then they write problems on their whiteboards and ask the applicant to solve them. When each interview is finished, the interviewer sends e-mail to all other interviewers on the list, with a recommendation either for (hire) or against (no hire), along with a description of what sorts of questions were asked and how the applicant did in trying to answer them. At the end of the day, the votes are tallied.

The interviews are intended to test not only applicants' programming abilities, but also their psychological fit with Microsoft. Accordingly, a certain amount of pressure, both psychological and cerebral, is brought to bear on interview subjects. As the day wears on, the effect of this treatment begins to register on the faces of the applicants, with the ratio of dejection to anxious hope rising interview by interview.

Gammill treats his interview subjects with a mixture of courtesy and impatience. He is as formal as he can manage—which is to say that his behavior differs from its norm by little more than a subtle change in facial expression. He is relentlessly skeptical, particularly of impressive-looking resumes. "I've seen a lot of *great* resumes," he said dismissively one day, looking over a four-page list of accomplishments and awards. Examining the resume of an applicant who had just received his Ph.D. from the University of Waterloo (Waterloo, the University of Washington, and the University of Texas at Austin are the three leading sources of developers for Microsoft), he was dubious. "Academics," he said, "they just don't think the same way we do." There came a knock at the door

then, and a gentleman in a gray suit—the applicant with the Ph.D.—
was ushered in. Gammill leaped to his feet and came around his desk,
extending his hand. He was wearing a baggy striped T-shirt, boat shoes
without socks, and oversized shorts made by tearing the legs off a pair
of sweatpants. Looking at the two of them, you would have sworn that
Gammill was a beggar, his interview subject someone he was trying to
hit up for spare change.

After a brief exchange of pleasantries, Gammill returned to his seat
and his guest sat down opposite him. With the local rock station KISW
broadcasting in the background, Gammill asked a few "codey questions"
about the man's dissertation. "Why didn't you write your code in C?" he
asked at one point, C being the language of choice at Microsoft.

"It doesn't have enough flexibility."

"I agree."

After two more such exchanges, Gammill, clearly eager to move on to
the more exciting portion of the program, said, "Now, I assume that you're
familiar with the procedures here? That we like to write problems on the
board, ask you to work on them? Will that be all right?" Without waiting
for an answer, he stood up and stepped over to his whiteboard. He wrote
out two columns of complex code, then asked, as he handed the pen to
his guest and sat down again, "What's wrong with this statement?"

"Well, you . . ." the man's voice trailed off.

"So what happens?"

The man stared at the problem in silence. As the seconds ticked by,
Gammill grew increasingly impatient, tapping a foot and manically clicking a ballpoint pen. He waited three minutes, then leaped out of his chair
again and pointed at a single line buried in the middle of his code. "It's
an infinite loop!" he shouted.

The infinite loop is one of computing's worst nightmares. Easily stum-
bled into, it is a function that repeats itself eternally, either because of
careless code-writing or because a programmer does not fully understand
the nature of the function he is calling for in his code. Once a program
enters an infinite loop, it stays there, performing the same task over and
over until finally the program crashes. Developers like to highlight the
difference between the world of computing and the world outside of computing by citing the common directions on a bottle of shampoo—"Lather.
Rinse. Repeat"—as an example of an infinite loop. In the everyday world,
common sense tells you not to keep lathering and rinsing forever. In the
world of computing, where there is no common sense and where every-

thing must be rigorously defined, such an instruction is careless and dangerous. "You can just see some poor software developer," Gammill said one day, laughing, "standing in the shower, lathering over and over again until he finally runs out of shampoo!"

His failure to find Gammill's loop left the applicant visibly dispirited. Gammill, erasing the first problem, wrote out two lines of new code, then asked his guest to "write a function called 'target string to long,' that will take any string and convert it to a bit value." Suspicious and hesitant, the man took Gammill's pen again and stared at the board, muttering under his breath. After two minutes or so, he wrote out a couple of numbers, turning to Gammill to explain what he thought he should do. "Okay," Gammill answered shortly. "Can you write it?" Uncertain, as if suspecting a trap, the man wrote slowly, asking questions over his shoulder at virtually every line. Spying a mistake at one point, Gammill offered a helping hand: "Don't forget you have to skip that first T there."

"Oh yeah! Right!"

With that, the man's confidence seemed to return, and he began writing more rapidly. But nearly twenty minutes had gone by, and Gammill was out of patience. His foot was tapping and his eyes were flashing angrily. Suddenly the tapping accelerated and he began madly clicking his pen again. Then he jumped up before his guest had finished. "Yeah," he said, "that'll work. Now let me show you what we did, just for comparison." Next to his guest's thirty-five lines of code, he wrote four. "Now, which one do you like better?"

The answer should have been obvious, the rule in programming being that "smallness is goodness." Gammill's code, being far shorter, should therefore have been preferable. But instead of answering, the applicant kept staring at the board, muttering noncommittally. On the radio, Nirvana's Kurt Cobain muttered too, endlessly repeating a refrain about someone who can't figure out what something means. Just as the man was about to admit that Gammill's was the better code, Gammill interrupted: "It's hard to say what is faster, because this"—he pointed to one of his lines—"is a black box." By that, he meant that the line was calling on something with an unknown internal structure. The programmer activating it, then, would have no idea how long the black box—a set of previously-written code, or a chip buried somewhere in the computer's hardware—would take to complete its task.

Question number two, then, had also held a trap. As Gammill began writing the third problem on the board, his guest looked crushed. All of the good cheer he had exhibited during the discussion of his dissertation had vanished. "So let's say there are integers in this array, and they're sorted," Gammill was saying. "And we want them entered into a binary tree," a binary tree being an arrangement of numbers in tree form, with a given number having two branches, the left extending to a lesser number, the right to a greater number, and each of those numbers in turn having two branches, and so on. The man stared listlessly at the problem for less than a minute before Gammill interrupted again. "Ah, we're out of time," he said, rising to lead the man away. Then he added the session's lone note of sympathy: "I got asked that one when I came here, too." As he left the room with his guest in tow, the man's face was slack, and his shoulders slumped.

A few minutes later, when he came back alone, Gammill rendered his verdict. "He did poorly," he said. "His solution to the first problem was inelegant. He couldn't understand! I don't know . . . academia is weird. . . . I've interviewed three Ph.D.'s . . . they're just different." As similar feedback came in from the man's subsequent interviews, the verdict was unanimous: no hire.

A few days later, Gammill received a twenty-one-year-old woman from Wellesley, who looked impressive on paper. Her grade point average had been 4.0 in high school, and 3.9 at Wellesley. "She taught a class," Gammill said as he was waiting for her to arrive. "That's unusual for an undergraduate. She has impressive skills . . . skills that she *claims* to have, anyway."

The woman proved to be eager, cheerful, and quick to understand Gammill's questions. To the tune of Led Zeppelin's "Whole Lotta Love," she glanced at the code containing the infinite loop and saw the loop immediately. The next question, the construction of a binary tree, proved more difficult. She set to work. Led Zeppelin's Robert Plant, still on the radio, was alternately exhorting his lover to gyrate, promising to deliver unprecedented pleasure to her, and moaning and exclaiming orgasmically. The woman, as if trying to placate Plant, was writing hastily and anxiously, hesitating, erasing, going back to insert new characters. Suddenly Gammill's computer let out a deafening shout: *"Presto!"* The woman jumped and looked over at him. "I just got mail," he said, laughing. She turned back to the board and wrote seven more lines of code. Gammill leaped up, corrected one character, then said, "Okay, you're close. Now, draw the tree to see what it looks like, and you'll see . . ." She did, looked at it for fifteen seconds, then exclaimed, "Oh! It doesn't tell how to end it."

"Right."

She added a few more lines of code and paused. Gammill said, "Okay now, continue through." She began mumbling instead of writing, working through the problem out loud. "You're close!" Gammill said again, by way of encouragement. Then, getting impatient, he said, "I'll give you a hint." He went on to show an error at the beginning of her writing. She seemed confused. "Is it too dark in here?" he asked solicitously. He sat down again, made a minute adjustment in his blinds, then fell to fidgeting, twirling and clicking his ballpoint pen, scratching a note on a pad.

"This will work, I think," she said hesitantly, a few minutes later.

"How will that improve it?" Gammill asked.

"Make it faster, more efficient."

"Well, there is a way you can—I won't make you do it right now—you can clean up the stack. . . . Move this down."

Seeing that she was lost, he moved on to the next problem. Just as she turned to begin working on it, Gammill's computer screamed again, and his frightened guest dropped her pen. Moments later, after staring at the board, she turned and described to him how she would solve the problem. "Exactly!" Gammill answered, with a grin. "Code it!"

She wrote something very close to the correct solution Gammill had put on the board during his earlier interview. "Okay, that's good," he said. "I'll show you what we did, and you can talk about the differences. It's very similar, though." He wrote his solution on the board. "Do you prefer one over the other?" he asked. When she answered, he seemed pleased and impressed.

"Okay!" he said enthusiastically. "Let's do another one! Isn't this fun? Just like exams!" She didn't answer. He asked her to take a linked list —a list of values, each pointing to the next one on the list—and reverse it. After writing the problem on the board, he sat back and waited. She wrote a few tentative lines, sighed, began fidgeting, leaning against the board at arm's length. "You want some help?" Gammill asked.

"No!"

"Okay."

"Okay, I think I have it," she said, after a few long minutes. "I think you need to keep three points here . . ." She went on to explain what she had written, and Gammill listened in silence until her voice trailed off, as she began to understand that it wouldn't work. "It's not as easy as it sounds, is it?" Gammill asked.

On and on they went, she proposing, Gammill disposing, until finally her shoulders slumped and Gammill took over at the board. "The hardest part is the boundary conditions," he said, referring to the setting of upper and lower limits in a given range of values. She had skipped an obvious step, forgetting to define the smallest possible list as one with nothing in it. "Which is . . . but we're out of time."

Although she had done far better than his previous interview subject, Gammill gave her an immediate thumbs down. "Verbally," he said, "she knew how to do the binary one . . . but her code was terrible. It was full of syntax errors, there were lots of mistakes and omissions." As even tiny errors—the omission of a single semicolon, for instance—can cause programs to fail, her numerous small mistakes would have added up to hours upon hours of bug fixing, had they been committed on a real project. "I'm gonna give her a 'no hire.' Her code was really inadequate." So went the rest of her day.

The interviews seemed to put Gammill in the mood to reminisce. Recalling a developer or two who had been given offers that they immediately accepted, he said, "You have to lowball them when you make an offer. You hate to do it, but you have to! Applicants don't understand that they don't have to accept the first offer they get, but they always take it." His loyalties in those situations were to Microsoft first. "You want to tell them that they don't have to accept the first offer, but you just can't."

At the same time, he made no secret of his distaste for Microsoft's Human Resources department, with which, in his view, he had been doing battle from the day he came to work for the company. In detailing his grievances with HR, Gammill made it clear that there are two kinds of people who come to work at Microsoft: winners and losers. Winners are those who can fight the company on its own terms, and losers are those who cannot. Gammill humbly held himself out as an example of a winner.

Jobs at Microsoft are highly prized, and when the company offered, under federal duress, to move Gammill from contractor to full-time employee, he jumped at the chance. He was outraged, however, when they tried to cut his salary. After paying him $50,000 the year before, they wanted to start him at $32,000. He held out angrily, and they eventually settled on $37,000. Gammill figured that periodic raises and other benefits—stock options, kitchens and cafeterias stocked with free beverages, and free membership in a health club among them—went a long way toward making up the difference.

Still, the cut in pay rankled. And when Gammill finished college, he was outraged anew when Human Resources tried to cut his pay again rather than give him a raise, the rationale being that new college graduates are paid a lower salary than Gammill had been getting. This time, instead of complaining, he decided to get even. He lined up job interviews with two Silicon Valley companies and left a note on Craig Bartholomew's desk telling him he would be interviewing down there for the next couple of days. "When I came back two days later," he says gleefully, "there was a new offer on my desk."

After four years as a full-time employee, Gammill said, his salary had crept back up to what it was when he was a contractor being paid overtime. But he was quick to acknowledge that Microsoft has compensated him so well that his salary was almost incidental. Stock options, tendered to him and his wife periodically at extremely favorable prices during times when Microsoft stock was rapidly rising, had made him wealthy. "I used stock purchases to start a college fund for Cassidy," he said one day, wonderment in his voice. His daughter was nearly a year old at the time. "Now, she could go to college for the rest of her life if she wanted." The options have been made all the more valuable by his wife's skillful selling of some Microsoft stock and the buying and selling of stock in other companies. While Gammill is somewhat cagey about his exact worth—"As long as money comes out every time I go to the cash machine," he says, "I'm happy"—he was living well. He estimated that he owned somewhere between 7,500 and 10,000 shares of Microsoft stock. He and his wife owned three cars and two houses, had a diversified stock portfolio built from the sale of some of their Microsoft holdings, and were investors in a small espresso shop in New York City.

Generally, when he attended developers' conferences elsewhere in the country, Gammill was offered jobs that would pay him upwards of $20,000 more than Microsoft payed him. On several occasions, competing companies had offered to double his salary. "But then I start thinking about the other things here," he said. "I get to live in this part of the country, there's the stock, the health club, the free soft drinks."

Angry as he was at Human Resources for what he saw as unfair treatment, Gammill harbored no grudges. Instead, he seemed to regard the department as a strong and skilled adversary, like a worthy opponent in sports. He had no patience with those who whined, to no avail, about the way the company treated them. The secret to success at Microsoft, Gammill said, is simple: "You have to learn how to be an asshole back."

While Gammill wallowed in contentment, Lindsey Smith sat in her office down the hall cataloging her growing roster of grievances. She had been noting for some months now the subtle and overt ways in which she and her fellow contractors at Microsoft were treated differently from full-time employees, and she was finding it increasingly difficult to keep her resentment at bay. Now, Carolyn Bjerke's move from design into program management, forcing Smith into a burdensome and ill-defined new role, seemed to provoke her to outright anger. Accustomed to suffering in silence and given by temperament to resignation, she decided to move against the grain of her character and complain directly to Bartholomew.

Smith is a pale, shy, softspoken blond who gives the impression that she would put up with anything as long as it didn't draw attention to her. In a company full of aggressive, hard-driving people, she had a tendency to fade into the background. At first glance, one would have thought her in an enviable position, one attained in spite of her instincts and character. Only twenty-three, a recent graduate in art from Western Washington University in Bellingham, a small town 85 miles north of Seattle, she had worked for a few months as a graphic artist at Seattle's Woodland Park Zoo before being tracked down there by another Western graduate, Scott Randall. An artist at Microsoft, Randall was looking on the company's behalf for similarly talented, computer-literate artists. With a degree in a field whose graduates expect only occasional part-time work and more or less constant starvation, Smith suddenly found herself under contract to a corporation with bottomless pockets. She was making as much money in a month as many of her former classmates might make from art in a year.

Yet Smith's good fortune in finding work at Microsoft coincided with misfortune: she had come to the company at a time when management was mandating a dramatic slowdown in the growth of its workforce. Microsoft had wholeheartedly joined the nationwide corporate trend toward hiring as many contract laborers and as few full-time workers as possible. This was both out of standard bottom-line concerns—contractors received no benefits or perquisites, and could be released by the company with none of the costs of laying off full-time employees—and out of a determination never to go through the cycles of layoffs that had hit every other hardware and software company in the world. Gates was particularly adamant that contractors not be turned into full-time hires, as every such move drove the budget of the project in question intolerably higher. "I think there's a misconception that a lot of freelancers have," Bartholomew said, "that freelancing is a way of getting your foot in the door; get this job at Microsoft, there's all this security and things like that. But we haven't converted a freelancer in over a year. We do it very, very rarely. And we're encouraged not to do it." From his point of view, a manager had nothing to gain by converting contractors to full-time employees. "What magical transformation comes from being made full time?" he asked. "Where does the productivity rise?"

So now, a year after coming to Microsoft, having won Bjerke's esteem and having cemented her position at MM Pubs for the foreseeable future, Smith felt cheated. "I find it frustrating here," she said. "I'd like to be hired on. That was my goal when I started working here." Now, being moved into the lead design position on a product deemed to be one of Microsoft's most important, she felt entitled to a full-time position. "It seems odd to me," she said with some heat, "that they can give me so much responsibility without having me hired on."

Smith felt that Microsoft employees treated contractors with undue disrespect, discounting their input because it came from temporary workers. Bryan Ballinger, for example, constantly resisted her directions, often going over her head to Bjerke. Smith also felt that management's practice of excluding contractors from all meetings where budgets and headcount were discussed was discriminatory and demeaning. Contractors often did not learn of important decisions made at certain meetings, or of news sent out on e-mail to full-time employees only. And no matter how hard contractors worked on a given project, no matter how good their work was, they were denied many of the rewards that routinely went to employees. "They say there isn't any difference between an employee and a contractor," Smith said, "but there's always just this fine line there."

More vexing was the difference in compensation. "I want stock and I want health insurance," Smith said emphatically. "If anything medicalwise were to happen to me, I'm just covered to the minimum. And I need to be in a 401(k) plan—I need to start saving for the future. I just have to start thinking about that kind of stuff."

Her distress was exacerbated by a dispute between Carolyn Bjerke and Jayleen Ryberg over her status. When Bartholomew had asked Bjerke to take over for Ryberg as program manager, Bjerke agreed on the condition that Smith be made *Sendak*'s lead designer. Ryberg objected, saying that the product needed a more experienced designer. The argument between the two was complicated somewhat by Bjerke's conviction that Ryberg was not letting go of her program management responsibilities with sufficient enthusiasm. With every question Ryberg asked, or every opinion she offered on Bjerke's decisions, Bjerke felt she was being second-guessed.

The disagreement between the two finally grew so heated that they stopped discussing it with one another and withdrew to their adjacent offices to continue the debate via e-mail. For two days, they sat some twenty feet apart, their backs to one another, sending opinions back and forth. Eventually, Bjerke prevailed—to a degree. The two agreed in principle that Smith would take over interface design on *Sendak*, although exactly which of them would be supervising her, and what her full range of responsibilities would be, was left up in the air.

Ryberg's skepticism and Bjerke's enthusiasm about Smith were to emerge again and again as a source of friction on the *Sendak* team. This was particularly troubling to Smith, as all art production people were to be supervised by Ryberg, while people working on *Sendak* were working under Bjerke. As far as Smith was concerned, which part of her work was to be directed by Bjerke and which by Ryberg was never made particularly clear to any of them.

After two weeks of increasing dissatisfaction with her status and of conflicting directives from Bjerke and Ryberg, Smith went to Bartholomew and complained. With some surprise, he watched the color rise in her cheeks and heard her voice quaver with anger. She told him she wanted a full-time position, that she had earned it, and that contractors should not be excluded from so many meetings and parties. "I know that full-time positions can't be made available for everyone," she said, "and I know I shouldn't be talking about one for me. But not everyone really expects one, and it's been a goal of mine for a long time."

Bartholomew told her that a full-time designer position for children's products would open in July and that she would likely be hired then, as her performance on *Sendak* had been good. He also promised to set up a new e-mail alias that would include Gandalf's freelancers, so they would not be left out of the loop so often. Smith left, satisfied, and Bartholomew sent Ryberg and Bjerke an e-mail summary of their conversation.

Bjerke, pleased to see that Smith was finally getting the recognition from Bartholomew that she deserved, now felt that Smith's hiring was assured. She was glad of this not only because she believed in Smith, but because the designer for *Sendak* and future children's products would be someone Bjerke herself had trained and brought along. Ryberg, however, was angry. If she was to supervise *Sendak*'s production resources, she wanted a voice in who was to be hired. While *Sendak* was Bjerke's project, art direction—coming under production—was Ryberg's territory. Now Bartholomew had all but promised a production job to someone Ryberg felt was unqualified. "She doesn't have much experience beyond what we've been able to give her here," she said. "She's got great potential, but if Gandalf can only hire two new designers, would she really be one of them?" She also was worried about Smith's personality and commitment to work. Newly married, Smith had made it clear that she would move to wherever her new husband, just finishing college, found a job. "She rides the fence too much, and doesn't like upsetting anybody," Ryberg said. "And long-term, I'm not sure how career-oriented she really is."

She also felt that Smith had breached protocol. "It happens a lot around here that contractors feel they deserve to be hired," she said. "Lindsey feels like she's worked a year or more, so she deserves a full-time job. I have a little trouble with that. I guess I don't feel like because you've devoted a year to a company that you deserve anything. It behooves you to work as hard as you can and certainly if you want to be full-time somewhere, that's your goal. But you can't sit around waiting for Microsoft to help you make that goal. It's the 'deserving' part that I have a little trouble with."

Three days later, in a meeting with Smith and Ballinger at which Ryberg sought to explain how the two artists' roles would change under the new Gandalf structure—with Ryberg as producer and Bjerke as program manager—she explained that Smith and Ballinger would split up Bjerke's former design responsibilities. "Wait a minute!" Smith objected. "I thought I was going to be hired as the designer in July. So I should take over the design responsibilities now." Then she went off to talk with Bartholomew again.

"It got kind of awkward," Ryberg said later. "Craig promised her too much, and Carolyn probably was overencouraging her." She sent mail to Bartholomew and Bjerke saying that Smith's responsibilities and expectations needed to be more strictly defined and that the future children's designer position should not be promised to her when there might be more talented designers available. "This transition for Carolyn from design to program management has to be clean," she wrote, "so that everyone is clear about what their roles are." And in any event, she added, Smith's motives for wanting the design position were not optimal: "Lindsey doesn't want the design position as much as she wants a full-time position here."

Bartholomew, backtracking, met with Ryberg and Bjerke, with Bjerke arguing strenuously that Smith should be the design lead on *Sendak*, whatever her corporate status, and Ryberg arguing that Bartholomew had erred in virtually promising her a full-time job. Bartholomew agreed with both of them, then talked again with Smith, scaling back her expectations dramatically and telling her that she had to prove her worth to Ryberg before Microsoft could consider hiring her full time. Smith was dejected. "You feel like you're always being judged or whatever here," she said. "You feel like your performance has to be at a very high level all the time. Like right now I feel like I have to prove myself now in this designer role to Jayleen in order to be hired on. But dammit, I've already proved myself! I've worked so hard since I've been here! And they already know what kind of employee I would be! It's frustrating, just to hear that continuously."

Added to her frustration was ongoing confusion over whether Bjerke or Ryberg had authority over her. For the next two weeks, Smith felt like someone with two jobs and two supervisors. While Bjerke continued to direct her artwork and pass on design responsibilities to her, Ryberg continued to feel that Bjerke's design supervision responsibilities had been passed to her, as production lead, when Bjerke became program manager. So Smith often would leave a meeting where Bjerke, she said, "treated me as the designer," then would enter a meeting where Ryberg "presented things to Bryan and me as if we were codesigners. It went on like that where both Carolyn and Craig were treating me as designer, but Jayleen wasn't." Finally, angry again, she complained to Bartholomew, and was surprised next day to hear Ryberg tell Ballinger, "Lindsey's in charge of all art direction, she will approve everything, and everything that deals with design is in her field. You will be the lead illustrator."

"It was like Jayleen was totally into me being designer, all of a sudden," Smith said. Yet she was more dismayed than delighted. "That's totally frustrating to Bryan. I mean, I feel bad about it."

Still, she felt that in the long run Ryberg's change of heart would do more good than harm. She was convinced that Ballinger, for whatever reason, had continued to treat Bjerke as *Sendak*'s designer and his supervisor, and Smith as a peer. "It helps a lot that Jayleen is seeing me in this role now," Smith said, "because it meant she enforced it with Bryan. So now he'll listen to what I have to say, and consider it a valuable opinion. Where before he used to always go back to Carolyn."

Suddenly morose again, Smith said, "It's like a soap opera around here." Bartholomew had forced a solution on everyone that would ultimately prove nothing more than a stalling action. The underlying problems—Smith's unhappiness with her status as a temporary worker, Microsoft's cultural bias against contractors, and the profound disagreement between Ryberg and Bjerke over Smith's abilities—remained unresolved. Although assured by her three managers that she had real authority and control over her part of *Sendak*, and that she quite possibly had a good future at Microsoft, Smith saw nothing but confusion and intrigue as she contemplated the months ahead. She was to report formally to Bjerke and take direction from her while having all the time to prove her worth to Ryberg. And Ballinger, she feared, would never allow her to direct him properly as long as she was a contractor. As far as she was concerned, nothing had changed.

In Which the Author
Comes Up for Air

I had come to Microsoft to describe, up close, unprecedented success in action. Instead, as Smith pointed out, I had landed smack in the middle of a soap opera. The more I watched the process of creating *Sendak* try to unfold, the more confused and disillusioned I grew. These people were hardly the crisp, precise, unerring, and ruthless Microsoftoids of popular legend. Listening to them dither through meeting after meeting, hearing them grow more and more frustrated with one another, and watching them drift into helplessness, I found it difficult to sit through meetings and conversations without supplying what I saw as the obvious answers to their questions.

I was struck at every turn by how *young* these people were, and how inexperienced. Their greenness seemed to render them terrified of making a mistake—with the result that they were unable to commit to a decision and move on. For more than three months, I had been attending meetings, reading corporate documents, engaging in steadily longer and more emotional conversations with team members, measuring their ever-increasing distress, and still the product being designed had no . . . *design.* As far as I could tell, nothing had been done, and I could see no signs on the horizon that the team was on the verge of any kind of breakthrough.

This state of affairs stood in jarring contrast to the confident air Craig Bartholomew and Tom Corddry presented to Bill Gates. To leave a meeting room where *Sendak* teammates yet again were wallowing in despair and confusion, then to walk into Gates's boardroom, where managers were presenting reports and spreadsheets demonstrating that *Sendak* and its companion products in Multimedia Publishing were on track to create and dominate the next new world of software, was profoundly disorienting. Perhaps some magic process was at work here that I had yet to understand; perhaps Gates was far more indulgent than popular myth would have us believe; or perhaps Multimedia Publishing was setting itself up for some kind of grand group suicide a few months down the road.

So I watched and listened in growing amazement as work on *Sendak* kept moving on a variety of fronts, in a direction deemed by all but me to be forward.

You could look at any individual part of the project and convince yourself that things were going well. Sara Fox's two contract editors, Meredith Kraike and Abigail Riblet, were making their way briskly through *Sendak*'s Civilization and Nature topics, editing text down to Fox's specifications. Ballinger, Smith, and Shelly Becker—the contract artist who specialized in scripting animation—all were hard at work getting a second *Sendak* prototype ready for the next usability tests, to be conducted near the end of March. Work on the prototype was progressing rapidly, and team members constantly dropped into Becker's office to watch her display some new working feature.

It was one thing, though, to come up with good edited text, or to put together a short animation script that showed a single *Sendak* scene appearing to work properly; it was another thing entirely to assemble so much material, in so many different media, and get it to perform adequately. The complexity of the project, as reflected in the number of issues to be tracked through *Sendak*'s production and the difficulty of bringing all the disparate elements together by the project's deadline, began to loom ever more menacingly—not only in my mind, but also in Carolyn Bjerke's.

Whenever Bjerke sat down to plan a step-by-step building of the encyclopedia, she ran into a welter of dependencies. No one element of the product, it seemed, could be finished before some other element was completed. Everything both trailed and preceded everything else. Editors of the text were waiting for design questions to be answered before they could complete their editing; Gammill was waiting for all design and editorial issues to be resolved before he could begin writing code; the whole team was waiting to see when Phil Spencer's core tools group would have a sprite engine available for *Sendak* to use, and how good the engine would be, before they could design animation into the encyclopedia; Spencer was waiting to hear exactly what *Sendak* wanted from his group before designing and beginning work on the core tools; *Sendak*'s editors and designers were waiting for Gammill to pass judgment on the feasibility of their designs and editorial ambitions; and the designers were waiting for final editorial decisions to be made.

In other words, the project was at a complete standstill. It was a corporate M. C. Escher drawing, with each team member looking anxiously toward someone else, in the hopes that he or she could do something to get the rest of the team moving. The arrangement of anxious glances came around full circle in a devious way, as is typical in Escher's drawings, that could be seen only after intense scrutiny.

Even so, as if determined to believe that *Sendak* was in plannable shape, Bartholomew insisted that Bjerke plan out a set of milestones, six to eight weeks apart, stretching from the beginning to the end of the project. Each member of her team was to have specific goals to be completed by each milestone. The team was to have milestone check-in meetings every two weeks to ensure that they were on track for the coming deadline. If a given task fell behind schedule, Bjerke was to eliminate some future feature to accommodate the slippage. There was to be no belief, as there had been throughout the *Encarta* project, that lost time could somehow be made up. "You have to be completely ruthless on schedule," Bartholomew told her.

Bjerke's first attempt at ruthlessness came to a rueful end almost as soon as she attempted it. Early in February, she had laid out milestones stretching from February 15, 1993, to September 1, 1994, with tasks to be completed at each of the first four milestones entered into a spreadsheet. Now, at the beginning of March, she saw that none of the February 15 milestone-one tasks had been completed. It was fast becoming obvious that the beauty and practicality of *Sendak* plans decreased in direct proportion to the span of time between the description of a task and its deadline.

The most striking example was the team's multimedia database, Merismus. As described in planning documents written months before by Gammill, it worked perfectly, bringing together the encyclopedia with awe-inspiring efficiency and power. But now, in practice, entry of *Sendak* elements into Merismus was proving to be endlessly complicated, and getting more difficult with each attempt.

Merismus was an entirely different tool to almost everyone who used it. Every piece of writing in *Sendak*, and every photograph, video clip, animation, credit, activity, and sound recording was to be entered into

Merismus and assigned a number. Subsequently, every approval or rejection by an editor or designer of every element in the encyclopedia was to be recorded there. *Sendak* editors planned to use Merismus to track a given topic through the editorial process, looking up topic titles in Merismus to see if their text had been edited and approved, their illustrations acquired and approved by editors, and the whole package of text and graphics assembled in final form and approved. Those acquiring art for *Sendak* did it entirely through Merismus, getting from the database lists of illustrations requested for *Sendak*, then tracking the arrival of a given illustration and its subsequent passes through editing and production. Art production people used Merismus to keep track of requests for their resources and of the progress of their work. And for Gammill, Merismus was the means by which he could arrange all of the encyclopedia's parts within the elaborate structure of his code.

The editorial work in Merismus was intended to ease Gammill's burden significantly. Eventually, much of his program would consist of lists of elements, entered by Merismus number, with each number linked in the list to all other related elements. The arrangement in Merismus would cut Gammill's workload by several months and would make his program, once completed, run far faster and more efficiently.

This circumstance afforded scant consolation to the rest of the *Sendak* team. Two things made Merismus enormously complicated for everyone but Gammill to use. One was its evolving nature; the team was to begin its project using Version 1.0 of the tool, and eventually move over to Version 2.0—a move that amounted to moving on to an entirely new product, with a new interface and new rules and procedures for users to learn. Version 1.0 had been relatively crude, and rushed into production for use by editors near the end of the *Encarta* project. Version 2.0, with a more detailed user interface and far more ways of indexing, arranging, and finding items stored in the database, was to be infinitely more powerful. Unfortunately, it also was infinitely harder to use.

The other, far more difficult issue was Gammill himself, who insisted that the rest of the team use Merismus essentially as a development tool. Asking artists and editors to understand how to use Merismus, and why it was being used in the way Gammill demanded, was like asking developers to understand why the Macintosh palette was better than the Windows palette, or why a colored border around a window was better than a simple black line. Just as designers were helpless and uncomprehending when it came to software development, so were developers helpless and uncomprehending when it came to design.

Gammill wanted everything in *Sendak* to fit into one of eighteen Merismus classes. Every sound effect, piece of text, illustration and animation, along with any other element *Sendak*'s editors could dream up, had to fit into one of these classifications, which were strictly defined. And every one of these elements was to be labeled and tagged with a Merismus number in a way that showed its place within the elaborate hierarchy of elements stretching through the encyclopedia from beginning to end, top to bottom.

Each Merismus class in *Sendak* had a label represented by a three-letter abbreviation. An animation that stayed in one place was an ANI, an animation that moved around on the screen was an SPR (for "sprite"), audio pronunciation of a word was an APR, a pop-up was a POP, its text a TXT, and so on. *Sendak* team members always referred to these classes by their abbreviations, generally pronouncing each letter individually. Meetings at which Merismus was discussed often sounded like arguments consisting of nothing but letters of the alphabet randomly flung around the room: "Is this T-X-T attached to this O-B-J or what?" "Should this be a C-I-M or several I-M-Gs?"

In Gammill's scheme, *Sendak*, as seen in Merismus, was an array of parents and children. Each of the eighty-five or so scenes in *Sendak* was, in this metaphor, the progenitor of a family of elements. Every figure in a given scene was one of the scene's children. An early version of the desert scene, for example, was the parent of seventeen children, each depicted in the scene: an antelope, a palm tree, an eagle, a date palm, a desert pea plant, a scorpion, a dromedary, a saguaro cactus, an eagle, a gila monster, a roadrunner, a rattlesnake, a yucca plant, a dust devil, sand, a shadow, and a long-eared hedgehog.

Each of the desert's children was nearly as prolific. The eagle had four children: an animation of the eagle flying around the scene, and a stack of three pop-ups. The whole generation appeared when the user clicked on the picture of the eagle in the desert scene. The eagle would fly off its perch and circle the scene, and a stack of pop-ups would spring up when the animation was finished. The first pop-up in the stack was the parent of four children: the phonetic spelling of the word *eagle*, which appeared at the top of the pop-up; an audio pronunciation of *eagle*, which was activated when the user clicked on the pronunciation icon on the pop-up; the pop-up's text; and another picture of an eagle, contained in that pop-up. This picture of the eagle in the pop-up had two children: a CPU, or child pop-up, of text about the eagle's head, which popped up when the user clicked on the head in the picture, and a CPU with text about the eagle's wings, which appeared when the user clicked on the wings.

In all, the eagle alone had eighteen descendants. Assuming a similar number for all of the desert scene's children, there were 323 descendants of the desert scene, each with its own Merismus number and type to be catalogued and arranged in the hierarchy of *Sendak* elements. Early on, then, it was clear that *Sendak*'s editors would be making some 27,455 entries into the database. They saw their task as 27,455 opportunities to make critical, if not fatal, mistakes, and were constantly pleading with an unsympathetic Gammill to somehow simplify their end of the Merismus bargain.

To the editors writing *Sendak*'s text and specifying what sort of illustrations and other accompanying materials should be displayed or played along with it, the class structure in Merismus was incomprehensible. Editors' notes on *Sendak* topics looked like genealogy projects run amok: little boxes, connected by networks of lines, filled page after page of topic entry notes, as editors tried to get everything arranged correctly in relation to everything else before actually entering text and image requests into Merismus. An incorrect Merismus entry could eventually result in incongruous combinations of text and graphics: an eagle's picture appearing in a pop-up with text about a mouse, a sockeye salmon sitting forlornly in desert sand.

In one editor's attempted Merismus arrangement, ultimately rejected by Gammill, a jumble of crooked lines pointed off in every direction from the IMG of a fighter airplane. When you deciphered all the boxes, crossed-out boxes, arrows, connecting lines, and crossed-out lines, there were eight CPUs—children of a single proud POP—and one of them had four children of its own. "You can't have a CPU of a CPU," Gammill said after the arrangement was described to him. He didn't deign to explain why.

"Keviiiiiiin!" screamed the editor.

Gammill generally left these meetings in a high dudgeon, rushing back to his office to profess bewildered anger at the dim-wittedness of his colleagues. "It's so simple!" he would say, over and over again. "It's so obvious!"

Editorial notes on Merismus entry tended toward incoherent attempts at self-instruction. "ANE Audio w/controller does NOT auto-start," read one notation. "((Can only be child of CPU) A) w/CPU when clicked on CPU will pop-up with a controller in the CPU that has to be clicked on to start Audio. POP-IMG-OBJ-CPU-ANE (can also have . . .)—Always a CPU in this class." Arranging text and graphics for Merismus entry took more editorial work than did the actual writing and editing of the text. In order to turn a two-page Dorling Kindersley entry, "Ships and Boats," into a single screen of information in *Sendak*, for example, Microsoft's editors had to produce twelve pages of their own work: five pages of pop-up text and verbal descriptions of the illustrations that would accompany it; and seven pages of Merismus-entry information.

In doing her first pass at a schedule for *Sendak*, Bjerke, anticipating endless problems with entering *Sendak* topic information into Merismus, had planned on each editor being able to write, edit, and get fully labeled for entry into the database two *Sendak* topics per day. But then she met one day in March with Meredith Kraike and Abigail Riblet to see how their editorial work was progressing. "We have a gazillion questions," Kraike said. "Merismus specing takes a really long time." Added Riblet, "It's definitely going to add time to our schedule." They told Bjerke that Merismus-related thought and work slowed them down from a planned two topics per day completed and marked up to one and one-half per day, a change that would extend a 382-day schedule for the completion of editorial work another 127 days.

In addition to misunderstanding Gammill's hierarchy, the editors kept dreaming up things that didn't seem to fit into his classifications at all. Kraike wanted pop-up text about the automobile to be accompanied by a picture of a car's interior. When the user clicked on the radio, she wanted music to play; a click on the windshield-wiper button should activate the wipers, a click on the horn should play a honk, and so on. How, she wondered, was that to be classified? Bjerke didn't know. Riblet wanted to know whether to file a topic in Merismus under the topic title or the name for the object representing it. How should she file "chemistry"—under that name or under "barbecue," since the user clicked on a barbecue in the Civilization scene to get the chemistry entry? Again, Bjerke didn't know.

The more Bjerke tried talking through the problem with her editors, the less they—or, for that matter, she herself—understood what she was saying. "These two would be the children of the container," she said to blank stares at one point. And later, silence came flooding into the room in the wake of this pronouncement: "So in that case, that child would be a hot child, whereas these container children aren't . . . they're just a dead end."

The longer Merismus conversations went on, the more bizarre they sounded. A stranger walking into a Merismus meeting of editors would conclude that the meeting was about family dysfunction. "We need to have it so that if the child is rejected, so is the parent . . . and vice versa"; "We need to have the child inherit the code of the parent"; "So if you reject a child, you reject the parent but not the other children?"

In contrast, work on the design side appeared to be positively flying along. Ballinger, Smith, and Shelly Becker were all hard at work readying two new *Sendak* prototypes—one based on the spaceship navigation model, the other on the magical room—for the upcoming usability tests. Day after day, the three worked far into the night, with Smith and Ballinger getting artwork drawn and colored, and Becker incorporating it into *Sendak*'s MacroMedia Director animation scripts.

The main purpose of the usability tests was to determine whether children had a marked preference for either the ship or the room. Ballinger had drawn a ship interior with a huge window through which could be seen four globes—one each for Civilization, Nature, Geography, and History. By clicking on any one of the globes, the user triggered an animation of the globe spinning and zooming in until it filled the screen. A dissolve effect turned the spinning Nature globe into a picture of the guide standing in the Nature unit's forest scene.

Ballinger had also drawn an eerie, cavelike magical room, with four globes standing on pillars. When the user clicked on one of them, the guide suddenly shrank down and flew into the globe. After a dissolve, the guide was standing in the Nature unit's forest scene. While Ballinger, perhaps hoping to overcome his own bias in favor of the spaceship, lavished far more care and attention on his drawing of the room, he added a few touches to the spaceship as well—particularly a soft drink, with straw, that popped up out of the dashboard. When the guide sidled over to sip on the straw, the computer emitted loud, luxurious slurping sounds.

Smith, meanwhile, was working on new pop-up designs and on a more direct navigational tool, called a "find gadget," for users who wanted to look up specific topics or pieces of information. This gadget, which popped up out of the guide's backpack and looked like a portable computer screen with various buttons arranged around it, was a combination verbal and visual index to the encyclopedia's contents. It was to show miniature pictures, called "thumbnails," of all the pop-ups. If the user typed *camel* in a narrow window along the top of the gadget, the gadget's main screen would scroll through its rows of thumbnails until it was filled with the first camel pop-up and its "children" all in a horizontal row to the right of it, and the pop-ups and their CPUs for the topics preceding and following *camel* in alphabetical order arranged vertically above and below. Each topic would be linked, in a hidden list, with certain keywords, so that—to cite Bjerke's favorite example—if a child typed in the word *humps*, the main find gadget screen would scroll to the camel miniature. Then, by clicking on any of the miniatures on the find gadget's screen, the user immediately jumped to the appropriate pop-up or CPU itself.

When Becker had assembled all of this new material into a more or less finished prototype—this one with two scenes in it instead of one, and with more user interface features—Bjerke and Smith brought Gammill in to look at it. Since the prototype showed an example of the main navigational features they wanted included in the final product, they felt it best that Gammill see it so that he could begin thinking in earnest about his code and what it would have to do.

While Bjerke, Smith, and Sara Fox—who had come in from her maternity leave to look at it—ooohed and aaahed, Becker ran the prototype through its paces. Gammill watched in stone-faced silence, occasionally asking questions: "How big is that window?"; "We're taking this to the offsite, right?"; "Why is the scroll bar on the left side instead of the right?" After watching for ten minutes or so, he got up to leave.

I had spent enough time with Gammill to see behind the cryptically angry expression that was spreading over his face as he watched the demonstration. He constantly complained to me about the inability of designers to see beneath the special effects they could create for small product demonstrations to the underlying problems of implementation in large compact-disc products. He could never get them to understand architectural issues—as far as he was concerned, all they cared about was the façade on the screen. Watching Becker play through the prototype, he saw example after example of things he had told *Sendak*'s designers would be unworkable.

For now, he kept his opinions to himself, although he left abruptly enough to have raised a warning flag in the mind of anyone who noticed. While the rest of the *Sendak* team watched Becker run through the prototype a second time, he walked out of the room and down the hall, wagging his head dejectedly from side to side, stretching his neck and shrugging his shoulders like a boxer entering a ring. Safely back in his office, with the door closed, he sat down, looked into his monitor, and shouted, "Fuck! Holy shit! I mean, it's okay to let them think and play . . . let this run its course. . . . I better get ready for the offsite, that's all I have to say." He had left the room out of fear that he would say something intemperate. "I have to think about it before I react," he said.

Fear and Trembling

Sara Fox ushered Carolyn Bjerke into her house and over to her dining room table, littered with pages of *Sendak* text. Henry, her baby, was sleeping in a nearby crib hanging from hooks in the ceiling. "We need to do a group review of all topics," Fox said as Bjerke was sitting down. "When I saw them, I was shocked and horrified."

Bjerke swallowed hard and blushed. Fox had spent her maternity leave, now nearly over, monitoring *Sendak* from afar, her fears rising minute by minute. In each call from a friend or subordinate, she found new cause for alarm. As her leave wore on, she came into her office more and more often on weekends, to leave worried e-mail messages for Bjerke. Increasingly, Bjerke felt that she was calming fears in Fox that were based on misconceptions. Contract editor Abigail Riblet had been talking almost daily with Fox, as had Jayleen Ryberg. Bjerke felt that Fox's tendency to worry under the best of circumstances was rendered virtually uncontrollable by her having to hear all *Sendak* news secondhand. "She's talking to Abby and Jayleen all the time," Bjerke said one day. Then she added, sardonically, "And Jayleen's got her more confused than ever."

Fox's anxieties were heightened by her attachment to *Sendak*: she felt it was the project she had been born to direct. Children's education had been a preoccupation of hers for most of her life, and now, with *Sendak*, she had been given her first shot at developing a children's reference product entirely according to her own vision. She had a nearly limitless budget and infinite resources at her disposal. Editorial direction of the project, she felt, presented her with the opportunity of a lifetime.

But now she felt the opportunity slipping away. More and more of *Sendak* was being developed outside her reach, by people with less expertise than she, and who, in her judgment, were liable to make critical mistakes. The farther along *Sendak*'s design moved during her leave, she feared, the greater the likelihood that it would turn into a poor product.

To an extent, Fox's fears were justified. She was the only *Sendak* team member with expertise in children's education. She was the only one to have previously helped create children's software products. And of everyone on the team, with the possible exception of Bryan Ballinger, she was the only one with a firmly held vision of how the entire product should look, and what it should have to offer.

Unfortunately, Fox was such a chronic worrier that she didn't even trust her own judgment. Arguing with her proved particularly frustrating for her teammates, as Fox often would take an argument full circle, savagely attacking the position she had taken at the beginning of the discussion. For Bjerke, dealing with her was a constant battle to determine whether Fox was advancing an argument out of her expertise or her neurosis.

The way both women reacted to *Sendak*'s predicament highlighted the essential difference between them. Bjerke saw a challenge that could be overcome only by the power of her intelligence and analytical skill. Fox, on the other hand, felt that the greater the challenge, the more obvious it was that Bjerke and the rest of the team would fail. She had a way of poking holes in any solution that anyone, herself included, could dream up.

So, as the two women now sat down to talk, Bjerke couldn't wait to show her teammate the solutions they had been devising while Fox was away. But Fox sat down with the look on her face of someone expecting —hoping, even—to hear the worst.

Bjerke began by explaining Merismus to Fox, and showing her the diagrams and notes Fox's editors had been making in the course of their Merismus entry. Since both women wanted as much of *Sendak*'s work as possible done on line—with text and graphics entered into the computer system—rather than on paper, they wanted to have topics organized in Merismus and stored on computer as early in the process as possible. Accordingly, Bjerke had sketched out a plan in which editors wrote and edited text for a given topic, listed the accompanying graphic elements they wanted, assigned Merismus numbers to all of the topics' text blocks and graphic pieces, then entered it all into the database. Once it was entered, acquisitions could begin buying photographs, video clips, and other illustrations, getting editorial's requests for these elements from Merismus. Production also could begin creating animations and drawings, and editorial could edit copy and review the ensuing production of text-and-graphic compositions. All of the work would be done on computer, all through the medium of Merismus, and the status of each element would be tracked in the database as it moved through editing.

To Fox, the process was perilous. "I can understand how this works from Kevin's point of view," she said, "but it's a real pain for us. If it's hard for Abby, who knows it best, and she's drawing these little pictures to make sure she's got it right, we've got a big problem." The way Gammill wanted to use the database presented her with a dilemma: in order to enter everything properly into Merismus, an editor had to be intelligent enough to make difficult decisions constantly, and anyone that intelligent was going to be hopelessly bored by what was essentially a data-entry task. "Anybody who can do editorial work really quickly and well," she said, "is not going to want to do this." Furthermore, she reflected, Merismus use was to be much more complicated in *Sendak* than it had been for *Encarta*; and Fox had spent four months cleaning up *Encarta*'s Merismus mistakes.

Fox was particularly unhappy with Bjerke's plan to have editors write copy, mark it up, and immediately put it in Merismus, as nearly all of it would have to be rewritten, necessitating another round of Merismus entry. She insisted that Bjerke direct her contract editors to "stop putting things into Merismus right now." Then she immediately regretted her decision, as it meant a more primitive means of editing and tracking *Sendak* topics. "I hate to go to paper."

Bjerke, seeing that Fox was about to set off on another worried loop, hurriedly changed the subject. Picking up drawings of her favorite new *Sendak* feature—the find gadget—she began explaining how it was a combination contents window, verbal index, and visual index. "See, that won't work," Fox interrupted, pointing to the miniature CPUs stretching out horizontally behind their miniature pop-up parents.

"What's wrong with it?" Bjerke asked, blushing.

"First of all, we should test it. I'm not sure we need to label every tiny piece of extraneous information."

"Well, the philosophy was to give an index to the entire content, and then to show a relationship of one thing to another."

"I'm wondering if we're giving too much, getting to a level here where—"

"See, with this, you type in *humps,* you get types of camel. . . . What about the scenario where the user finds value in some CPU?"

"Yeah, *Gothic,* buried in types of architecture, is a case in point. . . . You can argue either side on this."

Then, as if on cue, both women started fluttering their hands, remarking on how quickly time was passing—particularly since Henry was due to wake up. "Okay, Okay," Bjerke said eagerly, "let's move on to the next thing."

Sendak's design had begun with a single simple idea: to come up with an overriding metaphor that was appealing to children and that would make the encyclopedia somewhat gamelike. The team had settled immediately on the metaphor of exploration through a landscape, and set about mocking up nature scenes through which the *Sendak* guide could travel in search of information. Since the design proved an immediate success in the eyes both of team members and children seeing a forest scene prototype in usability sessions, Bjerke and Fox had embraced the exploration metaphor without thinking much about how it would work throughout the encyclopedia.

Now that they were turning their attention to History, Geography, and Civilization, though, they were running into unexpected obstacles. In Civilization, for example, the user was to navigate through various urban and rural scenes—equivalent to the forest, desert, grassland, wetland, and ocean scenes in Nature—clicking on objects and creatures to get textual information to pop up. But many of the Civilization scenes, Fox now pointed out to Bjerke, were inside of larger scenes. The operating room and emergency room, for example, both scenes in themselves, were inside of a hospital, which in turn was part of an urban scene. So some mouse-clicks would bring up information and others would only admit the user into buildings. Instead of having a single layer of scenes, the user sometimes would have to find his or her way to a second layer of scenes within scenes, and thus would never know what to expect in response to a mouse-click on an object.

Fox had sent e-mail to Bjerke outlining her concerns for Civilization some six weeks before. For now, Bjerke's solution to the problem was to find an undefined way to raise the user's consciousness. "We need to get the user used to the notion of dimensionality," she said. "Not only do you go sideways from scene to scene, but also into things within the scene." But to Fox, this was hopelessly confusing. She wanted consistent, predictable behavior throughout the product. "The problem is," she said, "what if you click on the sports stadium intending to read about it, and find yourself inside the stadium instead?"

As often happened in conversations between Fox and Bjerke, Fox's question brought both women up short. They stared at one another in silence for a moment. Neither woman particularly relished confrontation, unless they were confronting someone who was less able than they were at arguing. When points of disagreement surfaced between them, they tended to turn away after the first exchange or two failed to resolve their differences. Consequently, they often put off the most difficult decisions facing them if they could not come to immediate agreement. This habit, while preserving their friendship in the short term, threatened their progress down the road by postponing the most difficult issues until they became real obstacles.

Now, the possibility that their only option lay in abandoning their exploration metaphor entirely and starting over with the search for something completely new came looming up before them; out of panic, they moved on to Geography.

Since the intent in Geography was to have a stack of pop-ups for each country, the problem posed there by the exploration metaphor was twofold: how to divide the world into fifteen scenes or so, to make it consistent in number with the other units; and how to make information on each country accessible by clickable objects. How, for example, was the user to find, in a landscape of France, access to the entry on its wine industry?

By now, Henry was awake, and Fox explained her scheme for Geography while she breast-fed and changed him, then worked at trying to find a way to keep him happy and distracted while she worked through her agenda with Bjerke. She had come up with a plan in which the world was broken up into fifteen clusters of countries. By clicking on a given country, the user would either bring it to the foreground of the scene, with the bordering countries fading to gray, or would bring up a stack of pop-ups, with the first pop-up containing a more detailed map of the clicked-upon country. The map would be decorated with little illustrations and the names of cities and major geographical landmarks. A click on the picture of a cow would bring up a stack of pop-ups on agriculture, a click on a factory would bring up a stack on the country's industry, and so on. One of the illustrations in each country would be of a visitors' center, on which the user would click to get a stack of pop-ups on the country's history and culture.

Fox also was considering a pen pal idea for each country's pop-ups. "Say there's a little pen pal on each map that you could click on," she said, "and get a stack of postcards." She showed Bjerke a sample post-card for France. It was postmarked and had a picture of the Eiffel tower on one half, with the other half filled in with the text of a letter:

Dear_____,

My country is called France. It is the largest country in Western Europe. France is a land of green, open spaces dotted with colorful towns and small cities. France also has many industries and is very involved in the European Community (EC). The EC regulates trade between France and other countries in Europe.

France is a democracy. French people vote to elect the president and other members of the government. When I am older I will be able to vote too!

Ton ami,
Pierre

The postcard was to be the first of six in a stack, with each being yet another message from the user's friend, Pierre. It was one of the ways Fox had come up with to make the encyclopedia more entertaining, more like a game and less like a printed book. Moreover, it was an easy way to get a spiffy special effect that only a computer could help deliver: the computer would automatically address the letter by name to the user, who would have logged on when *Sendak* was first turned on and brought up on screen.

Bjerke was enthralled with Fox's idea. She peppered her colleague with questions about the types of map they might employ, the style of art for the clickable objects on them, the means of navigation, the ways of incorporating video and animation into the scenes, and so on. But even as they talked, Fox grew more and more fearful. "What should be our way in here?" she asked. "You could have a package shooting out of the wall or something . . . a globe with people all over it? Pen pals to click on? . . . You're in a hot-air balloon over a region, you click on a country, get a map to pop up. . . . I don't know, maybe we should bag this letter idea. . . . I just feel like Geo's just such a chore, and I feel like the user's going to think it's a chore, too. . . . We're like, 'Dammit, we can make this creative and fun in some way.' "

Finally, it came time for Bjerke to leave. As she gathered up her things, she and Fox ran through the long list of unresolved issues remaining before they could begin production of any of the elements in the encyclopedia. This subject always seemed to cheer her and depress Fox. Where Fox was happiest discussing her vision of the final product, and unhappiest when thinking about the details of implementation, Bjerke was happiest when she could focus on the process. Now, by her reckoning, production was at least a month away, and when she told Fox that "Craig's date for starting production was March 1"—nearly two weeks ago—they both laughed.

A heartened Bjerke headed back across Lake Washington to the Microsoft campus while Fox sat down with Henry and worried about her eventual return to work. She found the prospect of abandoning her new baby for the sake of her job unthinkable. "I'm vacillating between hysteria and panic," she said. With her return to work now only two weeks away, she contemplated the future with dread. Her mother-in-law was planning to move to the Seattle area, renting an apartment near enough to Microsoft for Fox to drop Henry off on her way to work, go there at noon to breast-feed, and pick him up on her way home. While it was an arrangement that earned her the undying envy of her fellow Microsoft mothers, Fox saw in it endless potential for unhappiness. She and her husband, Pat, both worked at Microsoft, and not until she was staying at home did Fox realize how many hours each day they spent at work. "We used to work late, then go grab dinner somewhere on the east side," she said, "and come home at eight or later. Now, it gets to be six or so, and I find myself staring at the clock, wondering, 'Where is he? Why is it taking him so long to come home?' " She couldn't imagine spending that much time away from Henry. "I really feel like it's very important for people to be able to spend time with their children if they want to. I think that's why you have children. I think kids learn from the very earliest of ages and are picking up things all the time. And so having to be away from Henry for long blocks of time doesn't seem like the best answer." Standing at her living room window, holding her baby in her arms, she looked at once anxious, contented, and restless. "Daycare is a *huge* concern at Microsoft," she said. "Nobody is happy. You'd think they would have solved this problem by now."

Determined optimist that she was, Bjerke found it hard to endure the fears and doubts of her colleagues, particularly Fox and Gammill. As more and more tension crept into the air around *Sendak*, Bjerke felt that she was constantly being buffeted back and forth from the anxiety of one to the bristling skepticism of the other. Fox bleated in fear whenever Bjerke talked with her about *Sendak*; Gammill growled with hostility and impatience. The scale of the team's ambitions for the project was proving to be far beyond anything its schedule could accommodate, and as each day went by, the pressure around Bjerke and her teammates was turned up another notch.

A few days after her visit with Fox, Bjerke held her first substantive meeting with Gammill. Sitting in one of the Microsoft cafeterias, she tried to describe the salient features of *Sendak* and elicit concrete answers from him about their feasibility.

As often happened to editors and designers who met with Gammill, Bjerke found him perversely vague, particularly when it came to the features dearest to her heart. It was of vital importance to her, for example, that scenes in *Sendak* be layered, so that sprites could move in front of and behind objects on the screen. But when she brought this up to Gammill, he immediately objected, insisting that the effect was not worth the effort it would take to create it. "This layering thing," he said, using one of Gates's favorite terms, "I don't see the value added." When Bjerke tried to explain that an apparently three-dimensional scene was infinitely more appealing than a two-dimensional one, Gammill shifted his line of attack to the extreme and time-consuming difficulty of coding the appearance of a third dimension. Since the effect would give *Sendak* better sprites, Gammill felt that Phil Spencer's core tools group would have to make it part of their work. "There's no way I can do this layer architecture if the sprites don't support it," he said. And since none of the other upcoming Multimedia Publishing products would need layering, Gammill doubted that Spencer would make it a high priority: "I can just see him saying, 'No way!' "

There was considerable doubt in Gammill's mind that Spencer's group would have even an elementary sprite engine done in time for the *Sendak* team to be able to use it. When Bjerke asked him, "What's your strategy for getting a sprite engine?" Gammill answered, "My strategy is to bug Phil." Then he added, lugubriously, "They don't even have a schedule yet." The one hold he had over Spencer was the charter given the tools group to meet the needs of as many product teams as possible. Gammill resolved to remind Spencer at every turn that he was being judged on his ability to deliver to all MM Pub teams, and that his future at Microsoft depended largely on how many products benefited from the core tool group's work.

After trying halfheartedly to pin Gammill down on a timetable for *Sendak*'s sprite engine, the layering of its scenes, and the text layout engine that Richard Hobbs was building, Bjerke agreed with him that they would have to schedule *Sendak* with qualifiers about those dependencies. Every report they submitted on the project would mention that these features were being developed elsewhere, and that *Sendak*'s schedule ultimately depended on the timely delivery of them.

Moving on to features Gammill himself would be doing, Bjerke began showing him examples of effects she wanted included in *Sendak*'s pop-ups. Most important to her was a "Related" icon—a button on a pop-up that would allow the user to jump immediately to related information contained in pop-up stacks elsewhere in the encyclopedia. A user cruising through a Nature scene, for instance, might be reading about whales, and a click on the Related button would immediately call up a pop-up stack on the whaling industry from the Civilization unit. The system of Related buttons was effectively a third way of navigating through the product, and called for yet another level of organization in *Sendak*'s code. It promised to be a tremendous amount of additional work for Gammill. He stared at Bjerke's drawing of the button.

"Uuuuuuhhhhhhh," he moaned.

"Just think about it!" Bjerke pleaded.

"I said no before, but . . . okay, I'll think about it."

On and on they went, feature by feature, with Bjerke outlining her designs, showing Gammill sketches and examples, and Gammill either registering no reaction or muttering objections. "I think this easel's a little flaky," he said of a backpack tool that was a combination word processing and drawing-and-coloring application. Most often, he waved his hand dismissively at her requests, saying, without elaboration, "Version 2 . . . Version 2 . . . Version 2."

"Can sprites run across the top of pop-ups?" Bjerke asked.

"No."

"Think about it."

"Okay."

Watching Bjerke add a series of features to her list of things to be scheduled, he finally yelled, "You're filling this in, and I'm not buying off on this stuff!" Looking over a set of topics for which a contract editor had designed short animations that were turned on and off by users as they read pop-up text, Gammill objected strenuously. Since these were animations in pop-ups rather than in scenes, and since they behaved differently from sprites, they would require the writing of a separate engine. "She's going gung-ho on these animations," he said, "and we don't even have an interactive animation engine!"

No less disturbing was Sara Fox's determination to have *Sendak* include activities for users to complete in order to find certain pieces of information. Throughout the encyclopedia, her editors had designed pop-ups that posed problems to users, asking them to do such things as drag plants with a mouse pointer into their correct habitats, to type answers to questions posed by anthropomorphized squirrels, to drag *X*s and *O*s onto a tic-tac-toe board, to search for answers to questions, and so on. "I need to figure out the feasibility of these activities," Gammill cautioned Bjerke.

Then he went on to explain to her that editors designing activities needed to think in generic terms—that while there was no limit on the number of activities that *Sendak* could include, there was a definite limit on the number of *types* of activities that could be included. Each type of activity had to be separately classified and coded. Any activity that differed in any way, however insignificant, from all other activities required the writing of an entire classification, set of rules, and code unique to it. One hundred activities all of the same type would require Gammill to write only one set of code; activities of one hundred different types would require the writing of one hundred different sets. "They need to think in terms of templates," he said emphatically.

When it came to *Sendak*, Gammill's greatest fear was the lust for features. He had learned when working on *Encarta* that his teammates were prone to ignore schedule constraints. Then, when it came time to figure out what to cut from the product in order to get it finished on time, no one knew where to begin. So he asked Bjerke to come up with a features priority list. He wanted her to devise a way to rank every feature in the encyclopedia, in order of preference, so that he could start eliminating features from the bottom of the list and work upward in reverse order of preference as *Sendak*'s deadline approached.

While Gammill's replies to Bjerke's questions tended toward playful banter, his demeanor and posture were undeniably hostile. He sat with his back ramrod-straight, tapping one foot frenetically on the floor while he drummed the table with his fingers. He gave the impression that he would rather be anywhere else in the world. You could gauge his reaction to Bjerke's questions by the increase in the rate of his finger- and foot-taps; they accelerated in direct proportion to the difficulty of the feature in question.

Gammill's agitation resulted from a long series of frustrating encounters with designers. They steadfastly refused to take developers seriously. He was particularly disgruntled over his treatment during the final months of the *Encarta* project. Because the design of Microsoft products and the editing of their content is done in advance of the writing of their code, missed deadlines in design and editorial are forgotten by the time a product ships. These are not the deadlines that directly hold up the ship date. But development is the last work done on a product, so a slipped ship date is invariably seen, unjustly, as a developer's slip. Gammill was convinced that *Encarta*'s slipped deadline had gone down in history as development's slipped deadline. Looking hard at Bjerke now as he got up to leave, he said bitterly, "In *Encarta*, editorial would slip, but we weren't allowed to." Bjerke was weary of hearing this sort of complaint from Gammill every time they talked; now, defeated and depressed, she let her shoulders slump, and she stared glumly down at the table until he had gone.

To look closely at Bjerke's emerging plans and schedule was to come face to face with the quantification of a fantasy. Never in her life had she invested in a project the emotion she now had invested in *Sendak*. In fighting off Bryan Ballinger's infectious gloom, Fox's contagious worry, and Gammill's enraged skepticism, and in order to concentrate on the product itself, Bjerke had worked herself over and over again into a frenzy of enthusiasm. She was thoroughly enchanted with *Sendak*. Every design meeting during March ended with a declaration of her ecstasy: "Too cool!" "This is great!" "I can't wait to get to the offsite, we have so many good ideas!"

This design enthusiasm sustained Bjerke through the seemingly end-less weeks (during which actual work still had not begun) before *Sendak*'s offsite. She spent much of March amassing a pile of spreadsheets and other planning documents that showed in proper Microsoft language and syntax exactly how she planned, week by week and task by task, to fulfill her vision.

A Microsoft program manager has the world's shortest job description: to find a way to meet a project's deadline. For Bjerke, this meant coor-dinating the plans of teams and individuals who essentially were working on eight separate endeavors—the results of which eventually would be assembled into *Sendak*—and arranging them all on a spreadsheet in such a way as to make it appear that everything could be done on schedule. Added to Bjerke's job description—in her own mind, at least—was the mandate to prove to Microsoft that a designer could step into a managerial position, from which designers had traditionally been excluded, and suc-ceed on the company's analytical terms.

The mode of operation that emerged for *Sendak* called for its editors to research and write the encyclopedia's text, to list the objects to be drawn into each of *Sendak*'s scenes, and to spec—write descriptions of —the art that was to accompany the pop-up text. This work was then to be entered into Merismus either by the editors themselves or by Merismus-entry specialists working under Sandy Dean, a Microsoft proof-reader who had evolved into Multimedia Publishing's only Merismus expert.

Once enough *Sendak* topics were entered into Merismus, Multimedia's image acquisition staff could search the database for *Sendak* media re-quests and begin buying whatever still photographs and video clips the editors had ordered. Multimedia's audio and sound-effects editor could begin buying *Sendak*'s music, narration, and other audio material; and Multimedia's producer, Ryberg, could retrieve requests from Merismus for animations and other original artwork to be done by a combination of Microsoft staff artists, contract artists, and freelancers, all of whom would be working under her direction. Ballinger, meanwhile, would get from *Sendak*'s editors lists of creatures and objects to be included in the en-cyclopedia's scenes, and would begin drawing and painting them.

While this effort was underway, Lindsey Smith would continue de-signing *Sendak* interface features—the pop-up display window, the find gadget, the dialog boxes, and various icons. Artists would be creating thumbnail versions of the pop-ups, which also would be entered into

Merismus, for eventual use in *Sendak*'s find gadget. Bjerke would write the encyclopedia's design specification and eventually hand it over to Gammill, who would use it to write his technical specification. Once Gammill's document was finished, he could begin writing *Sendak*'s code.

As content in various media came in from all of *Sendak*'s sources, Smith and Fox would direct the assembling of it into scenes and pop-ups, and keep track in Merismus of their review and eventual approval of everything. Once Gammill had written enough code to get the appropriate *Sendak* engines running, the pop-ups, with their text and illustrations, would be pulled from Merismus into "proofing builds" of *Sendak*. These builds would be proofed both for the accuracy and quality of the encyclopedia's content—just as galley proofs are reviewed by book and magazine publishers and editors—and tested for proper performance. As each batch of *Sendak*'s topics was completed, it would be added, build by build, to the rest of the encyclopedia, each build being a larger compilation than the one before.

Scheduling uncertainties cropped up everywhere in *Sendak*, even where Bjerke expected work to be easiest. She had counted on text editing, for example, to be the one predictable and trouble-free phase in the project. But Fox, she knew, had a habit of abruptly making decisions without regard for the scheduling problems they might cause. Already, Fox had decided that the Dorling Kindersley text upon which *Sendak* was to be based was incomplete and inaccurate. Editors were falling behind the schedule they originally set for themselves because Fox directed them not only to tailor the DK text to *Sendak*'s pop-up stack format, but to rewrite and augment virtually all of it. Because this directive was relatively recent, Fox and her editors still could not tell Bjerke how long it took to finish an average topic, and Bjerke could not reliably extrapolate that number out over *Sendak*'s total content.

Further, because every phase of *Sendak*'s construction depended upon some other phase for completion, a delay anywhere in the chain of events caused delays everywhere else. It was a precarious arrangement. There was also the danger that other Multimedia product units would be making demands on the division's Merismus and media acquisitions resources at the same time *Sendak* would be needing them. Bjerke knew that at times *Sendak* would have to wait in line at acquisitions and Merismus entry's doors for *Encarta* 2.0, or for titles from the Mercury, Variety, and Jurassic product units, to be finished.

After a series of meetings with everyone on her team, and hours upon hours spent alone in her office going over spreadsheets of *Sendak* numbers, Bjerke came up with a detailed production plan and schedule for pop-ups that did little more than call attention to the difficulties confronting her group. She broke down pop-up production into twenty separate steps, and drew up plans for producing 17,000 pop-ups—the estimated total content of the encyclopedia—covering 1,133 topics. She divided her team's tasks into seven categories—editorial, design, Merismus, acquisitions, production, development, and proofing—and listed each of their tasks week by week, from "Week 1: Apr. 19–23" to "Week 34: Dec. 13–17." Once production was in full swing, there would be six batches somewhere in the task pipeline each week, each batch numbering between 240 and 960 topics, with the batches growing in size as more contractors were hired. Each editor, according to Bjerke's formulation, could write and edit 130 topics per week, and she predicted that each batch, once ready for production, would take six weeks from its first design review through its incorporation into a *Sendak* proofing build.

Bjerke brought her team together on March 15 to review her schedule spreadsheets and help make revisions in them. For two hours, she and her teammates threw time estimates back and forth, only to come up short of time over and over again. "So, cool," Bjerke said sarcastically, "it takes eight weeks from spec to proofing. We're already slipping." At the end of the meeting, looking mournfully down at her papers, now completely covered over with handwritten revisions, she said, "I'll go back and do a new version of this spreadsheet. And we'll all laugh about it later."

There seemed to be a conviction throughout the group that anything was preferable to saying outright that Bjerke's schedule was a fiction. "So far," Ryberg said after the meeting, "I'm really not willing to say that we can't do it. We'll have to see how we do in finding resources for all this." Still, she could see that the plan was patently impossible. "When we first did the schedule," she continued, "we were projecting February '95, we just said, 'This is how long it will take.' We started at the beginning, which is the right way to do it, starting out, finding out, and then that's how we come out in February '95. So I think it's kind of hard to believe that you can pull it all the way back to September '94 and not pull out any features. In fact, we probably have more features now than we ever thought of when we started."

The night before, she had talked with Bartholomew, who reminded her about the politics of missing deadlines at Microsoft. "Craig told me last night that if we have to slip it's better to do it sooner than later." Bartholomew's message was, "Make sure you say something, if you really think the thing can't be done. Don't just sit back and say, 'No problem, we'll do it somehow.' "

She was most worried at the schedule's assumption that nothing would go wrong. "It always takes longer than you think," she said. "So even if you have a pessimistic person giving time estimates, you still have to add another 20 percent." She remembered vividly a morning during *Encarta*'s production when the editors arrived to discover that nearly all of the encyclopedia's captions had vanished from the computer system. "That was one of those unforeseen catastrophes," she said, "and they wasted several days. Those are the kinds of things you just can't plan for. Morally, you're just destroyed by something like that."

Nothing had happened thus far to ease Ryberg's fears about *Sendak*. Not only had five months been lopped off her schedule before the team got started, but now four months had gone by and the *Sendak* team had nothing to show for it. No production had begun and no plans for production had been made. The encyclopedia hadn't even been *designed* yet. Gammill was growing angrier by the minute; Ballinger was lapsing into unproductive depression; Fox was gone; and Bjerke and Smith, it seemed to Ryberg, were lost. Ryberg had originally estimated that it would take twenty-six months to create the encyclopedia. Now they had only seventeen—and had yet to get started.

Even so, Ryberg was careful to voice her doubts out of Bjerke's hearing. Gammill, however, was less given to diplomacy. Three days later, at a meeting with Bjerke, Smith, and Ballinger, he either dismissed Bjerke's requests or mocked her viciously every time she brought up a *Sendak* feature for discussion. "If you think it's important just say so now," he said curtly at one point, cutting her off when she asked again for layers in scenes. "I'll go back and think about it." Later, when Bjerke said that a certain amount of narration could be included "if we have disc space," Gammill laughed sarcastically and said, "Which means no."

"Can we have this dialog box that—?

"Sure—and we'll ship in ten years."

"How do we handle misspelling?"

"We don't."

The meeting turned into a kind of verbal softball game, with Gammill swatting pitch after pitch of Bjerke's out of the ballpark. "That's a lot of work for something that doesn't seem that valuable"; "May I interrupt?

This is basically a combined word processor and paint application. This is a *huge* problem, a huge technical hit"; "Right now, if I were to schedule this, I would put it at a man-year, easy"; "This could be a product in itself"; "This is too ambitious for this timeframe"; "I can tell already that this offsite's going to be brutal."

Near the end of the meeting, in what he intended as a conciliatory aside, Gammill said, "I'm playing devil's advocate here—"

"So what's new?" Smith interrupted.

Sensing that tempers were getting frayed, Bjerke ended the session by handing Gammill a list of features she wanted him to think over. "Now, is 'L.A. Law' a rerun tonight?" Gammill asked, looking down at it. "Because that will determine whether I read this tonight or not." His teammates couldn't tell whether he was being playful or contemptuous.

Salish

The Salish Lodge boardroom is a cozy space outfitted for corporate brain-storming and decorated in a way intended to be both rustic and genteel. Its walls are covered in a mix of fabric and old growth cedar paneling, and the furniture—a conference table surrounded by chairs—is ornate and comfortable. The *Sendak* team, convening there a few minutes before nine in the morning, was treated to a sumptuous Continental breakfast laid out on a sideboard. Team members sat down at places set with linen, silver, notebooks, printouts, and pencils, and looked over the day's agenda.

Salish exerted a mystical hold over the minds of those in Multimedia Publishing. They were convinced that the place held magical powers of inspiration. Product teams often fled there when beginning a project or trying to get a stalled one moving forward again. The *Encarta* 2.0 team had met there the month before, and the *Sendak* team had first roughed out its vision of a children's multimedia encyclopedia at a Salish offsite the previous September. The *Sendak* team expected to emerge from this visit with a complete plan of attack, free at last from the dithering and doubt that had dogged their project for the past four months.

The lodge is perched just south of the top of Snoqualmie Falls. On its west side, the boardroom affords a spectacular view over roiling mists rising from the bottom of the falls, down the Snoqualmie River valley toward distant Seattle and its suburbs. To step outside onto the small balcony overlooking the falls was to step from a warm room into a wet, oddly comforting chill.

The offsite's agenda called for three hours of brainstorming, to be followed by lunch in another private room, to be followed by three more hours in the boardroom. At the end of the day, the Microsoft visitors would trek a half-mile or so down a switchback trail to the riverside and gaze thoughtfully back up at the falls. The post-meeting walk—a pleasurable, tranquil trek through the woods—was a symbolic exercise in self-congratulation. It was regarded as the celebratory end to a rite of passage. Long-established custom dictated that a Microsoft team reward itself with the walk after a rejuvenating and productive day of inspired work in the boardroom.

Bjerke, sitting at the head of the table, began this day's session with a brief and brisk pep talk, intended to remind everyone in the room that this was to be a pivotal day in the history of *Sendak*. "We're here to work through the big big issues of the product," she said, "and to prevent new features creeping in, study our change of vision. Over the next couple weeks, there will be lots of meetings, lots of decisions. We're putting our stake in the ground, going over the waterfall. This is the setting of our vision, from which we can't be dissuaded—even by senior management." With that, she directed her group to begin work on formulating a goal statement for the product.

The offsite was of sufficient importance to interrupt Fox's maternity leave. She was sitting directly opposite Gammill now, to Bjerke's right, with an anxious look on her face. It was as if she had never been gone. Bjerke had no sooner gotten the meeting started than Fox interrupted, to share troubled impressions she had gathered at evening usability sessions the previous week, during another break from her maternity leave. The sessions had tested, among other things, a leveling switch that allowed users to set *Sendak* at one of three levels: the lowest level, where clicking on objects triggered sound or animation but brought up no text; a level where text and pictures alone popped up whenever objects were clicked upon; and a level that displayed everything—animations and sound effects first, then the pop-up stacks.

The results had left Fox tremendously worried. Ever since *Sendak* first was tested, she believed that the biggest challenge to its designers lay in getting children to read its text. In order to reinforce the notion that users should read the entire stack of pop-ups on a given topic, Lindsey Smith had designed an illustration, to go in the upper right-hand corner of each pop-up, consisting of a hand pointing its index finger forward, another hand pointing its thumb backward, and a number in between the two hands indicating which of the stack's pop-ups was currently on top. If a user was looking at the third pop-up in a stack of six pop-ups about bears, a click on the finger pointing forward would bring up the fourth pop-up, while a click on the thumb pointing backward would bring up the second pop-up.

After watching the newly designed stacks during usability, Fox had decided they didn't work. "Ten-year-old boys," she said, "were bored. They kept switching it to the baby level"—the level that played sound and animations without bringing up any text. "They weren't turned on at all. They didn't read the pop-ups. They didn't even figure out these were *stacks* of pop-ups." She paused, then set off on a worried ramble. "Girls, though, went through the stacks and read stuff. . . . Except for one ten-year-old girl. . . . Every time she clicked on something and something happened, she'd say, 'Dude.' Every time. *Except when text popped up.* Then she didn't say anything. . . . Boys need a task orientation to hold their interest. . . . I do think that one of the problems we need to address is pop-ups—it just looks like text, a book! We need some way to make it look interesting. . . . Somehow, we're losing them. I like what they look like—and adults do—but we're losing these kids. . . . They just aren't *readers.* We have to decide whether we'll pander to that, go 'Info Lite,' or direct them with missions to read."

"We're trying to design to two extremes," Bjerke said, "eight-year-old boys and ten-year-old girls who like to read. Is an 'education product' different from what we want to do?"

"Teachers want supporting material, a defined pedagogical rationale, and a way for it to fit into their curriculum," Fox answered. "And they're particular about readability levels and how it fosters critical thinking. But if you break all the rules, and teachers, parents, and kids love it, they'll go for it." She felt that *Sendak*'s best strategy was to go after the home market. "You're successful that way, and you can get in through the school's back door."

"So," Bjerke said, getting back to the vision statement, "we should say, 'Our market is the home, our secondary market is education.' "

Gammill chimed in, saying—in what was undoubtedly a paraphrase— "Craig's attitude—at least his attitude yesterday—is 'Screw the education market, we're a consumer product.' "

"The main decision for us," Bjerke said, "is whether to be deep, broad, or both in content." But Fox felt that the problem was more complicated than that. She had come away from the last usability sessions convinced that *Sendak* faced a potentially insoluble marketing problem. She now understood that she and her teammates were trying to realize three conflicting visions: of a children's encyclopedia that would appeal to teachers and parents because it was sufficiently educational; of an education game that would appeal to kids because it was as much fun to play as computer games and other entertainment software; and of a product that would address the team's own agenda, which involved pushing computer technology as far as it could be pushed, and making legitimate learning such a fun prospect that *Sendak* alone would reverse the downhill trend in American literacy and education.

So far, Fox believed, *Sendak* was failing on all three fronts. Now she commenced a long, anxious monologue, the release of a maternity leave's worth of brooding. She began by proposing that *Sendak* incorporate far more missions and activities, so that children could be tricked into reading its text. "Should we," she asked rhetorically, "make them play our game by forcing them to use missions and tasks to find the information they want?"

The problem with that strategy, she continued, as if arguing with herself, was that no matter how deep the content, parents and children didn't notice. No one was taking time to read the text. People looking at *Sendak* saw only the special effects and were putting the encyclopedia in the same category as such children's storybook computer titles as *Just Grandma and Me* and *Arthur's Teacher Trouble*. No matter how good or deep the reference material in *Sendak*, no one would regard it as a real reference product, which meant that there was no commercial justification for an encyclopedia's worth of text. "So we need to slash our content by half," she said suddenly.

Since the rest of the team had been enduring Fox's crusade on behalf of text for months, this reversal came as a considerable surprise. Now Fox proposed having an activity, animation, sound effect, or video clip accompanying text on every pop-up. "If we have eight pop-ups," she said, "and can think of animations or something for only three of them, we should get rid of the other five." She believed that everything should be "high-interest," with *Sendak*'s disc space going almost exclusively toward media elements other than text. Under its current design, *Sendak* was to be 70 percent text and 30 percent other media; in effect, Fox now was proposing that they reverse the ratio.

Before anyone could advance much in the way of an argument against this proposition, Fox said, worriedly, "This approach—fewer, better pop-ups, more activity—sinks our levels." Then she floated the dread word *random,* noting that an increase in the number of activities inevitably would lead to repetitiveness. "We need to avoid any semirepetitive nature of activities," she said, and went on to suggest that randomness somehow be programmed into the encyclopedia, so that when a child clicked on a given object a second or third time, he or she would elicit a new, surprising response. "Bryan," she said of Ballinger, "was talking last night about going back to randomness, because the kids in usability were so bored."

"So, what if a kid sees something," asked a disgusted Gammill, "has a friend come over, says, 'Look at this!' It could take twenty clicks to get it again. Random's random."

"But kids were using the find gadget to navigate," said Ballinger.

"Are we convinced that randomness is what makes for replayability?" someone asked. "I'm thinking about expectations versus surprise—"

"We're saying that they like the surprises the best," Fox added, "and they're not reading the pop-ups."

"And then you get a pop-up—"

"A *random* pop-up," said Gammill.

"Well," answered Fox, cryptically, "random or not random is the question."

"Are we done with this?" Gammill asked.

They weren't. The conversation sped on and on, in an endless spiral of dread. Bjerke noted that *Sendak* was supposed to be positioned in a product line that made it a stepping-stone to *Encarta.* Sonja Gustafson, *Sendak*'s marketing lead, pointed out that something called a "Children's Encyclopedia," priced at $195, carried with it the expectation that it would have a reasonable amount of text and information. Others feared that it was too late to change the nature of a product with a fixed deadline. Fox ecstatically described an animation she had seen on the behavior of the atom, then undercut herself by observing that an animation that long and complicated would take up far too much disc space. "So are we saying this is a learning tool to help prepare kids for school?" Gustafson asked.

Deciding that the ensuing moment of silence amounted to a growing consensus, Bjerke said, "So our goal is to have deep content, with value added in the form of multimedia elements to make it interesting." With that, the conversational circle closed: it was decided to leave *Sendak*'s content intact, keeping pop-up stacks at their current depth.

"So we just wasted an hour," Gammill muttered.

Bjerke seized that opportunity to turn the floor over to him, asking him for a "development update."

Brandishing a Bjerke-composed spreadsheet listing all of *Sendak*'s features, Gammill answered, "I'm just gonna take this feature list and give it to Phil and say, 'We need an answer by April 30.' "

A few days before, he went on to explain, Spencer had taken enough time off of his labors on *Dinosaurs* to write and distribute a preliminary document describing the sort of core tools set he expected his group to be developing, and asking for feedback from other product groups. Spencer had coined a head-scratching acronym for the new development tool: SPAM, standing for Sound, Picture, Animation Manager. It was the sort of witticism that delighted him and perplexed everyone else. To judge from the document, Gammill said, "SPAM is basically an authoring environment and run-time text handler for *Dinosaur* products. It's not efficient, it's slow. . . . Richard's text layout engine will probably be a module that plugs into this SPAM thing."

Gammill was depressed by this because it meant that SPAM, as it appeared to be envisioned by Spencer, would do almost none of the tasks the *Sendak* group needed. The *Dinosaur* titles, being far less ambitious, had no sprites or animations, and their text was bit mapped rather than live, meaning that a given block of text was simply a picture of words— a bit map—rather than searchable text. There is no possibility of indexing bit mapped text or of navigating through it with a Find mechanism. There also appeared to be no possibility of using SPAM to create animations, sprites, or layered scenes in *Sendak*. And Gammill was worried that SPAM's limitations would make it impossible to handle pop-up stacks the way Fox wanted them handled.

This news seemed too depressing for comment and was met with silence. While Gammill and his teammates sat there glumly contemplating the future, I began wondering how on earth I could ever reconcile the apparent reality of life at Microsoft with the company's public image of strategic brilliance. If Gammill's assessment of Spencer's plans was correct, Multimedia Publishing was more or less rudderless. How could the division's managers allow their workers to set off so unsupervised in so many different directions? How could Spencer have been permitted to define a mission so at odds with the vision Gates had for his group? Could things possibly be as confused as they appeared?

Looking around the room, I could find nothing by way of reassurance.

Gammill, like a stock villain in comedy, was reflexively contemptuous, constantly insulting his teammates and their ideas. Fox was so habitually worried that she even argued against her own ideas. Ballinger, glum and withdrawn, looked and acted like a sulky child. Jayleen Ryberg insisted time and again that whatever Bjerke and Fox wanted to do was impossible, given the constraints of *Sendak*'s schedule. Everything said in meetings now was greeted by one of her resigned, exasperated sighs. After four months of following these people around, I could see no sign of leadership. Where was the manager or supervisor who could come in and get this project moving? More to the point: Why did Bjerke seem so optimistic and excited? Either I was missing some vital secret to Microsoft's success, or I had managed to infiltrate the company just as it was on the verge of collapse.

Gammill went on to complain about all the effects *Sendak*'s designers were trying to include. By his count, there now were fifty-five separate features for which he would have to write new code. "Some of this stuff will be a huge development hit if we do it," he said, "but a lot of it I haven't even thought about yet." Singling out a particularly irritating feature—Bjerke's prized easel, the combination word processing and drawing-and-painting tool—Gammill insisted that "the simplest conceivable easel is extremely expensive, and we'll have to sacrifice considerably in other areas to include it."

"We need to firm down definitions of features," Bjerke answered, "so we don't have features creeping in."

"One thing we need to decide right away," Gammill continued, "is whether to have a dictionary or not." Bjerke wanted kids to be able to click on any word in the text and have a definition pop up. "I don't want to do all this work, then have it be for nothing."

This led to a discussion of Bjerke's plan to evaluate every feature in the encyclopedia in a purely analytical manner. Passing out a *Sendak* prioritized features list—the list Gammill had been asking her to make —she explained how her system would work. Each feature was to be rated twice, on a scale of one to five. One rating, by consensus, rated value to the user; the other, by Gammill, rated ease in developing. The two numbers then would be averaged, giving the feature in question an overall priority value. The ship or home, for example, was to have a photo album in which the user could copy sights and sounds from his or her travels through *Sendak*. If the *Sendak* team assigned the album a user value rating of two, and Gammill rated its difficulty of development at four, its overall priority rating would be three. Features with a priority rating of one would be ranked at the top, with others listed in numerical order, down to five. As *Sendak*'s deadline neared, features would be eliminated, one by one, from the bottom of the prioritized features list.

The team tried its hand at prioritizing a few features and—predictably enough—began arguing immediately. However scientific each team member tried to be, each came at the effort from a different set of values, and Gammill had a habit of assigning suspiciously high degree-of-difficulty numbers to features he didn't like. Further, many of the features were undefined—a circumstance that led to long discussions about what exactly was being rated. The home base? "Depends on what it is," said Gammill. The slide show? "I'd say three if we define our user as a home kid," said Fox. A VCR, for playing video? "How is it controlled?" asked Gammill. Caught between a general lack of definition and an inability to come to agreement on the value of specific features, the team before long lapsed into dreaming uncontrollably, no longer talking about prioritizing anything, each member taking a turn describing some treasured feature until finally it came time for lunch. I sat through the meal astounded at the happiness of the people around me—apparently they felt that the offsite was going fabulously.

The afternoon session included not only the *Sendak* team but others from Multimedia Publishing who would be helping build the encyclopedia: those who would be acquiring and editing *Sendak*'s illustrations, sound, and video, and handling Merismus—tasks they undertook for all MM Pub titles. Recapping the morning's events for the new arrivals, Bjerke laughed, pointed to the first page of the day's agenda and exclaimed, "We only got this far!" Then she decided to abandon discussion of *Sendak* itself and discuss instead the makeup of its team and the procedures she wanted in place for producing it. "Keeping in mind our vision now that it," she giggled, partly out of despair and partly because of the beer she had had with her lunch, "is much, much clearer to us, we need to move on the budget, production, and the spec."

Then Bjerke went on to define the roles of everyone on the team, explaining first of all that Lindsey Smith "essentially has replaced me" and that Gammill and Len Dongweck, head of Multimedia Publishing's testing department, would be attending all future design meetings. Without their assistance, she said, she could not finish the design specification by its April 30 deadline. "The spec," she said, "is to be an all-inclusive description of all features for everyone to read. This is a living document—it will be with us from now until the end of the project."

A postprandial stupefaction had settled over Bjerke's audience, and a meeting that in the morning had been a spirited exchange of opinions from around the room was now a monologue. While everyone else seemed sluggish, Bjerke was clearly energized. If she directed a comment at someone—as when she said to Fox that "activities should all be defined by April 30"—her listener would stare back in agreeable silence. On and on Bjerke talked, cheerfully shouldering the burden of the conversation, outlining her plan for the next eighteen months, stopping occasionally to ask questions of Gammill about technical matters.

For the next two hours, she took her audience through two more spreadsheets—one a disc-space budget, the other a monetary one. The first was an itemized list, by media type, of everything in *Sendak*, with an estimate of how much space on the compact disc each would take. Aside from the occasional fearful comment from Gammill, the disc-space budget was accepted uncritically, as was the monetary budget, with its estimate of "nine full-time person-years plus fourteen contractor-years," to complete the project at "around $3.3 million cost."

When Bjerke brought out her last spreadsheet—*Sendak* milestones—her audience suddenly woke up in a panic. Here they saw their specific contributions to the *Sendak* project laid out in detail along a timeline, with deadlines every two months, culminating in the ultimate deadline—the ship date. Bjerke's listeners all took careful note of how deadlines for their particular tasks dovetailed with the deadlines of people whose tasks had to be completed before their own could be. "It's real difficult for me to get my spec done when the design spec isn't done until the same date," Gammill said. With a note of dismay creeping into her voice, Sandy Dean—the MM Pubs editor who would be entering all of *Sendak* into Merismus—added, "So my whole flow chart is bogus now?"

To Bjerke, the milestones spreadsheet was intended not so much to lay out specific tasks as to establish a philosophical foundation for the *Sendak* project. "The basic philosophy of the milestone is that you agree up front to a no-trickle-over model," she said. "So if something moves from one milestone to the next, something has to go. That's what the milestones sheet is for."

It now was nearly 3:30 and the group had run out of ideas, mental energy, or both. It seemed a fitting end to an offsite that, as far as I could tell, had been an utter failure. Yet, incredibly, there settled over the *Sendak* team a general air of satisfaction, as if those at the meeting had come through a singularly emotional experience together. The meeting appeared to have wrought a transformation of sorts, as if Bjerke's unwarranted confidence, combined with the array of spreadsheets she had distributed, had made the *Sendak* project seem, for the first time, demonstrably doable. Reduced to a set of tasks laid out on a numbered grid, a product that for so long had been so vaguely defined took on a form with clear and manageable outlines. Bjerke had furnished a sort of mathematical proof that *Sendak* could be done on time. As they gathered up their papers and made their way out of the room, Bjerke and her audience looked as if they were moving from the planning of *Sendak* to the actual construction of it.

My own impression was of a team in the throes of disarray and self-delusion, but I decided to attribute my skepticism to ignorance. Somewhere undetected by me, the secret of Microsoft's success must be lurking, waiting to be discovered. Surely it was only a matter of time and more careful study before I could begin to see this process for what it really was.

Out in the parking lot, *Sendak*'s planners put their papers in their cars, donned walking shoes, and made their way in small groups down the path to the river. The trail, paved in some sections, covered over with gravel in others, was a series of switchbacks down a steep slope. It ended at a ramshackle Puget Power generating plant. Next to the plant was a concrete viewing platform with railings along the water's edge.

Everyone filed onto the platform, spread out along the railing, and looked up the river at the falls.

It was an overcast, nearly chilly day—typical for late March in the Pacific Northwest. The *Sendak* hikers wore flannel shirts, heavy sweaters, or lightweight parkas. The air was gray, the trees a dull dark green, and the ground moist but not muddy. From the viewing platform, the waterfall looked moribund. Its surface reflected the murky mix of surrounding color. The cliff face underneath, having endured centuries of waterborne abrasion, had long since collapsed into a pile of crumbled rock. The water no longer fell spectacularly down a sheer chute; instead, it came stumbling clumsily and haltingly down a broken spine. It looked defeated, debased, and drab. The *Sendak* team regarded it for only a few minutes before turning round and trudging back up the trail.

"So Where Are We Now?"

For all his teammates' delight with the offsite, Kevin Gammill only grew more disgruntled and anxious. The more he turned his attention to the details of implementing *Sendak*, the more heavily the project weighed on his mind. At every turn, he found himself confronted with infuriating obstacles. The encyclopedia's designers were piling on features even though Bjerke had said at the offsite that she intended to "prevent new features creeping in." Designers and editors alike were ignoring Gammill's pleas for stricter definitions of their ideas. So far, the product was so vaguely and incompletely described that Gammill could not even begin to write code for it.

Ordinarily, he would have appealed to his program manager for some disciplining of his projects' designers. But *Sendak's* program manager, Bjerke, was a designer by training, and still was acting as the encyclopedia's design lead, even though she professed to have turned design over to Lindsey Smith. It was a designer's assignment to try to pile on features, a developer's role to resist for the sake of meeting a deadline, and a program manager's job to mediate and render verdicts. Bjerke's bias for design made her incapable of reining in anyone's dreams or of taking Gammill's objections seriously.

So Gammill was reduced to attending meeting after meeting in which it seemed to him that *Sendak* was stuck in an endless design cycle. Not only could he not begin any real work, but he had to listen to the same directionless conversations over and over again. Bjerke and the encyclopedia's artists constantly revisited the same features, making subtle

173

changes in things that should long since have been finally designed or thrown out of the product altogether.

More and more, Gammill's frustration took the form of sarcasm. The mordant Gammill interruption became a constant feature of team meetings. Unfortunately, the result was the opposite of what he intended: instead of making his companions bring their imaginations back inside the boundaries he was trying to establish for them, his sarcasm and disdain made them more skeptical about him. What he saw as expert advice, they saw as an attitude problem. The *Sendak* team forged an infinite emotional loop: the more disgusted with his teammates' dreaming Gammill grew, the more acerbic his commentary; the more acerbic his commentary, the less attention his teammates paid it, and the more wantonly they dreamed.

Gammill's mood darkened even more when he considered Spencer's SPAM tool set. The greater the ambitions of *Sendak*'s designers, the more Gammill would have to depend on SPAM, and what little he had seen by way of documentation of the SPAM effort left him convinced that Spencer's tools would fall far short of the *Sendak* team's expectations.

Gammill believed that Spencer was willfully ignoring how complicated *Sendak* would be. Whenever I asked Spencer about *Sendak*, he drew a comparison with *Dinosaurs*. "Shoot," he said to me one day when talking about SPAM and *Sendak*, "I can do as many pop-ups as they want. The screen with the eagle flying around is kind of a level of complexity up from the pop-ups, but it's not impossible. I mean, it's just objects. You could lay out the screen and not have anything move, but when you click on the camel, the pop-up comes up for the camel. I mean, that's just *Dinosaurs*, that's exactly the way *Dinosaurs* is running now. You could build a static version of the product today."

Where Spencer was proud of *Dinosaurs*, Gammill was disdainful. "That *Dinosaurs* analogy," he said when I asked him about it, "is bullshit." He went on to list an array of features excluded from *Dinosaurs* that were to be part of *Sendak*, then concluded, "Sure, you could do a scaled-down version of *Sendak*, like *Dinos*, but it would *suck!*"

Just as *Sendak*'s designers felt compelled not to take Gammill seriously when it came to design issues, Bartholomew took a dim view of Gammill's attitude toward SPAM. To him, the political mandate to support cross-product tools development was unavoidable and it was up to Gammill to find a way to make SPAM work for *Sendak*. When Gammill, in a meeting with Bartholomew, objected to depending on Spencer's group at all, Bartholomew made it clear that he had no choice. After listening to Gammill recite a list of features SPAM appeared not to support, Bartholomew said, "We need to be cooperative clients—not standoffish. We don't want to be outsiders. I told Phil he had to think about Merismus, and he said, 'That's a good point—I hadn't thought about that.'"

"That's because he isn't doing his job," retorted Gammill.

"Cooperate with him, don't confront him. Stress that if he can do *Sendak*, he can do *everything*. We have to help leverage developers' work across products. Have you talked to him about how you author *Sendak* if he doesn't do the work you need?"

"His job is not to say he can't do stuff for us! His job is to service us!"

"It's good to have contingency plans, but our default position should be to use SPAM unless it cripples *Sendak*."

"I just don't think it can work."

"Well, you're going to have to prove to me that it can't."

Since Bartholomew had consistently told me that Gammill was his best and most trusted employee, the best developer in Multimedia Publishing, I was surprised to hear him treat Gammill so dismissively. I was beginning to think that he was fatally given to wishful thinking—that he only listened to those who assured him that they could meet deadlines handed down by management.

Yet I couldn't quite tell whether Bartholomew delivered his reprimand because the optimistic Bjerke had his ear or because the political mandate at Microsoft to use tools developed in-house left him with no choice but to ignore Gammill's warning. Bartholomew may have had no alternative to coming down hard on his prized developer.

Gammill fell silent. Uncharacteristically chastened, he did not revert to form until several minutes later, after Bjerke—her enthusiasm revived by Bartholomew's rebuke of her nemesis—told Bartholomew that *Sendak* was moving forward at a spanking pace, and that Sandy Dean soon would have a library of edited text making its way into the Merismus database. Bartholomew was surprised and impressed. "Sandy's entering everything into Merismus?" he asked.

Before Bjerke could answer, Gammill, his tactlessness restored, muttered out of the corner of his mouth, "Take this stuff with a grain of salt."

Gammill was not alone in his fears for *Sendak*. While sitting through the last week of her maternity leave, Fox had descended into a fog of gloom and endless worry. During the evening usability sessions just before *Sendak*'s offsite, she and Bjerke had gone for a walk across the Microsoft campus, talking about how something essential was missing from the *Sendak* package. Fox couldn't quite put her finger on what it was, although she was struck by Bjerke's comment that *Sendak* lacked a story to move kids through its landscape.

At home alone with Henry, she concentrated on *Sendak* as exclusively as she could manage, writing notes down more or less at random. It occurred to her that children should be able to play in *Sendak* by solving problems or going on information-gathering missions, then collecting some trivial reward. After a day or two passed in this manner, she looked down at the sum total of her efforts, as reflected in her notes:

Story
Solve mission in order to:
—slow down bad guy (slay monsters). too fantastic?
—clean up the world
—solve some other problem (like world spinning backwards)
Need to learn enough to do it
What do you need information for?
WISDOM will prevail
Restore seasons—make things right
Knowledge has been lost? Find it by gathering golden nuggets—makes
    the picture a little brighter each time.
Make your brain really strong
You're batman/supergirl/whatever you go to this place to solve a problem.
Bookburning!
All info is gone and everybody's really dumb?
World spinning backwards or leaves falling up. Too much to read?

"Why do you need to learn?" she asked herself, staring at her notes. "It seems so obvious. So you're not ignorant." Then there popped into her mind a single word: IgnorAnts.

Suddenly she saw these engaging yet villainous creatures infesting her encyclopedia, and kids being sent on missions to eradicate them. In a rush of exuberance, she swept Henry up in her arms and began dancing around their living room, singing, to her startled audience of one, "I'm so excited. . . . I just can't hide it! . . . I'm so excited. . . . I just can't hide it!" She spent the rest of the afternoon thinking through her idea in greater detail and coming up with a scheme in which these IgnorAnts would present users with a piece of misinformation, and the users would set off on missions to find correct information in *Sendak*'s text, which they would use to rectify the ant-generated misconception.

That night, a Friday, at a company party celebrating the shipping of *Encarta*, she tried to keep her idea secret, hoping to spring it on the rest of the team when she had worked out all of its details. In her excitement, however, she ended up telling everyone that she had a great idea for *Sendak* but that she couldn't describe it yet. Then she went home afterwards and spent the weekend writing a rambling, five-page argument, with crude sketches, for her plan. It began with a statement of *Sendak*'s philosophy:

Missions in *Sendak* can/should provide a synthesis between our interface and information. It can also justify our whole exploratory approach! In order for these to work up to their potential, however, there needs to be a purpose for the missions, and a story that integrates the two. There needs to be a **reason** for doing it that makes sense to kids, and a **reward** that kids will want. Optimally, the mission will make use of the information instead of just using it as a hiding place (i.e., for coins). And there needs to be some way we can make a magic room or magic ship make sense, and explain it other than as a device.

Besides, we need more FUN. And trying to turn all of the content into singing and dancing is a questionable solution to this. We will work to make the content as high-interest, accessible, and varied as possible, but that won't be enough. Intrinsic interest (beyond flashy elements like video) can only account for probably at most 50 percent of usage, judging from what I've seen so far.

What we need to solve these design issues like the ship/room/map/ etc. is a plot. That way we solve the design issues by figuring out what makes sense according to our storyline. Ideally, the plot and mission can lead to our replayability. (Varying the order of the pop-ups isn't a very elegant solution to replayability, because if you've seen the pop-ups and read them once, it's true that you don't really need to read them again.)

She went on to describe a dual-exploration model in which children could either look up specific topics in *Sendak* or explore the encyclopedia in "Mission Mode." Then she wrote:

> So the purpose of the missions is key. What would you (the user) be trying to accomplish? What purpose could be related to information? Trying to save the world?? Picking up space trash?? Neither of these relate to the product. No . . . , in a mission in an information product you are working to wipe out. . . .

> *the IgnorAnts*

> Now you are a needed kid (like a Superhero, Batman, Batgirl, whatever). You are desperately needed to help all sorts of towns, cities, countries, and organizations who will send you pleas for assistance. Your mission is to save them from the destructive IgnorAnts.

Once an inaccuracy was presented on some kind of missions sheet, she continued, the user would be sent into the encyclopedia to find the correct information and highlight it in some way. *Sendak* would make an entertaining, affirming noise when the correct answer was found, and when the user returned to the magical room or ship, he or she would see the misconception fade away and be replaced by the correct information. After a certain number of missions were accomplished, *Sendak* would present the user with a package to be opened, in which would be found a reward. These rewards could be collected and stored in *Sendak*'s home base.

On Monday evening, Fox drove across the lake to Gammill's house, where the *Sendak* team was assembling over takeout Chinese food for a brainstorming session. Her teammates thought Fox's idea was brilliant, and they spent the evening in a celebratory session that ended with Fox's concept being extended to include, in contract editor Abigail Riblet's words, "Intelligent ants . . . intelligent ants . . . IntelligAnts!" By the end of the night, they had decided to include in the guide's backpack a truth spray with which the user could transform IgnorAnts into IntelligAnts when he or she corrected a misconception. When the meeting broke up, *Sendak*'s team members went home more excited about the encyclopedia than they had ever been, and Bjerke resolved to consult Microsoft's legal department next morning about copyrighting the IgnorAnts and IntelligAnts and licensing them to toymakers and dollmakers, as was done with popular characters from books, comic strips, and cartoons. So convinced was Bjerke about the brilliance of Fox's idea that she swore team members to secrecy and directed that all written documents—including her design spec—would refer to the creatures not by name but as SLCs—Special Little Creatures. She wanted to ensure that none of the contractors working at Microsoft would learn of the idea and take it to a competing company.

Fox returned to work three days later, to find almost immediately that her euphoria had worn off. It took only two days for it to be supplanted by an almost hysterical anxiety over Henry. She immediately arranged with Bartholomew to work from 9:00 to 3:00 for her first month back, as compensation for time she spent at meetings during her leave. During that time, she talked Bartholomew into allowing her to keep her position at Microsoft while working part time, staying home on Tuesdays and Thursdays. It was her only alternative to quitting outright, as she found it impossible to be away from Henry five full days a week.

Her personal concerns aside, Fox also was worried about tensions on the *Sendak* team. Upon returning to work, she began hearing rumblings about battles shaping up between Bjerke and Ryberg, between Ryberg and Smith, and between Bjerke and Ballinger, Ballinger and Smith, Bjerke and Smith, Gammill and everybody. "This kind of stuff is *definitely* not okay," she said. Much of the tension had to do with who was to be in charge of what parts of the project. "I need to know what everyone's exact role is, what is their exact job. Who do I contact when I'm here?"

Indeed, it seemed that in her absence *Sendak* had grown far more complicated, and that responsibility for product vision and lines of authority over various aspects of composition and production had grown ever more blurred. Decisions that on a simpler product could be made by an author or editor were being left unresolved, or incompletely thought through, because no one seemed to know who "owned" them. "For example," she said, citing the whole problem of sound, animation, and narration in the encyclopedia, "with the narrator and the sprites and the audios that come up, well, who's going to specify those?" In her absence, it had been up to Bjerke, Ballinger, and Smith to make such decisions, which they did in a somewhat haphazard fashion. Now she felt that they were "probably editorial" decisions. But she wanted to consult with Ballinger before writing final specifications. "We especially need Bryan's input, because we need a creative person," she said. "We need a lot of creative people, we need more creative people for that kind of thing. Some of these things Carolyn probably considers design's responsibility. But when we look at it, they're going to be editorial. I mean, *I* see them as editorial, but we need to just get them kind of shifted over from design."

In general, she felt that Bjerke not only was not relinquishing design to the degree she should be, but was taking upon herself decisions that belonged to editors. When working at Davidson before coming to Microsoft, Fox had exerted nearly full control over the design of her products, working in concert with artists who took direction from her. She could not fathom the Microsoft method of carving a product into little provinces, with editors handling print content while designers handled all other media.

For some reason, Fox failed to see that part of her perceived loss of control over the vision for the encyclopedia was attributable to her leave, and to her returning only part time. She was back only a few days before Bjerke complained to me that it was hard to include Fox in decisions when she was gone half the time. She thought it odd that Fox was asking to be granted more authority while spending less time at work. While it was a measure of Bartholomew's regard for Fox that he was allowing her to keep her managerial responsibilities while moving to part-time status—it was the first time, Bartholomew said, that a part-time employee at Microsoft was put in charge of full-time workers—Bjerke was resentful. She saw Fox's move as yet another impediment to finishing *Sendak* on time.

Fox seemed blissfully unaware that anyone might suffer from her being on campus only half the time. Instead, she was distressed at the growing gap she saw between Bjerke's wishes and Gammill's assessment of what was feasible. More and more, she saw the two butting heads without specifically addressing one another's concerns. "This product can be incredibly great, but we have to stay vigilant, we're not there yet," she said. "And you know that things will have to be sacrificed along the way. Kevin makes these little asides, like, 'Oh, it will be slow,' and 'I don't think we can do that,' and Carolyn kind of seems to ignore them. But I think these things are definitely going to come back to haunt us. Three months from now, we'll have done all this paperwork that just led to people getting attached to ideas that Kevin won't be able to implement, and we'll be striking stuff, and it'll be so *painful*."

Four months now had gone by since the official launch of the *Sendak* effort, and Bjerke had nothing but wishful plans to show for it. Whenever she tried to make measurable progress by moving beyond planning and designing to the production of something concrete, she ran into obstacles. Now, in trying to write her design specification, she discovered feature after feature in the user interface that she could not describe in writing, as she, Ballinger, and Smith had not yet thought through how given features would behave and how the whole complex arrangement of user-interface details would work together. "I have been writing up the spec for all the features in the product based on discussions we have all had," she e-mailed to Smith and Ballinger on April 1, "and yikes, are there a lot of hard UI decisions left to make! . . . Just warning you that April will be a hard thinking month as well as a time to generate a lot of graphics." "I say we wing it as we go along," Ballinger mailed back, facetiously. To which Bjerke replied, "Ha, ha . . . that's what happened to us on Encarta, we forgot many of those little details that just happened to slap us right in the face when we weren't prepared."

That jovial exchange notwithstanding, Bjerke was reaching a breaking point, of sorts, with Ballinger. Both she and Bartholomew had intimated to him that his nature scenes were too cartoonlike and childish. They wanted to see work that would be more appealing to older children, on the theory that young kids would use a product that looked older more readily than older kids would use a product that looked younger. Bjerke also felt that Ballinger's scenes should be more realistic in style, as befits an information product. If parents and teachers were to take *Sendak* seriously as a reference source, the art, she believed, should reflect a certain seriousness rather than the pure playfulness and whimsy of a children's fiction product.

Her frustration with Ballinger had less to do with the specifics of their disagreements than with his manner of disagreeing. Ballinger never confronted people with his opposition; instead, he had a devious way of avoiding directives, perversely and with feigned innocence, turning in work exactly the opposite of what he had been directed to do.

Matters had come to a head during work on the prototype for *Sendak*'s second usability sessions. Ballinger had been told to render a magical room and a desert scene for the prototype, and to make them somewhat more realistic-looking than his forest scene. He registered no reaction or objection, then went off and did work in exactly the same style he had been employing from the beginning. By the time he showed his new work to Bjerke and Smith, it was too late to redo it in time for the tests.

He also had, as he put it, "snuck in" a feature he knew Bjerke would detest. In the desert scene, when the user clicked on one of the pockets in the *Sendak* guide's backpack, a video remote control device popped out. By clicking on the remote, the user triggered the following animation sequence: the remote jumped to the guide's hand and sat there pointed toward the camel standing in the scene's center; the hump on the back of the camel suddenly opened, as if it were attached with hinges to the camel's neck, and a huge television set came rising up out of the camel. By clicking "Play" on the remote, the user activated a video sequence on the TV set, showing a snake slithering across desert sand. When the video was concluded, the television descended, and the hump came swinging down again.

Ballinger included the animation without telling any of his managers because he knew they would make him remove it. Then it turned out to be one of the children's two favorite features during the usability tests—the other being the drink, with its exaggerated slurping sound effect, in *Sendak*'s spaceship. Bjerke's fury at being deceived was heightened considerably by the children's delight. She was angry enough to consider removing Ballinger from the *Sendak* team, but backed away from trying that because she knew Bartholomew would stop her.

The battle between the two was made all the worse by the hybrid structure Bartholomew had set up for Gandalf, which was organized along both team and functional lines. As a result, most Gandalf employees had two or three managers: one was the program manager; another (called the team lead) supervised a group of artists, editors, or developers working on a specific product; and yet another (the functional lead) was placed in charge of all artists, editors, or developers in an entire product unit. So Ballinger took artistic direction from Bjerke and Smith—his program manager and team lead, respectively—but was supervised by Ryberg, who as Gandalf's producer was the functional lead in charge of all artists on all products. Matters were further complicated by Smith's status as a contractor rather than a full-time employee. Not only did Ballinger tend not to regard her as someone entitled to give him orders, she herself found it hard to direct him, as she felt she occupied a lower rung on the organizational ladder. Then when she turned to Ryberg and Bjerke for advice, she got mixed messages from them—a circumstance that led to Bjerke's increasing resentment toward Ryberg because Ryberg was consistently sympathetic to Ballinger.

All of these personal relationships, increasing in tension and confusion, were making my head spin. The vaunted analytic image of Microsoft seemed to be only skin deep. And, as if to confirm my suspicions, Ballinger was hard at work on a document inadvertently demonstrating the futility of Bjerke's effort to shoehorn him into Microsoft's analytical culture. Asked to spec all the animations he wanted to include in *Sendak*'s nature scenes, Ballinger opted to write them on a spreadsheet, using Microsoft's *Excel*. The resulting document adhered perfectly in form to

Microsoft custom. Its content, though, was another matter. Ballinger's spreadsheet was seven columns wide, with the columns labeled from A through G, and headed—according to rules of capitalization known only to him—"topic," "object," "scene," "Section," "Television," "Sprites," "Sprite Audio." There were ninety-nine animations listed, the following five being typical:

topic	object	scene	Section	Television	Sprite	Sprite Audio
camels and llamas	dromedary	desert			Spits off screen-hear spitoon sound, looks down at Gila, gives big smile	spitoon ring
palm tree	date palm	desert			Palm tree gets pulled down close to the ground, then sproings back up and wubba wubba's back and forth a bit, dropping dates.	sproinging and wubba wubbaing sound
scorpions	saguaro	desert			pinch hedgehog	oop!
mosses and liverworts	moss	forest2	open coniferous		neon blinking sign pops up and says "Moss Vegas," porcupine puts coin in slot, pulls branch/lever	wayne newton Option B: slot machine sound
otters	otter	lake, river 1	above		takes out cloth, buffs top of hippo's snout, like buffing bowling ball	reeuh reeuh reeuh (buffing audio)

Ballinger spent a week working on his spreadsheet and on story-boards—pencil sketches—of new nature scenes. When he finished sketches for river, wetlands, and grasslands scenes, he brought them excitedly to Bjerke. As she leafed through them, certain creatures leaped to the forefront: she saw a kangaroo eating a melting ice cream cone, the drips landing on the head of a surprised rodent who was lounging in a sunbather's chair; a rhinoceros wearing a beanie with a propeller; an otter wearing a referee's striped shirt and brandishing a whistle; an alligator in collar and tie, sitting for a portrait being painted under water by a tortoise who stood on hind legs before an easel, brandishing a palette and brush, the paint from the brush bleeding upward in the water.

Bjerke exploded. Ballinger had taken her directive to make his work more realistic and set out to do exactly the opposite. Now, as she ticked off her objections to his work, he acted surprised and hurt, as if he had expected her to love them. She angrily sent him away and, as had become her habit when she was upset, sent anguished e-mail asking me to come to her office. After ten minutes of ranting at me, she said she was deter-mined to keep Ballinger from sneaking the new drawings into a usability test. "He wants to get it in front of kids," she said dourly "so he can use it against me with Craig."

Ballinger retreated into his office to nurse his dejection. Watching him sitting there in the dark, I was struck by how he wore the stress of the last two months like symptoms of a terminal illness: his skin was chalk-white, he was unshaven, and he had grown so gaunt that his eyes bulged out of his skull. He said that he felt betrayed by Bjerke, who had demoted him from coauthor of *Sendak* to a production artist cranking out uninspired work to order. "More and more," he lamented, "it's getting to be, 'Take this, do this this way, that that way.' It would have been better if it had been that way from the beginning—then I wouldn't be so emotionally involved in it."

On April 7, Bill Gates sat down to use *Encarta* at some length for the first time since its release, then dashed off an e-mail review to Tom Corddry, with copies to Susan Boeschen, Jabe Blumenthal, and two other Microsoft managers. Among other things, he said:

> I used this product more today than I ever had before. Maybe its because I am used to a higher level of quality now . . . but I just thought it was good not great.

The speed is the weakest part. There is something really WRONG with the speed of this thing. For example before you start it is so slow to show sample images—a taste of what is to come. . . . When it shows a small image and you ask for the big image WHAT IS IT DOING?? There is something wrong wrong wrong with this. . . . Multimedia elements should not be the slow part of a CD title. . . .

You want slow—try to use MINDMAZE—that is the slowest thing I have ever seen. . . .

The UI is weird in too many places. A weird setup. Weird dialog boxes. . . . Lots of weird UI things. . . .

Considering that *Encarta* was garnering extremely favorable reviews —computer publications consistently were rating it the best of the three multimedia encyclopedias on the market—Gates's mail seemed to me to be unduly brutal. Indeed, Bartholomew was devastated by it. "My first day back," he muttered—he had been gone on a week's vacation—"and that thing's waiting for me." He spent a day benumbed by the message, then fell prey to resentment. "Why am I working so hard, and for so many hours?" he kept asking himself. "For *this?*" By the third day, he was mentally composing furious rebuttals, finding flaws everywhere in Gates's arguments. What most angered him, he said to Jabe Blumenthal in an unguarded moment, "is this implication that we're dumb." What next most angered him, he continued, is that Gates had sent his mail not to Bartholomew directly, but to a list of other people—Blumenthal among them—first.

"You have to understand," Blumenthal said of Gates, "that he runs 100 miles an hour, then will take a minute to sit down with a new product and fire off a letter without thinking about who he's mailing or cc'ing. You shouldn't read anything into that." He went on to tell Bartholomew that Gates is beset by "constant angst that someone will catch Microsoft." It is never enough to produce the best product of its time—Gates wants any given Microsoft product to be good enough to be the best product on the market two years down the road. When he sends angry mail criticizing a new product, he does so solely to see whether the recipients are already aware of the most distressing weaknesses in their work. "He's worried about the tendency of people to relax, to stay on a plateau," Blumenthal said. "When you answer, you have to give him the impression that you're your own worst critic."

The more Bartholomew thought about Blumenthal's advice, the better he began to feel. "You read something like that mail," he said later, "and you just know that you can't relax. You just have to keep pushing higher and higher." Restored, he now forwarded Gates's mail to those who had worked on *Encarta*, knowing that he could console his troops if need be. "Don't get depressed by this," he wrote in a prologue to the message. He then assigned to different team members the task of responding point by point to Gates's mail. When he had studied everyone's responses, he sent back a long answer, the gist of which was that Gates's criticisms were justified, and that the *Encarta* 2.0 team was already hard at work making improvements in the very features that angered him.

When Bartholomew copied his answer to Susan Boeschen, he could not keep himself from complaining. "It's very difficult," he wrote to her, "for a team to get the kind of mail that Bill sent (I wrestled with whether to forward it on)." "Excellent mail," she answered after reading both his reply to Gates and his mail to the *Encarta* team. "I think you did the right thing and I think you did a very good job of putting his remarks in perspective. Bill unfortunately has no idea (in spite of the fact that I keep telling him!) the motivational impact he has on people when he praises and the demotivational impact he has when he whips off random criticism."

The only one who had seemed demotivated by the mail, though, was Bartholomew. Gammill felt that the criticisms were more than justified, given all the problems left in *Encarta* for the sake of rushing it out the door. And Bjerke, already so absorbed in *Sendak*'s problems that she appeared to have all but forgotten *Encarta*, wrote rather haughtily, in an e-mail answer to my question, "I am afraid I regard Bill as 'just another person' who deserves respect but is not to be worshiped or feared. He is not smarter than any of us, he does however have a lot of experience that should be valued."

Mid-April forced the realization upon Bjerke that her first pass at a schedule for *Sendak* was a complete fiction. Gammill was the first to sound an alarm, the day after he was to have received final guidelines for all *Sendak* activities from Fox. For several days leading up to that deadline, he had been enthusiastically preparing to go to work on *Sendak*. "Time to power up!" he told me one day as he was installing a new computer in his office. He had acquainted himself with Microsoft's C++ programming language, in which *Sendak*'s code would be written, and with its Foundation Class Library—a library of code modules, written in the C++ language, for various generic functions common to all Windows programs. Rather than write code for every feature in *Sendak*, Gammill could plug these modules into his code whenever he needed one. The research was part of his gradual focus on *Sendak*: having cleared his desk for the encyclopedia project, he had begun thinking in earnest about how he was going to go about writing its code and arranging its data on compact disc.

The first stage of Gammill's thinking about a product's code is an attempt to understand completely the parameters of every feature in that product. In order to guess at how much space it will take on the disc, and how much code he will have to write for it, he must know exactly how everything in it will look and behave, on all machines and under all conditions. He also must classify all product features, arranging them in groups: pop-up text in one classification, animations in another, sprites in another, sound effects in another, user-activated sounds (songs, pronunciation, narration, and so on) in another, and so on. Any feature that deviated in any way from others in its class would have to be separately classified and stored: a song, for example, that was to begin playing when the user clicked on an icon could not be delineated and accessed by the same code as that for a song that was to begin playing automatically when a given pop-up stack was opened. For most classes of features, hundreds of lines of code had to be written, and for all of them a separate address—a place either on the compact disc, the computer's hard disc, or in the computer's RAM—had to be set aside both for the features themselves and for the pathways to them.

Many *Sendak* meetings were devoted to Gammill's painstaking and decreasingly patient explanations to his fellows about why a given animation or other feature had to be changed, as it differed too much from others to be classified with them. Most troubling in this regard were Fox's treasured activities, to be included in *Sendak* so as to make it more engaging and replayable for children. Among the activities she envisioned was an exercise in which children were presented with pictures of three plants in one row, and with pictures of three different environments—a wetlands, a forest, and a desert, say—in another. The user would be asked to drag plants with the mouse pointer into their proper environments. Drag a plant to the wrong habitat, and it would spring back out again. Drag it into the correct one, and *Sendak* would emit a congratulatory sound.

These activities were particularly troubling to Gammill. *Sendak*'s editors seemed to be dreaming up a variety of them without thinking about the complexities of the underlying code. He explained to Fox one day that each new variation would have to be considered a new feature; in the case of this drag-and-drop model, for example, an activity in which you dragged objects vertically would have to be classified differently from one where you dragged them horizontally.

Gammill knew, of course, that no amount of pleading could dissuade Fox from designing a wide variety of activities. Since virtually all of the activities would use various media and require Gammill to invoke an endless number of engines, each one of them promised to pose difficult and unique code-writing problems. He decided he had to have thorough definitions in hand of all activity types by April 14, in order have sufficient time to code them. The definitions did not arrive; then Fox, when asked, was vague about when they would, leaving Gammill chagrined. "This is a pretty serious slip," he said to me. "I needed to start thinking about how to do these." Just as they had on *Encarta*, editorial and design were failing across the board, leaving development—Gammill—to make up the lost time.

Gammill took every opportunity to remind Fox and everyone else on their team that he regarded the missed deadline as a disaster. "How should we classify activities in Merismus?" he was asked one day. "I don't know—*because they haven't been defined yet,"* he answered, looking pointedly at Fox. By the time the meeting had ended, he had given that same answer to six different questions. Fox left early, visibly angered.

Deadline and feature issues involving Fox were complicated for Gammill because personally he liked her and had tremendous respect for her intellect. He regarded Fox as *Sendak*'s second-smartest team member, and never rejected a request of hers outright. He entertained fantasies about talking her into leaving Microsoft and starting a multimedia software business with him. While he tended to growl and snarl skeptically when presented with design or editorial ideas, he always listened intently to Fox's, thoroughly beguiled. When Fox asked him to come to her office one morning to listen to her explain a new activity—to be called "Hollywood Squirrels"—that she wanted included in *Sendak*, he followed her without hesitation. Fox drew on her whiteboard a tree with nine squirrels peeking out of its foliage. A question, she explained, would be presented to the user, and the squirrels would offer answers with which the user had either to agree or disagree. The goal, just as in the television show

"Hollywood Squares," was to win a vaguely intellectual game of tic-tac-toe, by correctly agreeing or disagreeing with three squirrels in a vertical, horizontal, or diagonal row. After her description was finished, Fox braced herself for the worst. But to his customary stock answers—"No" and "I'll have to think about it"—Gammill now added a third: "I can figure out a way to do this."

So it was a remarkable event when Gammill angered Fox. And ordinarily, Bjerke might have intervened. But she was busy trying to bolster the confidence of Smith, who was collapsing under personal tensions and unresolvable design issues. Smith now was convinced to the point of obsession that her status as a contractor kept others from showing her proper respect and from taking her seriously both as a designer and as a supervisor. Her resentment over her status grew to the point where she came to believe that she could hear a disrespectful tone in e-mail from elsewhere in the company—a tone occasioned, she said to Bjerke one day, by her e-mail address, which automatically included the name of her temporary-employment agency whenever she sent or received a message. She felt squeezed between Ballinger's refusal to take direction and Bjerke's refusal to leave design completely to her. Ballinger took questions either directly to Bjerke or on to Bjerke whenever Smith disagreed with him. She felt that she could never make a final decision without having Bjerke approve it in advance. Meanwhile, Ryberg, Smith said to me, "wants me to stand up to Carolyn, be more assertive with her." That mandate was further confused by Bjerke's confused feelings about Smith: on the one hand, she was pushing Smith to take over design and show the rest of the company that she deserved to be hired, as Bjerke believed she did; on the other, Bjerke seemed determined both to maintain her own authority over *Sendak*'s design and to continue in her role as Smith's mentor. So Smith felt entitled to assert herself only when her ideas coincided with Bjerke's.

In the storm that followed Ballinger's confronting Bjerke with his comic nature-scene drawings, Smith went to Bartholomew to demand a job description. "I don't have the authority or the respect that I need," she said. "All the decisions are still being made by Carolyn and Jayleen." Bartholomew talked with Ryberg and with Bjerke, who was furious. "I can't believe I have to deal with this *again!*" she said. She felt that the problem lay not with her and Ryberg but with Smith herself. "Lindsey keeps coming in to complain about Bryan and Jayleen," she said to me. "When someone bothers her, she feels really guilty. She's having trouble dealing with Bryan's personal issues, and with all these product issues. And she *thinks* she doesn't have authority when in fact she does. The real problem is that she doesn't believe enough in her own ideas. We'll give her input—the whole team will—but she still has the authority to design and test her own ideas. I'm tired of telling her this!"

Bjerke, who had grown up playing basketball, saw in Smith "the kind of basketball player who never was self-directed. They'd only act when their coach told them to. I *hated* those kind of players—'Don't do anything till the coach beats you up!' "

She called Smith into her office and told her that she needed to "be a tree and not a flower." In other words, Smith interpreted later with a laugh, she was to stand up for herself and believe enough in her own ideas to defend them in the face of criticism. When Smith complained that it was not the team's work so much as Microsoft politics that was holding her back, Bjerke snapped, *"Grow up.* It's a lot worse in other places."

Smith left the encounter with mixed feelings. "I'm going to try to be more confident in my ideas," she said, "even though it's not my personality trait." Yet she felt that Bjerke would never give in to her if they disagreed on anything. "She said that I can call design and everything, but she has the final say."

However confident she was supposed to have emerged from her talk with Bjerke, Smith still was tentative when presenting her ideas to her teammates. The previous weekend, she had redesigned the pop-up stacks so that they looked like pages in a student's notebook. Each pop-up had a numbered tab on the bottom, the tabs slightly overlapping in a row along the bottom of the pop-up window. A user reading the first pop-up in the stack could move on to any of the others simply by clicking on the appropriate numbered tab. It was a clever design idea that accomplished three things at once: the number of tabs told the user immediately how many pop-ups were in a given stack; the tabs afforded an easily understood means of navigation through the stack; and the notebook metaphor was one that children could instantly decipher. Yet Smith was afraid to show her design to Gammill. "I'm wondering what he's going to think about these," she said. "I don't know how it's going to fly."

At Bartholomew's direction, Bjerke tried to bolster Smith's confidence with an e-mail message to the rest of the team. "There are times when I have noticed people turning to me," she wrote, "and asking me a design question which should actually be addressed to Lindsey. We all know that I am more than willing to share my ideas but I am trying hard to not infringe on her role and her responsibilities. So in the next few weeks be extra attentive to asking Lindsey a design question directly. . . . Also to help everyone understand, Bryan's role is still Lead Illustrator but this role does not give him final authority on any design component of the project. Lindsey has final design approval on all visual elements of the product." In e-mail sent to me the same day, she wrote, "There are a few things I am going to do to help rectify the situation including hitting her over the head."

Smith's confusion—and Ballinger's too, for that matter—was further deepened by Bartholomew's occasional close interest in *Sendak*'s design. After months of leaving the product team to itself, he suddenly weighed in with a long list of concerns. Having looked at the latest *Sendak* prototype, he decided that it still was far too young in look and that there was too much grouping in the scenes of things that were not grouped together in the real world. The desert scene, for example, included both a camel and a cactus—inhabitants of different deserts on different continents. "This 'virtual world' metaphor—grouping together things inappropriately—isn't working," Bartholomew said one day. "They're mixing metaphors on the same screen." He told Bjerke to find a solution to that problem and to try again to get Ballinger to make the scenes appeal to older kids. "Kids want to be older—they don't want to reach down," he said. "I don't want to be pigeonholed by these style issues into too narrow a niche." He believed that parents would be put off by *Sendak* if it looked too juvenile, since "every parent thinks his or her kid is sophisticated."

Bartholomew was distressed to see that Ballinger's scene style had remained unchanged despite his complaint about their look two months before. He understood that the problem lay with Ballinger—"Bryan's a real creative guy," he said, "but he thinks too much like a little kid"— but he also felt that *Sendak* lacked a strong design leader. "This is a big issue," he said. "It's why I want to see art direction come into play." It was an oblique warning to Smith and Bjerke to get Smith's role straightened out.

The more strenuous Bjerke's efforts at writing *Sendak*'s design specification, the more distant its completion seemed to grow. As she tried to describe the appearance and performance of every one of *Sendak*'s features, she found herself reminded repeatedly of Indra's net, a Zen Buddhist allegory for the universe. The net is an infinite mesh of threads, the horizontal ones running through space, the vertical ones running through time. At each intersection is an individual in the form of a crystal bead. Every crystal, illuminated and suffused with the light of Absolute Being, reflects not only the light given off by every other crystal in the universe, but also that of every other reflection of every other reflection in the universe.

So it seemed in *Sendak*. In this little artificial universe, every feature was connected in some way with every other feature, and Bjerke had not only to imagine the look of a given feature on the screen, and how it would behave and how users might react to it—she also had to be careful not to design behavior into it that was inconsistent with behavior elsewhere in the product, or that would lead users to expect other features to behave differently from the way Bjerke and Smith were designing them to behave.

Bjerke was feeling particularly overwhelmed now because she was in the first weeks of pregnancy, and came to work each day feeling too sluggish and nauseated to think clearly or quickly. The more she worked at her document, the more unresolved issues she unearthed. But somehow she managed to finish a rough, or preliminary, version of the spec, and decided that the time had come to bash it by having Gammill and Len Dongweck, Gandalf's lead product tester, read it and meet with her to list its flaws and mistakes. So Bjerke scheduled a "spec basheroo," at a nearby pizza-and-beer joint one afternoon at the end of April, to go over the spec line by line.

This was a matter of considerable urgency, as the preliminary spec had been scheduled for completion by the end of April, and Bjerke's document was far from complete. Several pages of the spec had only headings on them, and nearly every page had at least one TBD—to be determined—feature. Throughout the document could be found such sentences as "There is a TBD header bar on it"; "TBD—there may be an exit app button here as well"; "Amount of functionality TBD."

Sendak's design spec was both a detailed description of the product and an accounting of the reasons behind its look and behavior. A typical example is the description of how a user logs on:

Since our product is somewhat customizable, it is necessary to know who is using the application at any time. Logging on is a step that is done at the beginning of the application or can be done during a session so that users can be switched. The only question asked during Log On is the user's name. . . .

Double clicking on the *Sendak* icon launches the application with the Log On dialog displayed on top of the Opening screen. The dialog asks the user for his/her name. The user must type something into the name field, if not they will get a prompt asking them to enter something when they single click on the OK button.

The meeting was a blizzard of questions and demands for detail. Turning first to her logging on page, Gammill said, "Define 'name.' Define 'home customization.' Is this a modal or a nonmodal dialog?"

Dongweck said, "I need as precise a list as possible of all the Macintoshes we're going to run on. Are we supporting any models with 68020 microprocessors? Some of this is controlled by marketing, and I have to pull their teeth to get anything, and I end up guessing—and I end up guessing wrong." Seconds later, he asked, "What platforms and video cards get tested? If we really want to test on a card, we have to buy it. . . . And for the Windows version, I need to know if you expect NT support. That will determine what we do, and how Kevin does things."

On and on it went, the first hour spent entirely on the spec's first four pages. Some of Gammill's and Dongweck's questions and comments could be easily dispensed with. To fulfill Gammill's request for the definition of "name," for example, Bjerke had only to add, "A name is defined as any standard character available from a keyboard, including numbers and symbols." But most others required long and careful thought, and many required input from several others on the team. Having begun at 3:00, they worked without stopping until well past 6:00, by which time they had been through less than half of Bjerke's document, which now was covered over with scribbled notations in red pen. Bjerke had arrived at the meeting hoping that it would lighten her workload by clearing up issues she had been unable to clear up on her own. Instead, it reopened hundreds of issues she had thought closed. Now, heading off into the darkness, she tried to imagine how she could have her final specification finished by June 1, the date called for in the schedule.

Among the principal obstacles to finishing the spec were two particularly alarming problems: general confusion about exactly what, and how much, *Sendak* could include by way of features—particularly animation and video—and an ongoing debate over the encyclopedia's style. Every time Fox or any of her editors talked either with Ballinger, Bjerke, or Gammill, they came away with new notions about what sort of art or animation they could include in the pop-ups. The more Fox brooded about *Sendak*'s graphic content, the more confused and worried she became, particularly when she started thinking about the encyclopedia's prose and pop-up art in the context of *Sendak*'s overall style.

At the beginning of May, thirty days before all design work was to be completed and thirty days after pop-up production, not yet begun, was supposed to have started, a worried Fox met with Smith, Bjerke, and Ballinger in Ballinger's office. "I showed Kevin some of the specs we have for pop-ups," Fox said, "and he was surprised that we had sprites in our content. Then I was looking at Bryan's spreadsheet, where he has a sprite for every object in the scene. But Kevin gives the impression that we don't have the disc space for that. Do we? I mean, has Kevin said yes to some total number of sprites?"

"Well," said Bjerke, "it's a question of tradeoffs among all the pop-ups and scenes. Right now we have 800 sprites budgeted . . . and I would guess there are 900 objects total, with plans for 810 sprites." She went on, though, to note that the word *sprite,* as being used by everyone on the project, was misleading. "We need to define the difference between animations and sprites," she cautioned. Animations were stationary—that is, they stayed in one spot on the screen and performed some action—while sprites were animations that moved about on the screen among other objects in a scene. A butterfly that flew across the forest scene, then, was a sprite, while a hedgehog that looked up and sniffed a flower was an animation. Bjerke also pointed out that a large sprite could take up as much as four times the disc space of a small animation. Somehow, she said, the editors would have to devise a way to measure the disc space hit of the sprites and animations they were designing.

Since this struck Fox as a practically impossible task, she moved on to the style issue, which had come to a head a few days before, when Bjerke decided to commission three freelance artists to draw versions of a forest scene and have them presented, along with Ballinger's work, to consumers either in focus groups or in mall intercepts. The latter involved setting up display stations in shopping malls and asking passersby to compare and rate the pictures. Bjerke and Ryberg told Ballinger that they were resolved not to use his current art for *Sendak*'s scenes, and that he should do a second version of the forest scene with a more realistic look. They would include both versions in the consumer tests, with the idea that if a clear preference for any of the five emerged, that would be the artist and the style *Sendak* would use.

For the moment, Ballinger kept his feelings to himself. Fox, however, was openly dismayed, particularly when she saw the other three artists' pictures. They looked like conventional children's book illustrations, with animals realistically rendered in peaceful, dreamy forest scenes. There was nothing in the paintings to suggest that children could have fun using the encyclopedia. There was none of the wit, mischief, or whimsy that characterized Ballinger's depictions and that had essentially directed the editorial vision of *Sendak* from the beginning.

In editing *Sendak*'s text, Fox and her editors had been guided by the style of Ballinger's scenes and animations. For months, they had been editing prose to make it similar in tone to his pictures, and had been designing pop-up activities, animations, and sound effects that would meld properly with Ballinger's art. Now Fox felt that the encyclopedia was about to undergo such a profound change that her editors would have to start over. "We need to get this style resolved," she said anxiously to Bjerke. "The humor quotient and the number of animations in our pop-ups is dependent on the scene style."

"Well," answered Bjerke, "we got money to do mall intercepts."

"You're kidding!" Fox was stunned. "We're doing *mall intercepts?* Can't we go into classrooms instead? Are we listening to kids or adults?"

When Bjerke didn't answer, Fox said, her voice heavy with sarcasm, *"It would be a paradigm shift."* Bjerke turned and left the room.

"So where are we now?" Smith asked Fox.

"Nowhere," she answered glumly.

The X/Y Gridlock

Of all of the changes she could have wrought to ease the pressures of work, Bjerke soon rediscovered, getting pregnant was not one of them. Any kind of sickness, even a mild cold, made her furious with frustration, as she could not abide feelings of weakness. Now, just as she had been during the *Encarta* project when she was pregnant with Troy, she was sick every morning with a narcoleptic nausea that found her struggling both to eat and to keep her head upright. It was not unusual when passing by her office to see Bjerke sitting at her computer with her head resting, face down, on a small pillow in front of her keyboard, a half-eaten bran muffin and an opened pint of nonfat milk sitting forgotten at her elbow. Sometimes she would type in this position; more often, she would sleep fitfully, her fingers poised on the home keys.

Intellectually, Bjerke knew that *Sendak* could be brought in on time only if her group attained the cohesion and purpose of a championship sports franchise. This is why she hammered constantly on her fellows to be team players, by which she meant that they must believe wholeheartedly in one another and in their project, buy into the same set of goals, and set aside personal satisfaction for the sake of the group's greater good. This ethic had been hammered into Bjerke by Craig Bartholomew during a series of meetings after he made her *Sendak*'s program manager.

Thus it was critical to Bjerke that everyone on her team trust one another and turn to one another for reassurance, advice, and sympathy. Most of all, they must never falter in their belief that they would succeed.

Like a determined coach, Bjerke refused to countenance negative input from anyone.

Psychologically, however, Bjerke loathed team spirit. She had always done far better at individual sports than team sports, and had taken far more pleasure in them. Throughout childhood, she had excelled as a competitive swimmer and played other sports with far less skill and joy. Even now, in Microsoft's volleyball league, her coach constantly harped on her for her selfish play—her tendency to freelance on the court rather than meld selflessly with her teammates. And when undertaking difficult projects, she drew inward just as she had as a swimmer. She believed that she performed best when she reached down inside herself for strength, motivation, and inspiration.

Bjerke felt most fulfilled and productive when she worked alone in her office devising solutions to design and schedule problems. During those long hours, she often would enter a state of frenzied analysis, from which she would emerge with a new plan in hand and a renewed sense of confidence in herself, her teammates, and their project.

Inevitably, though, she would be brought down as soon as she encountered anyone else from *Sendak*. It was a pattern opposite that of the ordinary athlete, who falls prey to doubt when alone, then is restored by his or her teammates when they are together. Bjerke was empowered when alone, and confronted by fear and doubt in the company of her teammates.

There were so many impediments to *Sendak*'s being done on time that it was hard to single out the most difficult hurdle. There was no model —no precedent—for anyone to follow, for no one had attempted such a product before. There was no real understanding of what was good or creative in multimedia computing. The emerging medium had no defined aesthetic and there was no sense among its creators of its limitations. No one knew how much consumers would be willing to pay for multimedia products, or what they would want to buy. Combined with the youth and inexperience of the *Sendak* team members and its managers, these obstacles made it difficult even to formulate a plan, let alone lay out a schedule for its fulfillment.

Yet it was clear by now that Bjerke had grown too estranged from her teammates for them to work productively together even under ideal circumstances. She and Ballinger had completely given up on one another; she had lost faith in Smith, who was rapidly losing faith in herself; she and Ryberg were increasingly at odds over the feasibility of Bjerke's plans; she was losing faith in Fox, who was chronically fickle; and Fox had lost all faith in her. Any time Bjerke met with her team, or with an individual teammate, they would retire to their respective offices afterward frustrated and angry with one another.

So it went when *Sendak* team members convened on May 3 to match their accomplishments with their May 1 milestones. Bartholomew, who had been professing all along to me that Bjerke was doing well, nevertheless felt compelled to attend this meeting because of complaints about her from Ryberg, Smith and Fox.

"Well, we made it!" Bjerke began cheerfully. She passed out copies of her design specification, noting that it was incomplete, with "a *lot* of TBDs." Then, laughing, she continued, "Our goal for the next one and one-half months is to solve all open issues. Some are tiny, some are big—like, what's the name of our product? So our goal is to reach something called 'closed spec,' and schedule the product." She paused. "Of course, the problem is that there's no precedent, no established look for these products."

By her best guess, she and her team had designed features taking up nearly 850 megabytes of space on a compact disc designed to hold only 680. Having been budgeted for fifteen person-years, Bjerke now estimated that it would take nineteen to finish the project.

Sendak was overbudgeted for disc space largely because its editors and designers hoped to load it with audio features, including songs, sound effects, a pronunciation for every topic title, and narration of at least every first pop-up of text. While they regarded sound as indispensable in a product intended to be used by preschoolers and children just learning to read, they also knew that it takes up tremendous amounts of disc space—a two-second sound effect, for example, requires as much space as it takes to store forty pages of text—and Bjerke was constantly trying to devise ways to clear more space for it on the disc.

Soliciting progress reports from her teammates, Bjerke heard nothing but bad news. Gammill warned her that Spencer's SPAM group was getting off to a bad start. "I sent mail to Phil, basically bitching him out," he said. "We're still up in the air about the sprite engine. The tools group seems to be scrambling. They don't seem to have a mission. Their ship date is the same as ours. That's just begging for trouble."

Smith reported that her first draft of the visual design specification, due that day, had slipped—in part because she was waiting for results of the upcoming mall intercept tests. Ryberg said that research on what sort of character, or characters, should serve as *Sendak*'s guide had "dropped off our list." When Bjerke asked if she had given any thought to what sort of help system *Sendak* should include, she shook her head gloomily. Listening to her and Smith, Gammill turned to Len Dongweck, sitting beside him, and whispered, "We're already slipping—that's not good." Then Bjerke, passing out a list of goals for *Sendak*'s next milestone, said brightly, "One year and four months before the product slips." Interrupted by laughter, she blushed. "I mean . . . *ships!*"

Discussion turned yet again to the thorny issue of *Sendak*'s style. "If we're spending more disc space than we have on every topic, that's a huge problem," said Fox. "And if the style changes too much, that's a huge problem. And the whole product concept is a huge problem!" She felt that everything was about to grind to a halt because no one could decide how *Sendak* should look. "It's hard to charge ahead with content when we have all these open issues."

Ryberg agreed. "We need to settle the style issue," she said, "because it affects our resources." The number of artists she could sign to contracts, the kind of computer equipment and technical ability they would have to have, and a whole host of other considerations could be determined only after she knew what sort of artwork, and how much of it, would be needed. She also was worried about the impact on *Sendak*'s schedule and budget of tests like the upcoming mall intercepts. For those alone, she pointed out, she had to contract with three freelance artists to draw and paint scenes, have Ballinger spend countless hours doing new artwork, hire consulting firms in Chicago and Los Angeles, and arrange to have some of *Sendak*'s team fly to both cities. "This mall intercept stuff," she said, "is a *lot* of work."

Now people all over the room were weighing in with objections to further testing. In addition to the intercepts, Bjerke was planning a long series of usability tests and an expert review session for which children's education and television experts were being flown from around the country to the Microsoft campus. It was not possible, she was told again and again, to keep to the schedule she had laid out when no one was likely to know for months how the product would look or behave.

These were reasonable objections, but they only served to stiffen Bjerke's resolve. "I'm trying to balance creative ideas from within and without the team," she said. "We just want to *do it*. But my biggest concern is our Achilles' heel—the style issue. We have to *decide*, true, but we have to understand what we're doing."

"But the longer we go before settling the style," Fox said, "the further back we go in terms of getting things done."

Bartholomew, growing increasingly impatient, brought the discussion to a close. "My issue isn't whether the style is appealing to kids, but whether it's a reference style," he said. "We're spending $3 million developing this product. We have to get it right, because we can't spend $3 million fixing it. And keep in mind the dual nature of the purchasing decision. It has to be not only appealing to kids but to parents, too. It has to be fun, yes—but adults are the ones who actually buy it." He also pointed out that the stakes in *Sendak* were particularly high for him: "If we have something wrong with *Sendak*, they don't come to you—they come to me."

Unwittingly, he had highlighted the most daunting problem of all: everyone was terrified of making a mistake. In a company where people had to make objective arguments for their decisions, and back them up with data, it was impossible to create products that you simply liked, that essentially were the result of a series of subjective judgments. *Sendak* had to be proven marketable and profitable in advance, and no one— Bartholomew included—wanted to take a chance on something that might be an aesthetic triumph and a commercial failure.

The meeting broke up a few minutes later. Bjerke retreated to her office and fell into her chair. "That was almost depressing!" she exclaimed. "This has been such a hard month—there are so many things to resolve." Incredibly, she found a reason to remain optimistic: "It's better to have a hard month now than later."

For her, the most pressing immediate problem was *Sendak*'s disc space overload. The easiest and most sensible solution to that problem would be to eliminate narration, she said, but Fox and parents of children who had taken part in usability sessions all singled out narration of the printed text as one of the most important features in *Sendak*. So now Bjerke was waiting for results of research by Steve Boyce, Gandalf's audio technician, into the latest audio compression technology before deciding what to do.

Data compression is one of the key technologies behind the multimedia revolution. By submitting all forms of digitized data—text, sound, video, animation, illustrations—to complex compression algorithms, developers can reduce the amount of space data takes up by anywhere from 50 percent to 90 percent, depending upon the medium and the quality of decompressed data required. (Compressed video images, for example, sometimes emerge from decompression as chunks of indecipherable, sparkling murk.) There was an endless, and endlessly changing, array of compression techniques available to the *Sendak* team. One form of text compression replaced a frequently repeated word—*the*, for example, or *which*—with a 1- or 2-byte symbol, saving at least one byte of space each time the word was stored. Another, for music, analyzed its patterns, eliminated as much of the digitized music as possible from a given song, then used logical analysis to replace it during decompression, when the song was retrieved from the disc and played. For *Sendak*'s audio and sound effects, Boyce was researching compression algorithms both for the amount of compression he could employ and for the quality of the resulting decompressed sound.

Such technical problems, though, paled in comparison with the *Sendak* team's emerging emotional problems. Bjerke was frustrated with the inability or refusal of her teammates to think of *Sendak* as a commercial product rather than the fulfillment of a pure artistic vision. "They're getting too caught up in aesthetics and vision," she said, "and forgetting that we're developing for the consumer market. The trouble with disagreeing with the person who's buying the thing is that you can't argue with them." She also felt that *Sendak* was at the most difficult stage in any project: the "transition from thinking and planning to doing." Indeed, when she looked over the milestone list that day, she noted that all deadlines for thinking and planning had been met, but that all deadlines for actual work on the encyclopedia had slipped.

Gammill was even more depressed. Walking into an office awash in papers, books, discs, cafeteria trays, and Diet Sprite cans, he swept his copy of Queaneau's *The Bark Tree* off his chair onto the floor, sat down, and began ranting. He was most angry about Bjerke's treasured find gadget. Not only would Gammill have to write huge lists for it—Bjerke wanted it to combine the functions of a table of contents, a verbal index, and an index to all illustrations in the pop-ups—but hardware constraints would make the gadget intolerably slow. A compact disc drive's head—analogous to the arm and needle on a record player—can only examine 2 kilobytes of disc space per search, with each search taking between

.25 and .5 seconds. The find gadget figured to occupy 19.5 megabytes, or 20,000 kilobytes, of space. So when a user typed in a word or clicked on a letter of the alphabet displayed on the gadget, the visual index would have to scroll through its array of thumbnails, just as a word wheel did through its array of words, until it reached the appropriate group arrayed around the requested letter or word. Gammill had been given a sample of a find gadget screen in which the user had requested *bats* and gotten a display of eleven thumbnail images. Each of those eleven thumbnails would have to be separately searched and retrieved from the compact disc. A search head moving two kilobytes at a time through 20,000 kilobytes of information could take up to seven seconds to find the right thumbnails, fetch them—2 kilobytes' worth at a time—back to the computer's memory, decompress them, compose the appropriate bitmap for the screen, then display the image. "I'm trying to think of alternatives to the standard way of implementing this thing," Gammill said. "Or I can develop it and let them see how slow it is. Then they can redesign it." He had asked Bjerke to build a seven-second delay into the current *Sendak* prototype's sample find gadget, so they could test it at the next usability sessions.

Gammill was constantly frustrated and often angry at Bjerke for ignoring his technical explanations. When he tried to tell her, as he did repeatedly, about the hardware limitations that made her find gadget impossible to implement, she seemed to look right through him without responding.

Bjerke never backed down from Gammill when directly confronted by him—a habit, it seemed to me, that was ego-driven and fatal. She could not concede points to him because she hated losing arguments and hated playing the typically subservient designer role to Gammill's all-powerful developer role. So she consistently turned aside his objections, which only served to fuel his anger.

Yet Bjerke did take Gammill's snarling to heart. By the end of that day, having worked *Sendak*'s multifarious tangle of disc-space, monetary, and scheduling numbers over and over again on her spreadsheets, and having forced herself to acknowledge the legitimacy of Gammill's objections, she finally concluded that she could never resolve its disc-space problems, include all the features she felt were indispensable, and still finish *Sendak* on time. So she came up with a solution that appealed irresistibly to the designer in her. Then she sent the following e-note to Craig Bartholomew:

OK, tell me what is wrong with this idea. First, sit back and get ready for a whacky idea. Is it totally out of this world to propose the creating and shipping of 5 separate products rather than 1? Are you still in your chair? The idea would be to sell nature, geo, civ, history separately with full narration of each area and then sell the 5th disc as the entire product that is a more "watered down" version without narration of the pop ups since we can't fit it all right now. . . . $3.2 million development for 5 products isn't so bad! Let me know, thanks.

In an effort to devise an objective means of evaluating the results of their upcoming mall intercept tests of *Sendak*'s style, Bartholomew and the *Sendak* team, *sans* Gammill, met to define and describe their aesthetic in the lingua franca of Microsoft.

"The question," said Bjerke as the meeting began, "is what makes a valid test of artists?" She and Bartholomew also agreed that the look of *Sendak*'s scenes, while appealing to children, should somehow give the impression of a reference product. To help them define that substantive but entertaining look, they brought to their meeting fifty or so children's encyclopedias and works of children's fiction by respected popular writers and illustrators. Gesturing toward the pile of these on the conference-room table, Bartholomew said, "We should look through these and see what people are doing."

"So, is this engaging?" Bjerke asked, picking up a book.

"We're only going by our own tastes," Fox said.

"What's 'engaging'?" asked Ryberg.

Fox stepped up to the whiteboard and wrote at the top, "Here's our perspective." Beneath that she drew a horizontal line, with "Realistic" written at one end, "Completely Stylized" at the other. Then she intersected that line with a vertical one, on top of which she wrote, "Generic/Impersonal," and at the bottom of which she wrote, "Personal Appeal." She had devised an x/y axis to measure their aesthetic. The idea was to pick up books from the table and write their titles in the position on Fox's chart that corresponded to the books' mix of style, appeal, realism, and impersonality.

The group regarded the chart in earnest silence.

"Are we trying to measure personal appeal?" Bjerke finally asked.

"I'm thinking more of a warm and fuzzy feeling a kid would get," said Bartholomew.

Then the group fell to picking up drawings by Ballinger and the other artists to be tested, along with books from the table, and trying to assign them positions on the grid. While Ballinger faded into the background, his face a mask, the rest of them shouted out comments and observations in a rush: "I find this somewhat endearing, but still realistic"; "Can you be gorgeous and still be fact?"; "Sometimes when you see things, you get a pleasing feeling"; "To me, that looks real, but it looks warm."

On and on they went, with Lindsey Smith writing a row of words down one side of the board (*Gorgeous, Endearing, Realistic, Warmth, Engaging, 3-D*), and Sonja Gustafson, *Sendak*'s marketer, writing a row down the other side (*Endearing, Empowering, Engaging, Exciting*). "What's scary," said Fox, looking at the board, "is that what kids loved in usability is Cute! Fun! . . . And those aren't in this test."

"But maybe they won't buy a cute, fun encyclopedia," said Gustafson.

The group gradually worked toward the conclusion that they should try to equal in x/y-measurement the Dorling Kindersley book, which they put just below the horizontal line, halfway between the realistic extreme and the vertical line. "We're starting with something already successful," Bartholomew said, referring to the book, which had sold some 300,000 copies. "We should try the same thing." Then, mindful of his own mandate to lift Ballinger's spirits by making him feel more a part of the team, he said, "Bryan, what's your take?"

"I don't know," Ballinger answered. "It's hard for me, because I'm extremely biased. I've already made it clear that I think we should go completely in the opposite direction."

Although no one responded, and everyone gave the impression that Ballinger had gone unheard, his comment dissipated all the group's energy. Talk died down, and the meeting ended a few minutes later.

Eating a late lunch at a patio table outside one of Microsoft's cafeterias that afternoon, Bartholomew told me about the previous weekend, when he had rented a videotape of Robert Altman's *The Player*. One of the running gags in the film is the endless series of movie ideas that are flung at the main character, a film producer, wherever he is—in a hot tub, at a restaurant, at his desk, on his car phone. "People were pitching ideas at this guy constantly," Bartholomew said. "And he would just say yes or no on the spot. What I realized from watching that movie is that that industry is very much a from-the-gut business. And multimedia is probably going to be a from-the-gut business, too. We're in this Microsoft analytical culture here, and we're going to have to learn to make decisions from the gut. It's going to be really hard."

It brought Bjerke considerable relief when Bartholomew, after a brief e-mail consultation with Sonja Gustafson, approved her decision to break *Sendak* up into five separate products. Bjerke's request, it turned out, coincided with Gustafson's discovery that CD-ROM products priced at $200 or $300 were being denied shelf space in retail outlets for the sake of products in the $50 to $70 range. Breaking *Sendak* into four discs, she told Bartholomew, would address her most pressing problem—the price point at which she tried to get Microsoft into the multimedia market. Gustafson also believed that narration was indispensable to *Sendak*. " 'The Encyclopedia That Talks to You'—I love it!" she would say again and again.

Tom Corddry and the rest of Multimedia Publishing's management looked upon Bjerke's decision as a strategic masterstroke. Instead of taking nearly two years to develop a single product, Corddry reasoned, the *Sendak* team now was giving Microsoft a whole series. The move also struck him as a brilliant marketing move. Not only could Microsoft sell far more units at a lower price, but the greater the number of separate packages on the shelf, the greater Microsoft's visibility in the marketplace.

No sooner did management approve, though, than Bjerke and her teammates lost themselves for a month in analyzing the implications of their decision. Gammill lobbied hard for breaking *Sendak* into four distinct products, each with its own features and each released on a different date. Bjerke, however, wanted *Sendak* to be seen as a four-part set, with all four parts released on the same day, and with a single environment and enough links to persuade consumers of the need to have all four. (The fifth disc was to be discussed with decreasing frequency and eventually eliminated entirely.) To that end, she wanted the find gadget on each disc to index the content on all four. She wanted each disc's video to include "Edumercials" about the other discs ("Visit History Land!"). And she wanted all of the Related and See Also features to remain intact, so that a user reading about the sun on the Nature disc could be cross-referenced to the solar power pop-ups on the Civilization disc.

Gammill constantly rebutted Bjerke's marketing and thematic arguments with technical ones. When a user loads a compact disc into a

CD-ROM drive and clicks on a program icon to start *Sendak* running, he explained, the computer loads indexes and directories to the disc into its RAM and configures itself to read, search, and interact with the disc that is in the drive at the time. Should a reader using *Sendak*'s Nature disc decide to eject it and replace it with *Sendak*'s Civilization disc, the computer would not know that a new disc had been inserted. Asked to find something on the Civilization disc, it would think it was still looking through Nature, and would begin displaying unpredictable and incomprehensible error messages. "I don't want it to where you ever have to change CDs," Gammill said insistently. "Because that just opens a huge can of worms."

Undeterred, Bjerke continued working out details for the design of an integrated find gadget. She was impelled in this direction not only, as Gammill believed, by her characteristic feature lust but also by Fox, who calculated that fully one-fourth of *Sendak*'s See Also references were to topics in other units.

Fox's first reaction to Bjerke's decision had been nearly ecstatic, as it solved what to her mind was *Sendak*'s most pressing problem: the shortcomings of its content. A one-disc encyclopedia, she had long feared, would raise comparisons with children's print encyclopedias, all of which were deeper in content than *Sendak* would be. "We're going to suffer if people compare our content head to head," she said. "This might help by taking us out of the comparative arena. We're not saying anymore that we're doing the definitive encyclopedia. Anything that takes away from that comparison is good."

No sooner had her teammates more or less committed to the four-disc strategy, though, than she began fearing it was a terrible mistake. Missions and activities, she said, would have to be greatly simplified, as users would be searching through one-fourth as much content for answers to questions. The more she worried, the more convinced she became that separating *Sendak* into four discs actually highlighted rather than concealed its content weaknesses. "Basically, you've split us up into four products that people can compete with," she said to Bjerke. "This makes our content even more vulnerable, easier to attack on the depth level. With one disc, the whole is greater than the sum of the parts. That's not necessarily the case when you break it up."

The more the team talked, the more its members began doubting the wisdom of their decision. They feared that they were abandoning their original vision of developing a product far more ambitious than anything yet on the market. They feared that they were losing the one feature—unrivaled depth of content—that distinguished them from Microsoft's other product units, particularly Jabe Blumenthal's Jurassic Unit. "How will we distinguish ourselves from *Dinos?*" Bjerke would be asked again and again. "Will we still be bigger than *Dinos?*"

Moreover, the mass of information and wealth of navigation features in a single-disc product seemed far more impressive to them than a relatively information-poor disc full of narrated content. Scheduled as sessions in which design changes could be made to accommodate the new four-disc product, meetings instead turned into exhaustive comparisons between a one-disc encyclopedia and a four-disc series.

To Bjerke, the comparisons were pointless. "When you look at this," she said one day, exasperated, "you have to pretend that you don't know what's missing. Buyers won't be looking at these with this reference expectation that we have, because they won't know that this huge one-disc reference idea ever existed."

Whenever they concentrated on the immensity of *Sendak,* and whenever they realized that they still had not begun actual work on it, team members began looking with increasing suspicion at one another. Gammill commenced reminding Bjerke and Phil Spencer that their reports—Bjerke's design specification and Spencer's SPAM architecture document—would soon be due. By his manner, Gammill made it clear that he expected both of them to miss their deadlines. Smith, after asking Ballinger to draw eight different IgnorAnt and IntelligAnt sketches, found instead that he devoted all his time to a single detailed drawing of each. Frustrated, she went to Ryberg to complain, only to have Ryberg tell her that it was her problem to solve. Smith instead went to Bjerke, who took the problem to Bartholomew. "We have a team member who's not a team player," she said, and went on to ask that Ballinger either be fired or moved to someone else's team.

When not fuming over Ballinger, Bjerke found herself more and more preoccupied with Fox. "You can never tell how she's going to react to anything," she said one day. For her part, Fox found Bjerke predictable to a fault. She felt that Bjerke was making decisions unilaterally and cutting Fox and her editorial expertise out of the managerial loop. Asked one day whether the team had decided once and for all to make *Sendak* a four-disc product, Fox snorted in disgust and said, "Not officially." It was her way of saying that the constant meetings over the issue were a sham. Bjerke, she believed, already had made up her mind.

By now, these constant complaints about teammates were wearing me down. They came about less from real faults and psychological impediments to progress than from the schedule pressures and technical uncertainties confronting the team. *Sendak*'s creators seemed to be turning more and more toward critiquing one another as a means of distracting themselves from the real problems they should have been facing. Rather than concede that they were at an impasse, or even say out loud to one another that they needed someone to force them to make a decision and move on it, they lost themselves in increasingly luxurious fits of back-biting. To everyone on the team, it seemed, there was one other teammate who was singlehandedly holding up progress.

Occasionally, a single event would highlight to the *Sendak* team how far it was from getting down to actual production. Bjerke convened a core team meeting at which she wrote out on her whiteboard sixteen issues to be resolved. They included such things as whether there should be a radio and television in the home for playing songs and videos; how many guide characters there should be and whether each should have a voice of its own; whether random events could be programmed into the scenes so that users would be surprised each time they clicked the mouse on certain objects; whether animals should be standing in a scene when the user opened it or should come walking into it while the user watched; and whether there should be a pronunciation-of-place-names feature, and how it would be implemented. Fifteen of these issues had been discussed in previous meetings. At this one, the team sat through nearly two hours of debate and was unable to come up with a definite yes or no to any of them.

I began to see signs that some on the team were looking, whether consciously or subconsciously, for a way to bail out of the project. I wondered about the timing of Bjerke's pregnancy, which would cause her to leave Microsoft for the first three months of 1994. And when Craig Bartholomew passed along the consequences one day of a directive from Microsoft's upper management to slow the company's personnel growth, it was clear from Lindsey Smith's reaction that she had in some sense given up on Microsoft, and on *Sendak*.

Told along with other product unit managers that new hires should be limited to positions deemed to be absolutely indispensable, Bartholomew couldn't think of any positions in his group, other than software developer and program manager, that couldn't be filled by contractors. After a long conversation with Bjerke, he also decided that *Sendak*'s design was close enough to completion to eliminate the need for a new full-time designer. So he had Ryberg tell Smith that she was no longer in the running for a full-time position at Microsoft, as the design position she had been aiming for now was not going to be filled. Ryberg explained to Smith that the company's new determination to contract out as much work as possible made it impossible for Bartholomew to hire her full time.

Smith was angry at first, then philosophical. As a contractor, she was paid $18.50 per hour—$27.75 per hour for overtime—and Ryberg explained to her that becoming a Microsoft employee would cost her in the neighborhood of $10,000 per year, as salaried employees are not paid more for working over forty hours per week. "I have to admit that I get paid extremely well," Smith said. "When I got out of college, I expected to be paid $7.00 and be a starving artist. And I like the flexible hours, the laid-back atmosphere, and I like working hard and being rewarded for it. So when I start bitching, I just tell myself to shut up."

Still, her contractor status kept rankling her. "You never get acknowledgment for working on a product," she said. "Like when *Encarta* shipped, everyone got their little Ship It awards. But the contractors got nothing. And I don't get a voice even in the hiring of people who end up working for me."

But in the final analysis, she felt that Bartholomew had given her a kind of emotional freedom. "It helps me become more disconnected," she said. "I feel like if they're not willing to provide me with a spot, then I'm not willing to go the extra mile. That's probably a bad attitude, but that's kind of how it hit me." And with that came a marked decline in the amount of time she spent working on *Sendak*, and in the quality of her work.

Two things kept Bjerke's spirits high in the face of *Sendak*'s immobility. One was her belief that the product was destined to be great; the other was the progress Fox and her editorial staff were making. While Bjerke and Ryberg struggled constantly to complete the intricate details of *Sendak*'s design and production, Fox and her editors kept writing and editing copy and speccing illustrations on schedule. "Whatever other troubles we may have," Bjerke thought as she walked into an early June core team meeting, "we at least are getting the encyclopedia's content done on schedule." She was convinced that the project would take off and run smoothly once she completed *Sendak*'s design and got art into real production.

But then Fox told her at the meeting that editorial work was going disastrously slow, and by the end of the session everyone—Bjerke included—was forced to acknowledge that *Sendak* now was a full month behind schedule, even under the most optimistic of scenarios. "We have an end date that we can't change anymore," said Fox. "What can we do?" Bjerke began juggling production schedules for July and August, and finally came up with a new work flow scheme that—on paper, at least—made up for the lost editorial time. But she was glum. She knew full well that production, once started, would bring with it a host of unforeseen nightmares.

While there was a general consensus on the team that something was seriously wrong, each team member had a different idea about what it was. To Bjerke, it was the inability of her teammates to approach problems analytically and dispassionately. While she was the first to admit that she had to struggle constantly against her tendency toward condescension—when her associates expressed fear or doubt at her initiatives, she forced herself to be patient, and she never raised her voice to a teammate or allowed herself to express unmediated anger—she still found it difficult to wait patiently for others to catch up to her. When trying to discuss complicated issues in *Sendak* meetings, she tended more and more often to roll her eyes, blush, or preface a reiteration with a heavily emphasized, *"Again."* Safe in her office after heated discussions, she often would say of her teammates, "They're not looking at the issue analytically—they're just reacting emotionally to it." In her mind, emotional attachment to an idea was a great danger. She and her teammates had to explore every option and think it through thoroughly before accepting or discarding it. "If we do this wrong," she frequently would say, "we've spent $3.2 million to do it *wrong*."

Bartholomew, who had taken recently to attending *Sendak* meetings in an attempt to diagnose its problems, was beginning to intervene. Alarmed at Ryberg's refusal to begin production of anything until all *Sendak* style issues were settled, he told her to at least start producing pop-ups that would be using art from the Dorling Kindersley book. Pop-up production originally had been slated to start on April 15, and now, at the beginning of June, Ryberg had no plans to begin anytime soon. "I don't seen any reason," Bartholomew said to her, "why we can't at least do DK stuff—it's not *all* dependent on the scene style."

Bartholomew felt that resolution of the scene style had been held up almost entirely by Ballinger, whose temperament was proving a tremendous liability. "I won't say we made a mistake in hiring Bryan," he said, his tone of voice implying the opposite, "but we didn't know enough about what we were doing when we hired him. I think what we learned from hiring him is that if we hire people too quickly, without really knowing what their job description is, we can either come up with the wrong person or coach that person in the wrong direction—which might be more the case with Bryan. From day one we should have been setting expectations for him as a full-time employee as moving more towards being a generalist illustrator as opposed to a specialist illustrator. It would have been nice if he could have taken a leadership role in this whole style issue, as lead illustrator. And he's obviously not been able to do that—he's kind of had to have been pushed."

But Bartholomew also felt that his biggest problem, and the main reason he had been attending so many *Sendak* meetings, was Bjerke. "Carolyn doesn't communicate with everybody," he said. "So some people are in the loop, and some aren't, and she creates a misperception that the team is kind of clique-ish or something, that there's an in-group and a not-in-group. That's something that has to be avoided at all costs. She also has a tendency to put herself at center stage too much. You hear the word *I* too much from her." Noting that at meetings Bjerke tended to stand at the whiteboard and lecture rather than invite discussion from around the room, he said, "She likes too much to be the center of things. A lot of times, you're in a position of leadership and everyone knows it, recognizes it, and it's your job to kind of diminish that notion of separateness or being above or whatever. She's got to remind people that the team doesn't work for the program manager—the team works *with* the program manager and the program manager directs them." He believed that Bjerke's tendency toward authoritarianism made others on her team afraid to confront her with unpleasant truths. Their fear was exacerbated by the way she handled her own emotions. "She takes things well," he says, "but she turns red as a beet, and sometimes I can see her start to get emotional, then check it." It was a reaction that tended to cut off discussion.

Indeed, others on Bjerke's team felt more and more estranged from the nerve center of the *Sendak* project. While no one blamed Bjerke outright, many complained that they no longer had a role in key decisions—or weren't even apprised of them. "I don't feel like we're a team anymore," Ballinger would lament in the privacy of his office. Fox was no less depressed. "I get really panicked when I think how everything is unresolved," she said. "I don't have a picture of the product we're working on anymore, because there are so many variables. And as for where the responsibility for the vision of a product lies at Microsoft, I'm really confused. Is it the program manager? Is it a consensus? For a while, it seemed like Bryan had the only vision . . . and now he's been shoved aside. I need to find out if I still like this product, because I don't know anymore."

Ryberg was more frustrated and angry than depressed. "There is *nothing* I can do," she said. To think that six months now had gone by, and that no work had begun or was likely to begin in the foreseeable future, seemed even more astounding to her than it did to me. "I mean, I feel like we're actually taking a step backwards in many ways," she continued. "To even reevaluating the whole goal of the product, whether it's an encyclopedia or a knowledge explorer or what."

Gammill stopped talking at meetings entirely, and spent more time in his office shouting curses and enumerating the shortcomings of his fellows. He saw someone letting him down everywhere he looked. Anyone wanting to talk with him would find themselves confronted by his closed office door, on which he had posted the front page of the June 6 *New York Times. Sendak*'s problems, he kept saying to me, were simple. "People get too emotionally attached to things sometimes, to certain features. They keep making things too complicated."

Ballinger, meanwhile, left alone in his office to draw and paint, turned contagiously tranquil as he set to work on a more realistic version of his forest scene. He began his effort by drawing a new bear that sat at the bottom of the screen, in the front and center of the scene. It sat, as bears often do in zoos, on its haunches with its legs extended in front of it. The bear was gripping one of its hind feet with a forepaw. Looking slightly off to one side, it wore a wistful and thoughtful expression. Ballinger had spent hours refining the color and texture of its fur, to the point where it had an almost photographic look. There was something tremendously arresting about the bear's gaze; it looked relaxed, expectant, alert, and a little puzzled. Where Ballinger's animals previously had been cartoon creatures, remarkable only for their cuteness, this one evoked powerful fascination and affection in the viewer. It struck me as odd and ironic that something so beautiful could arise out of so much pointless turmoil. Staring at this bear in the gloom of Ballinger's office, I wondered for the first time if I was misinterpreting all the anguish around me. It didn't seem possible that something as enchanting as this image on the screen could have resulted from such ridiculous misdirection. Either I was hallucinating, or the meaning of the *Sendak* team's struggles had eluded me entirely.

Beyond the Mid-June Milestone

June saw the *Sendak* team begin coming apart in earnest. Not a day went by that did not bring with it a new disappointment or cause for anger. At every turn, an opportunity to settle an issue or find the answer to a critical design question turned instead either into a colossal setback or a new cause for contention, or both.

Having decided against conducting the mall intercepts they had been planning for months, Bjerke's team instead convened focus groups in Chicago and Los Angeles to evaluate various potential styles of *Sendak* art. A total of sixty people—parents, children, and teachers—were shown pictures of Ballinger-drawn *Sendak* screens and of scenes painted by four other artists. They were asked to vote for their favorite, second favorite, and least favorite, rating the drawings according to how well they matched their expectations of the proper look of a reference product.

Only the *Sendak* team could have compiled the results into a set of hard numbers interpretable by nearly everyone in an entirely different way. Bjerke felt that Ballinger's work had finished behind that of three other artists; Smith agreed, but feared that the voting samples were too small to be considered reliable; Ryberg felt that the results were inconclusive; and Fox felt that Ballinger's work had been the clear favorite. Moreover, Fox believed that the tests had been rigged, as Ballinger's work was shown in black-and-white while the other artists' work was shown in full color. When Gammill was apprised by Fox of that procedural irregularity, he was livid, and not just at the sloppiness of the testing. He had

214

decided that Ballinger's work was perfect for *Sendak*. "If we end up not using him as the artist," he said to me, "it'll be a horrible mistake."

For Ballinger, the tests, their methodology, and Bjerke's interpretation of them all were further blows to an already battered psyche. Justifiably feeling persecuted, he withdrew even deeper into his office, emerging only when absolutely required to do so. When sitting in at meetings, he looked more like an apparition than a human being. Deeply religious, he turned even more devotedly, as he wrote me in e-mail, "to the Lord."

Just as Bjerke stood alone in her conviction that Ballinger should be replaced as the artist for *Sendak*'s scenes, so did she stand alone in her optimism and good cheer. Ryberg was convinced that Bjerke had willfully blinded herself to *Sendak*'s problems. Ballinger was resentful and depressed. Gammill felt that the project was doomed. And Fox was lapsing into despair. "This is fascinating," she wrote one day to me in e-mail, "in a horrible and scary sort of way. Part of me is amazed we even got this far in this marketing driven environment."

Into the midst of all this turmoil waded a group of children's education and entertainment experts flown to the Microsoft campus to look at the company's children's products. After studying *Sendak*, the group registered general approval, but delivered a parting shot at Bartholomew as they left. "Your group," one of them said, "could benefit by a bit more of the experience that age can bring."

Bartholomew relayed the comment to me in e-mail, with a terse "interesting perspective" as his only comment. Since I had for some time felt exactly the same way, I relayed the comment to Fox and Bjerke. As I expected, both women were dismissive. Fox professed to be too mystified to comment on it, and Bjerke was outraged. "I am all for experience, experience is a good thing," she e-mailed in response to my question, "but so is a certain amount of freshness and inexperience. . . . When I was an inexperienced swimmer, I had to rely on sheer natural talent rather than finesse and mental strength. And that's how I feel about now." Hers struck me as a classic attitude at Microsoft, where IQ is as prized as speed and strength are in football, where native intelligence is far more valuable than wisdom, and where experience counts for nothing unless it is experience in working at Microsoft.

Bjerke's self-confidence and her conviction that *Sendak* was headed in the right direction stood in stark contrast to her teammates' growing sense that it was headed in no direction at all. Everyone had expected by June to be well into production, with a single shared image of what they were building.

Finally, her team confronted Bjerke with its despair at their mid-June milestone meeting. She walked into the room, set a pile of papers down at the head of the conference table, and chirped, "Are we still having fun?" After a gloomy split-second of silence, Ryberg sighed and answered, "We're lost. We can't see the sidewalk in front of us. This product is no longer defined. I don't see a plan for resolving our questions. I feel like we're back to last December. We don't know what style we want. We don't know what direction we're headed in. We still haven't started production. We have no idea what to expect from SPAM. I'm worried! Our ship date is completely unrealistic. This four-disc thing . . . we don't know if it'll really happen. There's no end to our outstanding issues."

Bjerke, completely undone, stared at her in silence. No one spoke until finally Fox said, "Same with me."

"I'm frustrated," said Gammill.

"Looking at the spec," added Fox, "it's so unclear where we're going. This style thing is holding everyone up. Even if Kevin starts tomorrow, we'd have trouble meeting our ship date. And the way it is now, I can't move toward any of my milestones."

Bjerke was shocked. Her face red, she sat staring now at the table, now around the room. At a complete loss for words, she finally stammered, "It's not unusual for a product to do this." Then she tried to get the meeting back on track by asking everyone around the table to report on their milestones. Without hesitation, her teammates, unmoved by her attempt at reassurance, weighed in with grim reports: "I haven't done a thing"; "I haven't started anything"; "I feel like I can't move forward."

Later, safely back in her office, Bjerke heaved an enormous sigh and sat down in her chair. She was crushed. Her face still red, her eyes glazed, she said softly, "That was my worst moment as a manager yet. I keep asking myself, 'Do I need this?'" Then she closed her door, sat down again, turned to her desk, and put her head down on the pillow in front of her computer.

Bartholomew, meanwhile, had been writing a postmortem of the *Encarta* project and was struck by at least one similarity between what he had gone through on *Encarta* and what Bjerke was enduring now on *Sendak*. He sat down and sent e-mail to Bjerke, saying:

Carolyn, I've been digging through the Encarta schedule for the post-mortem and have noticed a similarity between our 10/14/91 usability feedback and the impact of the recent Sendak focus groups. Both provided fairly important/radical impact for the team to deal with quickly, since we were under schedule pressure in both cases. . . .

It's interesting that you folks are 9 months into Sendak now and are encountering some high-impact feedback. On Encarta, we were 6 months into the project when we got the input. In both cases, it seems that time is/was of the essence in coming up with responses. . . .

With this in mind, I very, very highly recommend that you get the Sendak team (at least Sara, Kevin, Lindsey, Bryan, and you—possibly Jayleen too in regard to scene/illustration logistics issues; possibly Sonja too for marketing input) off-site within a week to hash through these issues.

We should be starting Production very soon (the old schedule called for this to start two months ago), and I think that 1 day off-site will save you weeks of meetings and iterations internally. There is no question that input of this magnitude is going to slip things, and the goal is to minimize the slip while being realistic about the hit on the team. We can't repeat history in slipping design/editorial/production decisions that affect development and still assume we'll hit our ship date. . . .

For all of the trauma engulfing the *Sendak* team, Bartholomew occasionally fell prey to being pleased with the way its members were going about their work. His direct interventions in team disputes invariably were in support of Bjerke—an endorsement, it seemed to me, of the decisions she was making, particularly those about further testing and about Ballinger—and a sign that he was unworried by all the turmoil. But when he sent out his e-mail directing Bjerke to set up another offsite, I thought that he might be beginning to have his doubts, so I stopped by his office to ask.

Given what I knew about the team's morale, I found his answer mildly astounding. "By and large," he said, "I think things are looking pretty good. I don't care what the solution to the style problem is as long as they've tested it. The spec seems to be rolling along, although I know there're still some things to pin down. But by and large, I think things are in good shape. I think they have a really good shot at hitting their date. The team is pretty experienced, and Kevin is pretty experienced at the endgame, getting features completed."

Bartholomew's pleasure was reflected in his semiannual performance review sessions with *Sendak* team members, during which he assessed each individual's performance over the previous six months. As part of his review procedure, Bartholomew generally spent two hours or so in conversation with each of his subordinates before the two of them jointly filled out a "Microsoft Performance Review" form, which includes written evaluations from both employee and supervisor of the employee's work as measured against objectives and goals defined by the two of them at the employee's previous review session. Some of the goals are for projects—for example, "Finish and Ship *Encarta* by Sept. 29, 1992"— and some are for personal professional development, as in, "Become as fluent with C++ as I am now with C." The supervisor then assigns a numerical performance rating, ranging from a low of 1.0 to a high of 5.0. "Although," said Gammill after his review, "that's kind of stupid. No one ever gets a 1, no one ever gets a 5. Basically, it goes from 2.5 to 4.5."

Bartholomew's conversations with *Sendak* team members focused almost exclusively on teamwork and building efficient processes. He told Fox that she needed to work on her tendency to concentrate on the pleasurable parts of her job—editing and creating rather than hiring and supervising contractors—and on her habit of doing too much work herself rather than delegating responsibility. Her greatest failing, he added, was that she takes on too many priorities and ends up completing none of them. He told Bjerke that she needed to communicate better with her team members and other Multimedia employees who helped work on *Sendak*. He told Ballinger to work harder at taking direction and filling orders rather than fulfilling his own artistic vision. And he told Ryberg that she should push ahead with art production on pop-ups regardless of the state of the rest of *Sendak*.

Generally, the review sessions went smoothly, with Bartholomew's subordinates accepting his criticisms and advice without objection. The lone exception was Gammill, who pressed Bartholomew rigorously for specifics. Far more ambitious than his colleagues, Gammill was acutely interested in determining what exactly it would take for him to advance up Microsoft's career ladder. No matter how high his numerical rating, he always left his review sessions professing to believe that he deserved a higher one.

At his review session the previous December, Gammill had dutifully, if grudgingly, taken responsibility for his team's failure to ship *Encarta* on time. "Although not in my job description," he wrote in his review then, "I should have seen the signs of slipping long before I did and raised some flags. This will NEVER happen again." On that particular goal, Gammill had been given a 3.0 by Bartholomew, his lowest-ever rating at Microsoft. His overall rating had been 4.0, a high rating by Microsoft standards, but one that he regarded as a humiliation. Yet Gammill also understood the necessity for his confession and its attendant low number. In confessing to an error and suffering the numerical consequence, he had performed one of the ritual tasks essential to advancement at Microsoft: he had acknowledged a critical mistake and professed to have learned from it. So this time around, Gammill expected to be rewarded for his previous exercise in humility and for his hard work over the past six months.

Bartholomew was pleased with Gammill's work in all but one respect. When conducting his reviews, he always asked his employees, confidentially, to critique their teammates, and if the same criticisms came up from several sources, he would pass them along to the offending team member. In Gammill's case, three people had complained about his habit of saying no outright to their design requests, without appearing to think about the issue at all and without bothering to explain his refusal to them. Bjerke was particularly vexed because she felt that Gammill had promised her a feature one night, over beer, then reneged a week later. And whenever Smith talked with Gammill or communicated with him via e-mail, she came away demoralized at his obvious disdain.

Bartholomew, who regarded the melding of designers, artists, and editors—creative thinkers—into Microsoft's developer-driven culture as among his most important responsibilities, now took Gammill to task for his treatment of designers, particularly Smith. While explaining carefully that this issue would have no impact on his overall performance rating —this time around, it was to be a 4.5—he stressed to Gammill that better treatment of his teammates was to be one of his most important goals for the next review period.

Gammill took all this in impassively, saying little by way of objection. "I asked Craig what I had to do to get a five," he grumbled later. "He said, 'I'm not gonna answer that.' He was too smart about it." Gammill knew, of course, that his question had no answer, and he was appropriately resigned. "If I went home and wrote all of *Sendak* over the weekend . . . then maybe I'd get a five."

He left his review session both pleased and frustrated. His 4.5 ensured that he would earn at least 10 percent over his salary in bonuses during the year, and that he would be given a large pay raise and more stock options. But he was intent on two impossibilities: earning a perfect rating and moving up the salary scale from a Level 11 to a Level 12. To his knowledge, no one in company history had ever rated a 5, and no one had moved up a salary level in less than two years. Gammill had started out at Level 9, spent two years there, then spent two years as a Level 10 developer. He now was in his first year at Level 11. While he understood that company protocol stood solidly in the way of his ambitions, he felt held back by rules that were essentially subjective—a circumstance that infuriated the mathematician in him.

He was also furious about Bartholomew's critique of his teamwork. Gammill felt that the ruffled sensibilities of Smith and Bjerke were entirely their own fault. Why couldn't they be as straightforward as developers were? His summary of Bartholomew's criticism was characteristically crude. Striding through his door, he greeted me with a growled, "Craig says I say no like an asshole."

In the final analysis, though, Gammill preferred to play by Microsoft's rules rather than flout them. Two days later, he sent e-mail to Smith after she had sent mail to the *Sendak* team alerting everyone to a mistake in *Sendak*'s palette strategy. "Good job catching this," Gammill wrote. "I should have a long time ago."

Perhaps by coincidence, Bjerke scheduled the mandated offsite for June 21, when Ballinger would be visiting his parents in Vermont. So before leaving, Ballinger e-mailed a four-page lamentation "on some issues to be discussed at said offsite." The document was headed by a table of contents centered on the first page:

Introduction
1. Thoughts on LA. and Chicago focus groups
2. Implications of using a realistic style
3. Product definition and vision
4. The overall state of Bryan

Outwardly impassive and soft-spoken, Ballinger nevertheless is deeply emotional, and distress constantly came seeping through the mask of indifference he presented to his peers. Now, after seven months of enduring as best he could the constant disappointments and setbacks delivered him by Bjerke and Bartholomew, he lashed back, wounded and perplexed. From the attempted formal tone of his writing, the abundance of qualifiers, and his occasional use of the third person when referring to himself, I could see that Ballinger was trying to present a dispassionate argument. But the overall impression left by his document was one of wretchedness and heartache. "If you are thinking that Bryan feels that the data gathered from these focus groups is somewhat invalid then you are probably correct," Ballinger wrote. "But what really bothers me is the path of action that seems to be evident, based on the data that was received."

Ballinger's introduction consisted of two tortured and tortuous sentences: "I've put myself in the frame of mind that I will view the issues I'm about to discuss from the standpoint that someone else will be doing all the illustration on the product. This is to help distance me from any feelings I have about what kind of favorite style I may have." He then reiterated his conviction that the focus groups had been rigged to discredit his work. "I mean," he wrote, "none of the most popular elements from usability were shown or given in context." Then he pointed out what he saw as a glaring inconsistency in Bjerke's and Bartholomew's arguments against his whimsical scene paintings. In breaking *Sendak* into four separate products, they were making it less of an encyclopedia, yet their questions in the focus groups were designed to find a look for the product that would match what people would expect of an encyclopedia. Ballinger wrote:

> Is it just me, or does this seem wacky? Are we going to decide to make, target, or market Sendak less towards being an encyclopedia, but style it around what people expect of one? I am very unclear of the logic of this strategy. . . .
>
> I think perhaps part of what may be happening is that everyone is very antsy to get this whole thing moving, and having this style question come up after we'd done so much is probably facilitating a tendency to take whatever numbered data we can get, and just run with it. While this can help keep things moving, I think it can also be very dangerous.

There followed a detailed explanation about why realistic drawings were more difficult than cartoonish ones to animate on a computer, and how that effort would dramatically extend the time it would take to complete *Sendak*'s scenes. Then Ballinger devoted the end of his document to a series of complaints amounting to an assault on Bjerke's leadership:

> It has been very confusing, murky, and not a lot of fun for awhile on Sendak. . . . I also feel like I've been totally spinning my wheels for about 2 or three months. . . . I don't feel like I'm part of any team. . . . It feels like all the work I do, is just to show that something is being done, but won't ever be used for anything anyway. While perhaps I was once too attached to this project, I certainly am not comfortable with the current trend of detachment that feels like it is overtaking Sendak.

While Gammill viewed the document as "typical Bryan," he also agreed that the team was coming apart and had lost its sense of mission. Ryberg, too, was sympathetic, and Fox agreed with Ballinger completely. "I'm so incredibly frustrated with Carolyn," she said after reading Ballinger's litany of complaints. "She has no understanding of our problems. She doesn't understand the psychological implications of these changes she's always making. She has no people or communication skills. We've got organizational problems. We've lost our psychological balance. . . . And I can't believe the timing of Carolyn's pregnancy! How can she be gone at such a critical time in this project! There's just no backup for her for a program manager . . . for her to be gone. . . ." But then she stopped in mid-sentence, a confused look on her face.

Ballinger walked into her office. Brandishing his document, Fox looked up and said, "I bet you got an F in citizenship, huh?"

To Bjerke, Ballinger's mail "was the same old stuff. He just can't let go." Bartholomew, again, agreed with her. "It's great that Bryan expressed his opinion," he e-mailed to Bjerke. "All points are valid as his opinions, but I don't agree with all that many of them. Still, let's reinforce him when he speaks up and keep letting him know everyone is listening." Bartholomew also regarded Ballinger's mail as yet another warning Bjerke should heed. "You stand in danger of a serious fissure in your team unless you can bring everyone together," he continued. "When you're ahead of your team on conclusions, you don't leave much room for them to come along for the ride. The team just has to be more in the loop on these decisions."

But Bjerke found it hard to extend herself on Ballinger's behalf. Summoning him to her office, she asked him if he still wanted to work on

Sendak. Ballinger reacted with panic and Bjerke found herself consoling rather than disciplining him. Then the normally secretive Ballinger told Bjerke that his father, who was fifty-five, had just been diagnosed with leukemia. "If he dies," Ballinger said, "I'm trying to decide whether to move back to Vermont or move my mom out here."

Bjerke was stunned. She thought immediately of her father-in-law, also suffering from cancer, who was on his deathbed. Suddenly all the panic over *Sendak* struck her as pointless beyond belief, and she was horrified at how much she had heightened Ballinger's suffering. It seemed as if her life had veered drastically off course without her having noticed. She told him about her father-in-law and they talked for awhile about how they were coping. "This is ridiculous," Bjerke said, referring to *Sendak* again. "How can we get so worked up over something like this? It doesn't mean a thing!"

The two friends sat together for a moment, in silence. "Then," Bjerke said later, a note of wonderment in her voice, "we just went back to work."

On June 21, the *Sendak* team convened at 8:30 A.M. in the Bainbridge Room of Kirkland's Woodmark Hotel, on the east shore of Lake Washington. Bjerke and her partners invaded the room with their customary informality and gusto. In short order, they had lapsed into their habitual argumentation, which was to go on all day, ending in a fit of inexplicable exuberance.

Until nearly five, the group argued through every detail of the product, from whether or not it should be called an encyclopedia to what should be the tone of its content to who should be its principal artist.

It took two hours and one x/y graph to come up with a new vision statement: "To use technology and imagination to expand and improve upon the Dorling Kindersley Children's Encyclopedia in creating, on four discs, the most engaging, learning-oriented, malleable knowledge exploration game possible, for children from six to eleven, by September 30, 1994."

It took two more hours and one more x/y graph to decide that Ballinger's second, more realistic renditions of scenes would be used on *Sendak*. Had Ballinger been there, he would have been unsurprised to hear Bjerke suggest replacing him with another artist. He also would have been chagrined to hear Smith and Sonja Gustafson immediately concur.

And he would have been shocked and gratified to hear Gammill emerge as his most outspoken advocate. Gammill snorted contemptuously whenever Gustafson referred to the focus-group results as "data" or "data points"—something she did almost constantly. He insisted that the focus groups were too small to mean anything and that even if the numbers were to be taken seriously, the final totals were effectively even. By the time he was finished expostulating, Bryan Two, as Ballinger's more realistic style was known to the team, was selected.

Rather than bring any sense of closure to the group, or any feeling of relief, the decision only elicited more anxiety. Could they still include the kinds of playful animations Ballinger had specced now that the scenes were more realistic-looking and less whimsical? Would *Sendak*'s entertaining side clash with the new tone and feel of its scenes? "We have a pop-up," Fox said, "where you click on a portrait camera and a frog family in clothing jumps up and sits for a portrait. Is that appropriate in a 'realistic' product? How much should the content and scenes be directed by each other?"

It took the team an hour to decide to put off a decision until later, and another four hours in the afternoon to review and reiterate decisions that already had been made. By the end of the day, from what I could see, *Sendak*'s creators had nothing to show for their labors save for having decided yet again to do exactly what they had already been doing. Yet for some reason, they were as thrilled as they had been after the Salish offsite. They viewed the day and its labors as a great leap forward, as if the previous problems had been simple questions of communication and attitude. Even Gammill left in a good mood: "It was a great offsite," he said as he prepared to leave, "a *great* offsite."

Two days later, though, during a team meeting at Fox's house, Gammill started the proceedings with a bitter litany of complaints. Bjerke reacted with the facial expression of someone nauseated by a carnival ride—a loop-the-loop without end—and the team descended again into the same endless arguments over features and feasibility that had been dogging them from the first days of the project. They grew progressively more seized with disenchantment and panic in the days that followed, as they were forced to turn their attention away from the offsite's ethereal visions and back to the material details of building *Sendak*.

They also began dreaming of escape from Microsoft. Ballinger talked about all the future products he would design on his own, without corporate interference. Smith, who commuted for an hour between work in Redmond and home in Marysville, to the north, and was accustomed to doing most of her thinking about *Sendak* during the drive to and from home, now found that she spent the time crying instead. The MacroMedia animator, Shelly Becker, who had been working on *Sendak* prototypes, ran out of her office screaming one afternoon and took a new job at Continuum, another Seattle software company. (She was not to return until Microsoft bought Continuum a few months later.) Sonja Gustafson burst into tears at her employee review session when Bartholomew laid out the list he had been keeping of her errors and shortcomings. Eventually, at his prodding, she found a job elsewhere at Microsoft.

Gammill grew so much more impatient and contemptuous that he turned into a virtual caricature of himself. The day after the team meeting at Fox's house was a milestone day at which it was reported yet again that none of *Sendak*'s milestones had been met. Even so, Bjerke went ahead with a celebratory Milestone Beer Bash, held in one of the Microsoft cafeterias at the end of the day. Gammill declined to attend. "It's like one of those preauthored pats on the back," he said. "They just say, 'At this point, we'll have a party and tell everyone they're doing a good job.' It doesn't matter what we're doing."

He was, however, uncharacteristically solicitous of Smith. After she exhibited a new feature, called a slide show, to be activated by clicking on illustrations in pop-ups, I asked Gammill why he had not objected to it, as it was nearly impossible to code. "It's just her," he said, mindful of the rebuke delivered him by Bartholomew at his last employee review. "If it was anyone else, I'd say, 'There's no way I can do it.' Now I'll just wait till the next priorities meeting, then say, 'It'll take two man-months to implement this,' and that will be that." He laughed.

Having descended to new levels of dejection, Bjerke began fantasizing about giving up her job and becoming a contractor to Microsoft. "I look around here in this company," she said soberly, "and there's no one above me, older than me, who's happy." She was unnerved by the announcement that Susan Boeschen, the lone female among the company's senior vice presidents and an executive famed for her concern for employees' well-being and personal lives, was going to retire. Boeschen was in her mid-forties.

Bjerke's reverie was interrupted by Ryberg's announcement that she too was pregnant and would begin her maternity leave in mid-January.

"Great!" Bjerke said with a mirthless laugh. "We'll both be gone at the same time."

By mid-July, with Bjerke's design spec now a month overdue and his own spec barely begun, Gammill finally gave up on his hope of coding and building *Sendak* under ideal conditions. Instead of waiting for Bjerke and Smith to finish their design, he decided to isolate those few parts of *Sendak* on which he could conceivably begin work and write code for them while waiting for the rest of the design to be finalized. Gammill also decided the time had come to put together his detailed, task-by-task schedule for development of the whole product. With *Sendak*'s design unfinished, this was a near-impossibility, but Gammill reasoned that by distributing his schedule to his teammates he would force them to finish specific elements of the design by the time he needed them. If his schedule called for him to begin coding the pop-up window, for example, by August 15, Smith would know by looking at it that she had to have a full-color bit map of the window done and delivered to him by that date, with its position on the screen defined and all colors identified by their RGB values. Perhaps a written development schedule, with dates and times etched in stone ("16: Generic activity generation. 2 days. 10/21/93, 8:00am"), would be the key that could get *Sendak* started.

Gammill believed that he was being forced into a dangerous and haphazard approach to software development. "I hate Carolyn's spec," he said, "because I can't get the big picture." Without a firm understanding in his own mind of how the entire product would look, behave, and mesh its parts together, he feared that writing properly efficient code for it would prove impossible. Worse, he knew that it would be impossible to program *Sendak* to behave in the way intended by its designers if he didn't know exactly what the designers wanted. Software is a notorious minefield of what developers call "what ifs": scenarios in which users type or click on something expecting a particular result, and get an unexpected one instead. It was the developer's job to look for features in the design that might deliver a surprising or unintended response to the user. Looking over Bjerke's incomplete design spec, for example, Gammill noticed that there was no explanation of what was supposed to happen if a user clicked on a figure in a scene when a pop-up stack about another of the scene's figures was opened. Was the newly clicked-upon figure supposed to animate? Was a second pop-up stack supposed to open? Was the user supposed to get a message explaining that the first pop-up stack had to be closed before anything else could be done? There likely were hundreds more such unanswered questions lurking in the product. "A lot of times," Gammill said, "these things don't get fleshed out until it comes time for me to implement them."

Once he began directing his attention to code-writing, Gammill spent far less time in meetings and far more time in his office. By way of preparation for his labors, he augmented his office decor with a Chia Pet, a new computer for monitoring Merismus, a pocket chessboard on which he lovingly laid out the pieces in their positions after the forty-third move of his favorite chess game (Endon-Murphy, 1938), and a new stack of compact discs brought in from his car.

Working either at his computer, finishing the first draft of his technical spec, or scrawling notes and sketches on notebook paper, Gammill would sit at his desk for hours at a time, typing, scribbling, gulping Diet Sprite, and constantly muttering: "How am I gonna implement this fuckin' thing"; "Oooooh, God"; "Fuck . . ."

Gammill would be writing *Sendak* in the C++ programming language. C++, developed at Bell Laboratories in the early 1980s, is derived from C, a language written at Bell in 1972. Called a high-level language, or source code, it reads like truncated English mixed with math, as in: "if (IpList ->hCurHunk = _hGetHunk (IpList, OL));". Source code is translated by a compiler into machine language, which interacts directly with the computer's hardware.

Traditionally, a computer program was written in a top-down manner, with a programmer beginning by defining the major steps that a program performs, then proceeding down through layers of abstraction, descending through a hierarchy into areas of greater detail and increasingly specific tasks. The first thing a top-down programmer did was to sketch out a vision of the structure of an entire program, from the most general to the most specific parts, then work his or her way from the top, or most general levels of code, down to its most basic processes and subprocesses.

C++, though, is an object-oriented language. Rather than consider a program as a single set of tasks or procedures, the object-oriented programmer breaks a project down into independent objects, which in turn fit into classes. Each class must be identified, and its attributes and behaviors described. Where pieces of a traditional program are incomplete parts of a single whole, objects in an object-oriented program are miniprograms unto themselves: collections of data and routines or functions that interact with other, similarly self-contained objects.

Rather than write entirely new code for a given product, the object-oriented programmer invokes classes, or blocks of previously written code, for specific functions or tasks. In the case of *Sendak,* for example, a click on a picture of a bear in the forest scene activates a call to Windows, requesting a function for opening a window in which the text and pictures about bears can be displayed. Simultaneously, another function call goes out requesting that the engine for displaying stacks of pop-ups and their numbered tabs be activated; another goes out to MediaView, asking it to display a requested block of text in the appropriate area of the newly created window and its pop-up stack. Media-View, in turn, sends out calls to Windows in the course of fulfilling its instructions. Yet another function, meanwhile, is activated to retrieve and display the text's accompanying graphics, sounds, animation, or video.

In studying *Sendak* in its inchoate form, Gammill came up with a preliminary set of objects arranged in as coherent and efficient a structure as he could imagine under the circumstances. According to his plan, when a user clicked on an object in a scene, *Sendak* would call a function that would identify the hotspot by a number. "The function," Gammill explained, "says, 'Hi! I'm Number such-and-such. What do I do?' "

There would follow an elaborate series of requests and calls for actions and information. Part of the object's number would be an index, or pointer, into a hot spot list, which is stored in the computer's RAM. (Information stored in RAM is the most quickly accessed information in the computer; second-most-accessible is information stored on the hard disk; and least accessible is that information stored on the compact disc.) By means of a binary search—in which *Sendak* seeks out the middle number in a list, compares it with the pointer it has, then moves halfway up the list if the list's number is larger than the pointer, and halfway down the list if the number is smaller, then repeats the pattern over half the list, then a quarter of the list, then an eighth of the list, and so on —*Sendak* would search for the number matching the pointer. The correct number in the list, once found, would point to a larger list, called the *Sendak* action list, stored on the computer's hard disk. This second list is an index to the entire contents of *Sendak.* By means of another binary search, *Sendak* eventually finds the number in the action list that corresponds to the pointer from the hot spot list. Arrayed under this number is another set of pointers to file names containing all information and behavior associated with the clicked-upon object. If the user clicked on the bear and it had a pop-up stack, a song, a sound effect, a comment from the guide, and an animation all associated with it, pointers to files containing all of those bit maps and pieces of media would be listed directly under the bear's number in the *Sendak* action list.

The structure, then, is that of a series of indexes. The content of *Sendak* is stored in named files on the compact disc; the index to those files is stored on the hard disk; and the index to that index is stored in RAM. It was the quickest means Gammill could devise for getting to all of the information associated with the objects in *Sendak*'s scenes.

Once the appropriate number in the *Sendak* action list has been found, *Sendak* checks to see which of the available actions it is to take. If the user has set *Sendak* to show animations only, the program calls on SPAM, which in turn calls on Windows to retrieve and play the animation file named in the list. If the level has been set to show text only, *Sendak* calls on Windows and other functions related to displaying the appropriate pop-ups.

The whole set of procedures set in motion by the mouse-click is enormously complicated. To display a pop-up stack in a window, for example, *Sendak* must use information gathered from its action list in order to send calls out to Windows, directing it to create the window in which the pop-up stack will appear. The Windows function then defines and grays out the section of the screen designated as the window area in which the image of the pop-up stack will be painted. Another function, meanwhile, is retrieving bit maps for the outlines around the stacked pop-ups and for the tabs. Still another is retrieving, one element at a time, the text, graphics, sound files, animations, and whatever other material is to be displayed in the pop-ups themselves. All of these elements are retrieved by their various engines, brought together, and assembled in memory—by means of a process called bit-blitting—before the screen itself is painted with the collection of bit maps and live text that make up the whole display.

There was one more stage everything was to go through before finally arriving at the user's screen: decompression. All of *Sendak*'s information was to be stored in compressed form, and each piece would have to be decompressed on its way to the screen. Part of Gammill's mission was to integrate the decompression of information as smoothly as possible into the delivery process.

Speed was critical. Gammill hoped that a given retrieval-decompression-assembly-and-display cycle would never take more than four seconds. To that end, he sought to arrange and structure his data in as accessible and efficient a way as possible. The hot spot list would be loaded into the computer's RAM when *Sendak* was started. *Sendak*'s thumbnails would be stored on the hard disk in order to speed up the find gadget's performance. Each genre of content would be stored in its own sector of the compact disc: all sound files would be in one place, all text in another, and so on, with the pointers to those files containing genre-identifying information so that *Sendak* would go directly to the appropriate section of the disc rather than searching through all of it each time it was asked to retrieve something. "Among the problems I have to solve," Gammill said, shouting over the shrieks and pops and screams of Primus, "are speed and the order of display, so the transition doesn't look weird while the user is sitting there waiting. . . . I need to turn the music up so I can think better."

The difficulties of getting down to *Sendak*'s implementation made Gammill even less patient with his teammates. Now, whenever he emerged from his office to check in with them, he would come back outraged and appalled. To walk into any team meeting was to be confronted with another new feature—months after the design was supposed to have been completed. In mid-meeting one day, discussing the guide's backpack, Fox said, "When you click on this activity tool—"

"Activity tool! Activity tool!" Gammill shrieked. "What the hell's that?"

"It'll be specced, don't worry."

Moments later, Gammill was shown a new dimension to the find gadget: a network of "breadcrumbs" meandering through the thumbnails, forming a trail linking all thumbnails for those pop-ups that had most recently been clicked on. "Oh, fuck," Gammill said when he saw a sketch of it. "This is going to be a black hole . . . a six-month developer."

Bleak as Gammill's mood was, his days were not without their light moments. At a features priority meeting one day, Bjerke mentioned a proposed unit tool. Before she could explain what it was, Gammill shouted, "Unit tool! That's a redundancy!" He and lead tester Len Dongweck, looking at one another, laughing, whispering vulgarities back and forth, brought the meeting to a halt while their teammates either tried to figure out why they were laughing or looked tableward in embarrassment. "Unit tool . . . must be some new kind of joystick." "It's an ease of use issue—like, how hard is it?" "Heeheeheehee."

"Want me to say it again?" Bjerke said acidly. "So you can laugh again?"

While Gammill busied himself with actual programming, Bartholomew suddenly abandoned his unreasonable optimism about *Sendak*. He decided that the project was floundering dangerously. In e-mail to Ryberg, he broke the news that he had decided to remove Lindsey Smith from the project because he no longer had "much confidence that Lindsey's art direction skills are sufficient to get us on track." A day later, though, he decided that *Sendak*'s problems were attributable not to Smith but to Bjerke. She now seemed to him to have cut herself off from her teammates, spending longer hours in her office working on the design spec and emerging only for occasional team meetings or forays into Smith's office to help with design problems. Bartholomew felt that Bjerke and Smith were working out *Sendak*'s design on their own without inviting the participation of anyone else.

This ran counter to the way Bartholomew expected projects in his department to run. In his mind, a program manager was a manager of process rather than of people. He or she should direct discussion among everyone rather than hand down decisions. The program manager was to be an arbiter measuring the worth of ideas in terms of their ability to help meet a product's objectives and deadline. Rather than argue from the perspective of art direction or taste when questions of style or approach came up, the program manager was supposed to weigh alternatives suggested by other team members, assess their impact on a product's deadline and production process, then direct the team toward the proper choice. Questions of aesthetics or development methods were to be answered not by the program manager but by the workers themselves, in concert with their functional leads.

In the case of *Sendak*, Bartholomew expected style issues to be settled by Smith under the direction of Ryberg—who, as producer, was Smith's functional lead—with no direction from Bjerke, who was responsible for keeping everyone on her team informed of decisions and issues, and for keeping the project moving forward. "Note that you should be looking at this from a critical path/schedule/product objectives perspective," he e-mailed to Bjerke, "and Jayleen should be 100% in the loop and ultimately accountable for this (through Lindsey) from a creative/process perspective. . . . Just so you're aware, I'm holding Jayleen accountable on the style (as opposed to you) and Art Direction solution. This is consistent with my expectations for Program Manager vs. Design Manager/Producer."

At first, Bjerke was stunned. From the beginning, she had seen style and art direction both as her primary responsibility and as her favorite one. It was impossible to imagine giving up creative control of the project. Bjerke also had long felt that Ryberg was too hard on Smith. Further, Smith regarded Bjerke as her mentor and asked her advice on nearly everything she did. It was a role Bjerke relished. Now Bartholomew was asking her to sever that relationship.

She decided she must have misunderstood his mail and asked to have lunch with him. But when they met, he was even more emphatic. "Basically," Bjerke said later, "he told me to butt out. Then he brought up the fact that our schedule called for us to start production on April 15, and he wanted to know why we hadn't started yet." The question stung. "I *hate* being held accountable to that," Bjerke blurted out. "Because you just make it up!"

She did not fare much better at the following week's team meeting with Bartholomew. After a cursory look at the latest versions of Ballinger's scenes, Bartholomew decided that art direction was doing better than he had thought. He was less happy, though, with the psychological state of the *Sendak* team. The fact that he had had to call a meeting in order to find out that art direction was proceeding reasonably well was a signal to him that communication had broken down. He was even more convinced of that when he went around the conference table, asking every team member what he or she thought was the greatest impediment to *Sendak*'s shipping on time. Everyone had a different answer.

After he heard everyone out, Bartholomew said, "Look, based on what I'm hearing here, my gut sense is that what's going to happen is that you're predicting you will ship October 5, you'll probably ship somewhere between December 5 and January 30, something like that. You'll probably slip by two to four months, because there just are too many dependencies beyond your control. This kind of sets you up for short-term failure, possibly a long-term success, but it's a short-term failure, missing

Christmas. It's a really bad morale hit as well as a bad business decision, when Christmas is our biggest selling season." Then he suggested to Bjerke and her team that they think of *Sendak* as a series rather than as a set, and aim to bring out two discs first, followed by two more a few months later.

To Bjerke, the idea of shipping *Sendak* serially was the best news she had heard in months. But Bartholomew followed it immediately with bad news: since they now were shipping only half of the product they had planned, and since new Consumer Division marketing plans called for products to be available by August 15 in order to be part of the company's Christmas launch, the ship date for the first two *Sendak* discs would have to be moved up seven weeks.

Gammill, who was not at the meeting, was furious when he heard the news. Having just completed his development schedule, he had barely gotten started on *Sendak* work when he was pulled off of it to help fix bugs in version two of *Encarta*. Now entitled *Encarta 1994*, it was to ship on October 1. Gammill estimated that the *Encarta* effort would cost him three to four weeks of *Sendak* time. Now, seven more weeks were being taken away from him. The news that he would have to ship two discs instead of four furnished him no consolation. While editorial and production would have to do half as much work, the workload for him was unchanged, as the underlying code was the same no matter how much content was involved.

Ryberg, meanwhile, taking to heart Bartholomew's order that she begin art-directing Smith, e-mailed her a detailed critique of *Sendak*'s current look. "I feel like there is still a long way to go in determining what this 'home' is and how it relates to the content in both style and overall theme," she wrote. "I also feel like the product is too complicated: the backpack has too many tools to remember, the mission process is complex, there are lots of different icons, copy and print are confusing, there is this guide . . . adding clutter and there are up to twelve pop-ups per topic. I guess I just wonder which features actually add value as opposed to just being cool in our eyes." Then she went on to criticize specific elements in Smith's design.

For Smith, though, the mail was the goad that finally pushed her to a decision she had been mulling over for weeks. Looking ahead, she saw a bleak future in which she was effectively deprived of Bjerke's guidance. She told Bartholomew that she no longer felt capable of being *Sendak*'s

art director, and had decided to step down. Better, she said, to go back
to being someone's right hand and letting a more experienced designer
take over *Sendak*'s direction.

When she learned of Smith's decision, Bjerke was horrified. "This
constant flux of people," she said, "has really hurt this project." She felt
that a properly built product team needed a designer and editor who were
collaborators, melding form and content into a single cohesive unit. Ever
since Bjerke had become program manager, Fox had been forced by
Smith's inexperience and lack of confidence to write and edit *Sendak*'s
content without knowing how it would be packaged and presented to
users. As a result, she constantly panicked, second-guessing herself to
the point of intellectual paralysis. Still, Bjerke felt that she herself had
been able to compensate well enough for Fox's panic and Smith's weaknesses to keep the project moving forward. Now, just when it seemed that
everyone had adjusted and *Sendak* was about to move forward at last,
Bartholomew had swooped in and made changes that ultimately would
send the project into yet another unpredictable, wrenching turn.

Sure enough, the remains of the summer consisted of nothing more than
a constant revisitation of the same issues that had preoccupied the *Sendak* team from the beginning. It was an astonishing thing to watch. Everyone on the team knew that they were getting nowhere, everyone
decried their lack of progress, and everyone felt powerless to do anything
about it. Every new direction the team took eventually led back to its
origins. By well into August, nearly nine months after the official formation of the first *Sendak* team, Bjerke and her troops were still trying
to settle such questions as whether the guide character should be human
or nonhuman and whether the metaphor should be of a spaceship or some
kind of magical room. The more I tried to make sense of the project and
its perverse lack of progress, and the more I tried to reconcile what I was
seeing with the image Microsoft projected to the outside world, the more
surreal everything looked.

The low point of the summer came at image acquisition editor Carrie
Seglin's house, to which the team repaired in early August to try laying
out a clear production plan for all four *Sendak* discs. Bjerke's team spread
out a 20-foot long section of butcher paper on which Bjerke had marked
out the next fourteen months, through October 1994. She instructed her
teammates to take a Post-it note for the beginning and end of each task,

write on each note the name of a task, then stick them all to the appropriate places on the butcher paper. She also asked anyone who needed the completion of someone else's task before beginning his or her own to put a Post-it with that dependency on the schedule. Many tasks, then, would have three Post-its pasted down: one for when a task would begin, one for when it would be completed, and the third for when someone else needed it to be completed for the sake of his or her task. "Do your schedules individually," Bjerke said, "then we'll match them up and look for overlaps—a start that takes off before the end of something it depends on. And we'll look for critical paths."

"I'm really concerned about SPAM," Len Dongweck, the lead tester, said as they got started. "I haven't seen them do shit yet."

He and Gammill decided to go outside, away from the rest of the team, to work backwards from the August 15 ship date, so as to confront their production and editorial teammates with well thought-out deadlines. "Fuck!" Gammill said, as soon as they were out of earshot of everyone else. "August 15!" He and Dongweck began doing calculations. "How many release candidates do we need?" Gammill asked. A release candidate is a nearly final version of a product that is handed over to testing in the last days of a project, in order to find and eliminate the last remaining bugs. Testing typically spends a full day or two working on each candidate. "Well," said Dongweck, "I should have ten or twelve candidates per disc—"

"We only had eight for *Encarta*."

"You keep saying *Sendak* is more complicated."

Mumbling, the two did more figuring. "We'll need code complete by 7/7, with zero bugs," said Dongweck.

"That's gonna fuck my Fourth of July already, I can tell."

"We need a beta by the end of May—that gives us a month to get beta feedback." A beta is a rough draft of a product that is sent out to other software houses and selected users, who rigorously use and test it, looking for bugs that might have escaped Microsoft's testers during their work on the alpha version. "So they need a feature-complete alpha by April 15."

"So that's eight months for development," answered Gammill. "Including SPAM. There's no way . . . but that's okay!"

"What's SPAM done so far?"

"Pie in the sky. Some documents."

"No code?"

"No."

"Shit."

"Fifteen work-days a week, on average," Gammill said, looking down at his scrawling. "We're screwed!" They went back into the house and sought out Bjerke, who was looking in some confusion down at the butcher paper, now festooned with Post-its. "We've decided we need content complete by April 1," Gammill told her.

"Whew. I had the end of May."

"I have a feeling this 8/15 date isn't gonna stay for long."

"No, that stays—*we* have to change."

Bjerke walked over to Merismus lead Sandy Dean, who had just finished putting her Post-its in place. "They want this"—Bjerke pointed to Dean's May '94 Post-it for when she hoped to have all *Sendak* content entered into Merismus—"put here." She pointed to the end of March.

"Whoa!"

Now, as Bjerke surveyed the results of her team's labors, she saw overlaps everywhere. Virtually everyone asked for something before the person delivering it could have it completed. Guide narration depended on editorial to have all copy written and edited, acquisitions depended on Merismus, scene production relied on the SPAM team, various groups and phases throughout the project relied on design getting decisions made that Bjerke was nowhere close to making.

"This is all pie in the sky anyway," Dongweck said after a long silence. "I just wish we could get in there and start working on it."

"Look, we have to push this first test release out a week," Bjerke said.

Gammill answered immediately: "Then we have to push the ship date." Before Bjerke could answer, he went over to Seglin's refrigerator, angrily extracted a beer, walked outside, sat down in a lounge chair, took his shirt off and leaned back. "It's complete bullshit," he said to Dongweck, who had followed him outside and now was sitting on the grass beside him. "Chaos. Uproar. . . . At least it's a nice day." He drank for a few minutes, thinking, then turned again to Dongweck. "You might want to put 'Start testing . . . End testing' for each test release."

"You might want to suck my dick."

The two sat with a resigned air, knowing that the schedule would be reworked and reworked until it corroborated Craig Bartholomew's fiction. What he told Bjerke didn't really matter, Gammill believed. She would force him and Dongweck to move their dates around until the schedule could look "real." Then he would be slammed in future employee reviews for missing his development deadlines. "We're completely fucked," he said. Dongweck nodded.

Half an hour later, Gammill went back inside and slapped his set of Post-its across the second half of Bjerke's chart. Standing back, looking the whole thing over, he said cheerfully, "Magic numbers!"

"I have 145 days total for authoring sprites in scenes, using SPAM," Ryberg said.

"For that," Bjerke answered, "all the sprites and artwork would have to be done by October." The completion of those had been entered in December. "Jeez, I knew this would be interesting, but I didn't think it'd be *this* interesting."

"I have a feeling that the first pass at SPAM will be like Merismus—with a lot of problems," Ryberg answered.

"SPAM is such a huge dependency," Bjerke said. "We can't get over it."

Gammill finally dropped his mask of sarcasm, and pleaded with Bjerke to alert Bartholomew. "We need contingency plans," he said. "If they slip, we slip; if they slip, we slide; if they slip, we have no sprites or minimal sprites; if they slip, we slip the date, cut the sprites, cut content; if they slip, we push all four out to spring '95. Present the options to Craig, let him decide."

Bjerke didn't answer. Instead, she spent the next hour moving Post-its around, trying to get tasks aligned behind the completion of the tasks on which they depended. With each move of a note, her work seemed increasingly arbitrary and decreasingly based on comments of the teammates who would be doing the work. The mood in the room grew bleaker. Bjerke's blush deepened and her shoulders sagged. Looking at Fox, who was looking dejectedly down at the chart, she said softly, "Everything's critical path, basically." Then she dismissed her teammates, folded up her chart, and left.

The high point of the summer came to Gammill, of all people. A young software developer named Bill Sproule, newly graduated from the University of Waterloo, was brought to the campus to interview for a position elsewhere in the Consumer Division. Sproule was sensational. At the end of a long day of interviews, all but one of his inquisitors recommended that he be hired. Unfortunately, the lone "no hire" came from the man slated to be Sproule's supervisor.

Phil Spencer, one of Sproule's interviewers, told Gammill to look into trying to get him for *Sendak*. Gammill had the interviewers' feedback forwarded to him via e-mail. He was astonished at how well Sproule had performed, and he noted with satisfaction that the no hire recommendation had come from "an asshole." He interviewed Sproule that evening, sent in his hire recommendation, and waited at his desk while Human Resources tendered an offer to Sproule, who accepted it. Then Gammill went home astounded at his unbelievable luck. Let the rest of *Sendak* go down in flames—at least he now had one hell of a development team for it.

Autumn Light

Never having managed to come up with a metaphor to replace that of the spaceship, the *Sendak* team decided to test five storylines on groups of children. Each storyline consisted of an environment, a home base or vehicle, and a guide. The five to be tested were: the original spaceship metaphor; a theme park through which the user traveled in a little train; a world through which the user traveled in a time-space machine; a forest with a ranger station as the home base; and an attic in which sits a magical book.

The intent of the tests was to see whether any of the metaphors was significantly more intuitive and sensible than the others. For the sessions, the *Sendak* team set up six stations around a large room. At each of the first five stations was a set of pictures mounted on the wall. The first picture at each station was of a guide character as he or she might appear in *Sendak*'s opening screen, standing outside a vehicle or home—the spaceship, the time-space machine, the locomotive, the attic, or the ranger station. Next was a picture of the home's or vehicle's interior, with an overview map of *Sendak*'s scenes. (By clicking on the appropriate image on the map, the user, according to Lindsey Smith's design, would be "transferred magically" or "beamed" to the appropriate scene.) Next was a picture of one of the nature scenes with the guide character standing in it. Last was a picture of the missions poster or game board that was part of each storyline.

The children in the tests were to be asked a number of questions about the pictures. Could they tell how to get from one picture to the other?

What did they think of the character? Why did they think it was there? Did they like it? Could they tell from looking at the missions posters how the game was to be played? One *Sendak* team member would be a buddy for each child, taking him or her around the circle of stations and asking questions. Two more teammates were stationed at each set of pictures to record the dialogue. Once the children completed their cycle of the stations, they were taken to a final station, where they looked at drawings of the five characters and voted for their favorite.

Bjerke and her group particularly wanted to quiz the children on their impressions of the guide characters. The train was driven by a puppy in overalls. The time-space machine was controlled by a robot. An African-American boy, who looked to be eleven or twelve, was the guide into the attic. The spaceship was piloted by a green, antennaed alien who looked like a cross between a tubeworm and a tree trunk. The ranger station was occupied by a uniformed girl with pigtails. Would the children identify the character in each scene as a friend? As an authority figure? As themselves? Would they turn to it for help or would they dismiss it as absurdly out of place?

As they were ushered around the room, the kids displayed a maddening gift for randomness. The more earnest the question, the more playful the answer. With a succession of adults diligently noting down her every word, one seven-year-old girl delivered a series of assessments and proposed uses for *Sendak* that called, at the very least, for a rigorous reading between the lines in search of data. After registering her approval of the puppy-engineer and noting that it was a boy puppy because its coveralls were blue, the girl, when asked, said that the puppy "would answer questions for you and help you figure things out." When she moved on to the robot and was asked what she would do with it, she said that she would have the bear in the nature scene bite it, the moose fight it, the skunk spray it, and the beaver build a dam over it. As for the boy on the steps leading up to the attic, she thought it would be most satisfying to lure him up the stairs, then move a flowerpot from the floor to the middle of the staircase and have him trip over it when he descended. Once she was tired of that, she said, she would take him into the attic and push him through a trap door she saw there, to his death. At the ranger station, she saw the guide—a girl—as an accomplice who would help her "stuff the deer down the chimney. It would turn black and *smell* really bad." Her favorite guide was the alien, and her favorite vehicle his spaceship. But when it came to finding answers to questions, she said, she would have to help out the alien rather than turn to him for answers, "because he wouldn't know anything about Earth." If she didn't know the answer to the alien's questions, she added, she would ask the animals in the scenes.

These and similarly thoughtful observations from all of the children were duly noted down, tallied, and quantified. When their first and second choices were added up, and when all of their subjective comments were factored in, there emerged a single clear message: the overwhelming preference of the kids, boys and girls alike, was for the alien and its spaceship.

Ballinger had contrived to put himself at the table monitoring reactions to the spaceship-and-alien drawings. As the kids came through and declared their affection for the ship and its pilot, Ballinger documented his sarcasm, writing on little notecards: "Fancy that"; "What do you know"; "They really like the spaceship!" After the first session, Bjerke had him moved to another display.

A few days after the tests, Ballinger sent an uncharacteristically direct e-mail answer to one of my questions:

While at first it is a heck of a lot of fun, it is not always, when you are given the responsibility and creativity of a designer, but really none of the final say. I look at all this testing which quite frankly I thought from the start it would be useless, and I feel that is still the case. I mean, really, what was wrong with my original ship concept? Kids like it, both boys and girls, they understood the navigation, it didn't need a complex story to support itself, it facilitated exploration, it was fun, and was producable. Designing by committee, to me, is really goofy. But I was never in the position to push through my ideas, so ah well, you know. If we go back to the ship, I'm not sure if I'll be more happy, or frustrated. It would save a lot of time, rather than trying to fully develop another idea. My relationship to *Sendak* is much more distanced than it was, but I've latched onto the Nature scenes, and those will be fun. As to my relationship to Carolyn, I really like CB, but sometimes I think she only really listens to me when I'm not talking about *Sendak*, and design issues. Maybe my way of thinking hurts her head.

Ballinger nearly always kept these and other opinions to himself. Throughout the long meetings held in the wake of the storyline tests, he sat in silence, often curled up on the floor. "I get so fed up with him,"

Bjerke said after one of those meetings. "He just checks out, then gets resentful if we don't labor to include him."

More galling to Bjerke was the sympathetic reaction of her teammates to Ballinger's malaise. She took any kindness directed toward Ballinger as a personal insult, as if everyone else had taken his side against hers. What had begun months ago as a discussion between the two had turned into a clash of egos. The whole question of *Sendak*'s style, in Bjerke's mind, had turned into a battle to be won rather than a collegial quest for a solution. She may not have been aware of it, but her anger now was a sign to me that in her heart of hearts she sensed she had lost control of the project. Unable any longer to persuade the rest of the team that her instincts were correct, she began turning against them in a rage.

In matters of *Sendak*'s style and theme—particularly after the storyline tests—teammates most often agreed with Ballinger, more or less covertly, and disagreed with Bjerke. Fox in particular regarded Ballinger as the custodian of *Sendak*'s real vision. Although no one ever said so directly to Bjerke, she could see what was happening around her. "You have everybody else," she said angrily one day, "constantly trying to credit him for things. You have all these stories . . . and *Bryan's* story, *Bryan's* idea. . . . What a bunch of coddling females!"

At first, Ballinger's withdrawal had been entirely a function of his depression. But now it had become at least as much a function of his absorption in real work. Having hit upon a look that passed muster with Bjerke and held his own interest, he was hooked again on his art. It was now early in September and he had been hard at work on the nature scenes since the offsite at the Woodmark. "I'm just now getting into high-production mode," he said with satisfaction.

The nature scenes now were scheduled to be completed by December 22. Ballinger had sketched out all fifteen of them on paper and had three nearly finished. He was working entirely with Fox and her editors. He would begin a given scene by studying an editorial spreadsheet that listed all of the topics covered in the section to be accessed by that scene. Then he would do a pencil sketch of the scene, containing every creature or object that was to be clicked on, and would show the sketch to *Sendak*'s editors. They might call for a different arrangement of creatures or ask him to replace one with another. Then he would do a draft of the scene on screen, show it to the editors, and go through the cycle again.

The editorial exchange was not going as smoothly as Ballinger had hoped. Each scene had to be approved by three or four people, and in every draft of every scene *Sendak*'s editors made changes having nothing to do with the quality of Ballinger's work. He was making changes in each one and sending it back for editorial approval three or four times. Sometimes the changes were relatively insignificant. The replacement of one animal with another, for example, or the addition of a new, small animal, might call for re-creating only a small part of a scene. But most often a single editorial change threw the composition of a scene completely out of whack, and Ballinger would have to start the whole thing over.

These, though, were the kinds of problems Ballinger loved contending with. Almost forgotten now were the battles over *Sendak*'s style with Bjerke, Smith, and Bartholomew. And while control over most of the product had been wrested from him, Ballinger now was doing what he most loved—drawing and painting—and he was too preoccupied with his work, he thought, to care much about his earlier troubles.

Ballinger's argument with Bjerke had eventually maneuvered him into a kind of magic realism. While there was a photographic quality to his scenes, there also was something mystifying about them. His creatures were alive with a supernatural intelligence and emotional dimension that lent them the aura of human children. To catch the eye of any of Ballinger's animals was to be arrested by almost limitless charm. Anyone stopping by his office to see how he was doing would be stopped in mid-query by whatever image happened to be up on his screen. "Hi, Bryan, how are you do . . . Whoa!"

With Ballinger now working more or less contentedly alone, meetings over the direction and identity of *Sendak* continued to rage unchecked in the conference rooms and outdoor courtyards around his office. Bjerke, Fox, Smith, Gammill, and a new editor, Debbie Annan, met late one afternoon in the courtyard between Buildings 8 and 9 to decide once and for all on *Sendak*'s storyline. Talk immediately centered on the spaceship. Gammill preferred it because it was the most sensible metaphor: *Sendak* was a knowledge explorer and the ship was the only metaphor that brought exploration and adventure genuinely to mind. Fox preferred it because the children did, and because "there are no ship products out there to date. We're so different from other products that I'm not worried about the spaceship . . . unless we don't get the product out in a year. . . . Every time we test this with a ship in it, the kids love it."

Suddenly no one could believe they had ever considered any other metaphor. There was a brief, flustered silence before Annan asked, "Why did it change, anyway?"

"Well," answered Bjerke uncertainly, "because of the boy-girl thing, and I was concerned about the amount of artwork needed to support it and its transition effects. And the metaphor just didn't seem very imaginative. It was too simple. Would it give us a competitive advantage?" No one replied.

Bjerke looked weary and defeated. "I guess we could make it kind of sophisticated," she said hesitantly. "I guess if we think it's basically working, we can still do it. But the rendering will have to be extremely unique. The bar has to be high. Because the story isn't that high."

"See," said Fox, bridling, "here again you're not even thinking about the content! If you come up with a functional metaphor that works, no one is going to do a similar one. It's not uncreative!"

"No, no, I think the ship is *fun* . . . if we had more time . . . we could do better. . . . But . . ."

And with that, Bjerke decided to restore the spaceship to *Sendak*.

The decisive moment was surprisingly anticlimactic and the decision brought happiness to no one. There was no sense of resolution or relief. Instead, Bjerke's worries about *Sendak*'s schedule were heightened, Gammill felt even more dependent on the SPAM team, and Fox already was fretting about the spaceship's implications in the troubling guide character discussion.

It seemed to me that the only finely honed skill on this team was the ability to find flaws in its decisions. If team members had not managed until now to arrive at a decision on an exploration metaphor that would allow them finally to move ahead with actual work, it was because they were afraid to move ahead. Young as they were, inexperienced as they were, they found the pressure to succeed overwhelming. To begin actual work on the encyclopedia was to risk failure—and no matter how they looked at the project, failure seemed certain.

"At Davidson," a glum Fox said, already worried about the decision they had just made, "we resorted to an alien guide only because we couldn't think of anything else. And it's really hard to go with an alien character when I think of all the data." She was referring to the usability tests in which a child guide had piloted the spaceship. If the tests were to be believed, children seemed content when offered the choice of a boy or girl guide, and they were unconcerned about questions of race.

Bjerke, though, regarded the guide issue as an Achilles' heel for reviewers. She felt compelled either to have a racially and sexually diverse group of guides for users to choose from, or to have some kind of all-purpose creature in lieu of a human. "We could get slammed for the guides' uniformity," she said.

Fox disagreed. "It would be worse to have an alien guide and have to deal with the 'I don't get it' factor. It might bother adults to have a 'fictional' character as a filter for real information. I mean, here we are making our scenes more realistic and then we want to stick an *alien* in there."

"Yeah," said Bjerke. "I guess I am tending to lean toward a kid guide. You just get in your ship and go around. The kid gives you help and holds your backpack for you." She seemed resigned at last to the idea that any decision carried certain unknowns, certain risks. "The best we can do is say, 'It's a well-informed, calculated risk.' And you go on."

Now it seemed that after nearly a year of Bjerke trying to jettison their original metaphor, they were about to go back to it entirely, as Fox had wanted to do all along. But before anyone could say so out loud, Fox, looking stricken, objected. "But what if we test it and everyone likes the alien more?" she asked. "No *person* ever could be as endearing."

At this, Gammill, who had been trying with even less success than I to figure who was on what side of this issue, threw up his hands and snorted. He had been waiting since the project began for someone to make a decision, stick to it, and let him get on with his coding. "Are we almost done or not?" he asked, contemptuously. "I have to go to the bathroom, and I'm trying to decide whether to hold it, or go now and come back."

If he was intending to embarrass Fox and Bjerke, he succeeded. Fox stared at him, then said, "All right!" Getting up to leave, she laughed. "Kids and ship!" she exclaimed, throwing her arms wide. "We did it!" Then she recited a brief verse by T. S. Eliot:

> *We shall not cease from exploration*
> *And the end of all our exploring*
> *Will be to arrive where we started*
> *And know the place for the first time.*

Ballinger derived no more satisfaction from the spaceship's resurrection than did any of his teammates. He learned of the decision within minutes of the meeting's conclusion. As Bjerke and the others walked down the hall past his office, he stood in his doorway and watched them. They all stared down at the floor as they filed by. Had they looked up, they might not have survived the experience. Looming menacingly in the air to their right was a wholly expressionless face—in which, incongruously, were set the enraged eyes of an assassin.

While it was possible for those working on *Sendak* to persuade themselves that the decision to adopt the spaceship exploration metaphor would save the project, it was not possible to pretend that it could restore their battered psyches. Everyone, particularly Bjerke, worried and fumed incessantly in private. It had taken them too long to arrive at their decision; production, which should have started months before, could never get underway in time to meet *Sendak*'s deadline.

Yet Bjerke was careful always to wear an optimistic face in public. Whenever she sent out e-mail updates to her team and other interested parties, she struck an upbeat chord. She began her progress report to her teammates at the beginning of September with a typical, "Things have been progressing really well on *Sendak,* thanks to all!"

Bjerke next decided that the best solution to choosing between a human character, with its political risks, and a nonhuman character, with its aesthetic ones, was to opt for neither. Instead, she thought, Microsoft could either buy the rights to a famous character—a Bart Simpson, say, or a Bugs Bunny—or commission an established artist, cartoonist, or children's illustrator to create a *Sendak* character. She felt that the fame of the artist and the presence of one of his or her creations would help heighten *Sendak*'s profile. After talking it over with Bartholomew and telling him that such a course of action would likely cost at least $10,000, Bjerke secured permission to pursue the plan.

Meanwhile, the tension that people had been carrying around inside themselves for months began to break out whenever they communicated with one another. Ballinger's monthly report for September—a rather dry list of the status of his various tasks—included the comment, "I'm glad we're going back to the ship and characters like I originally had, and stressed so much over when it began changing." For Ballinger, it was an unusually direct statement of discontent, and all of his teammates remarked on it. Most succinct—and most angry—was Bjerke's reaction: "What an asshole."

By mid-September, the *Sendak* team had effectively split into two camps, with Bjerke and Smith in one and Fox, Ryberg, Ballinger, and Gammill in the other. Bartholomew was content to let the teammates sort things out among themselves as long as some kind of progress was made. Ryberg, after all, had been able at last to make the first tentative concrete steps toward production: she finally had contracted with freelance artists to do some pop-up illustrations for *Sendak*. True, there were only five pictures involved, but at least something was underway, and Ryberg now expected to begin pop-up production in earnest early in October. While that was six months behind *Sendak*'s original schedule, Bartholomew had seen a revised pop-up production plan that still showed *Sendak* coming in on time, and he remained optimistic.

It was not until Bjerke sent out e-mail outlining her plans for contracting a "well-known illustrator" to create *Sendak*'s guide character that Bartholomew finally felt moved to intervene. Ryberg immediately responded with mail detailing her fears that a new artist would be unable to meld his or her work with *Sendak*'s emerging style, arrived at only after months of agony and anger. Fox e-mailed a furious objection accusing Bjerke, among other things, of having deliberately left her, *Sendak*'s lead editor, out of the loop on this, one of the product's most critical decisions. She copied it to Bartholomew and to everyone else on the *Sendak* team.

Fox no sooner clicked her Send button than she regretted it, and went down to Bjerke's office to make amends for having copied her mail so widely. After apologizing for her indiscretion, she began lambasting Bjerke for her slight. She told Bjerke that in making such a crucial decision on her own about one of the primary components of an encyclopedia the two were supposed to be co-composing, she was perpetuating Microsoft's bias against editors. It was the same treatment, she pointed out, that Bjerke herself so resented when she was subjected to it by developers. Here Bartholomew was preaching "team-team-team" to them and constantly harping on Bjerke to keep the lines of communication open, and she turns around and makes this critical decision on her own.

"Come on, Sara," Bjerke finally interrupted. "You were at the meeting when we talked about this, and we left it hanging. What am I supposed to do? Who owns this decision? Someone has to make the decision and move forward."

"But we've already done all this work on the Nature unit," Fox answered. "What if the character art doesn't work with it?"

"Sara, that's the designer's job—to find someone who does work that matches."

Mollified for the moment, Fox began talking with Bjerke about their relationship. No sooner did she begin than I realized that she was talking about one of *Sendak*'s central problems. Fox had just attended a "Managing Microsoft People" seminar during the previous week, where she had heard a former program manager from a *Word* team speak on the pitfalls of having people manage their former peers. She realized that everything mentioned in the seminar had come to pass on *Sendak*. She and Bjerke had ceased being collaborators the day Bjerke became program manager, but never had formed a new relationship to replace the one that was lost. The problem had been made all the worse by Bartholomew's decision not to hire a new designer. Bjerke had been left doing both jobs, meaning that she was somehow supposed to be both Fox's supervisor and her peer. Then Bartholomew, hoping to ease Bjerke's burden, had kept his hands—intermittently, at least—on the *Sendak* project, violating another tenet Fox picked up at her seminar: "Never give responsibility without authority."

Bjerke, who was beginning to realize herself how ill suited she was for program management, began pouring out her heart to Fox. She explained that she had spent the last nine months trying on her own to define her program manager's job while also trying to fill the void left by Smith in design. "What does the program manager own?" she asked. "When can you tell? When is a decision owned by a designer, when by an editor, when by the program manager? We don't know the answers to any of those questions. So nothing gets decided, and eventually I have to do something so we can move."

Fox suddenly realized that much of her resentment toward Microsoft in general had coalesced and become directed almost exclusively at her friend. Now she believed that Bjerke was as much a victim of circumstance as she was. Bjerke had been forced by default into a position for which she was ill suited, and now she was being set up to take the blame for failings beyond her control.

Bjerke, of course, had been willingly forced into program management because it was the funnel through which nearly everyone wanting to advance at Microsoft had to pass. Considering her own future, Fox realized that her only hope for professional growth—for getting better at what she did best—lay in advancing up an editorial ladder and continuing to do the work she was born to do. But at Microsoft, there was no such ladder for anyone other than software developers, who could choose either to move into management or to advance along a guru track, free to work at their craft without having to manage anything other than their own minds.

It was the most endemic of the many subtle and overt forms of pro-developer bias built into the company culture. Developers who had no interest in managing others could opt to stay developers, refusing to supervise either people or processes, at no penalty to themselves. They still could advance up the salary-and-benefits ladder. A reclusive guru, as such developers were called, could be no less esteemed and rewarded than a senior vice president.

Editors, designers, and marketers, though, could only advance by taking on the risks and intimidating responsibilities of program management. Eventually, they had to choose between career advancement and professional satisfaction. Just as Bjerke had been forced to forsake a job—interface design—for which she had the requisite skills and which she loved, for a job she hated and for which she had little aptitude, so would Fox someday be forced to choose between advancement in the company, with its attendant trauma, and job satisfaction with no hope of advancement.

Now she suggested to Bjerke that rather than bring in a new designer, as Bartholomew and Ryberg currently planned, Bjerke should step back into design and the two of them should resume their collaboration and ask Bartholomew either to bring in a new program manager or allow them to muddle through without bringing in anyone new at all. That, after all, was the way projects had worked at Davidson when Fox worked there: an artist and an editor directed projects, bringing developers and marketers along as their ideas took form and flight. Moving in this direction, she added, not only would restore Bjerke to sanity, it also would eliminate the risk of a new designer coming aboard and making dramatic changes in *Sendak*, forcing it to slip even further behind schedule.

Fox was moved to these recommendations partly by something else she had heard at her seminar. She had sat appalled as a presenter suggested that his listeners read Machiavelli's *The Prince* to gain an understanding of how to succeed in management at Microsoft. "I couldn't believe he was *serious*," she said later. But now, sitting there with Bjerke, mulling over the dismal state of *Sendak*, she understood. Machiavelli, the lecturer had said, taught that the first move a new manager must make is to win his or her minions over immediately or get them into another group. Whether out of kindness, forebearance, or ineptitude, Bjerke had done neither. Now her team was so badly split that the damage was irreversible unless she were to move back toward design, becoming more of a visionary and less of an authority.

The more she imagined herself in Bjerke's position, the more sympathetic Fox felt. She understood how consistently Microsoft's environment undercut Bjerke's confidence and made it harder for her to direct her subordinates. "Our structure is really screwed up," she said later. "Carolyn's really in a jam. They keep telling you here, 'It's obvious your manager believes in you—that's why you were promoted.' But people at this seminar were all saying, 'No! We were promoted because there was no one else around!' "

A few days later, desperate for a way to restore the morale and cohesiveness of her team, Bjerke went to Bartholomew only to discover that Fox and Ryberg both had already spoken with him about her. Intending to bring him up to date on her plans, she found herself instead listening to him for nearly two hours. Bartholomew told her that she was both too *much* a leader and too *little* a leader. When it came to solving problems, he said, she came up with solutions on her own, then dictated them to her teammates rather than collaborating with them and coming to a consensus. And when it came to motivating her team, to telling everyone that the turmoil they were enduring would prove to be well worth it, she vanished. As a result, her teammates were doubly demoralized: they felt cut off from decisions affecting their work and their lives, and they no longer understood what it was they were working on, or why.

"I see the *Sendak* team as being an inch away from being a really effective team," he said. "They're just so close. It's just a matter of coming in and leading the product by distributing authority, communicating, keeping people up to date on what you're doing as well as what everybody else on the team is doing, making them feel like they're all contributing. In bad times you have to keep reminding people how cool the product is. Communicate, communicate, communicate, team, team."

Bjerke took all of this without objecting, suggesting only once that the real problem with *Sendak* was "that there are too many cooks," and abandoning that line of argument as soon as Bartholomew disagreed. But Bartholomew ended their conversation by suggesting that she had taken the program management position "for the wrong reasons": that she felt she had something to prove to Microsoft and that she wanted personal recognition for team success. She had been motivated less to finish *Sendak* on time as an end in itself than to get it done her way, on her terms, according to her vision, so that she could win a battle not only against the project's technical barriers but against a company that regarded people with her background as lesser creatures.

Bjerke realized that Bartholomew intended to lay the failure of *Sendak* at her feet, and she left the meeting in a fury. She felt that Bartholomew had singled her out for blame when in fact she had laid the groundwork for success. It struck her as ironic and unfair that she would be leaving to have her baby just as the project was about to take off. "I'll go on maternity leave," she said to me, "and a new program manager will come in, a new designer, and suddenly everything will work. And they'll blame me for all the problems." She felt she was being branded for the weaknesses of other, far weaker women. "I don't need personal recognition!" she insisted.

Still, she took seriously Bartholomew's directive to rebuild her team's morale. Over the next few days, she went around to everyone except Ryberg ("How can I talk to her about teamwork," she said, "when I know there's a performance problem?"), telling them that they had been so focused for so long on personal problems that they had lost sight of how marvelous a product *Sendak* was shaping up to be. She told Smith and Ballinger that it was their responsibility to find a way to work together and to shore up the rest of the team's confidence in design. She told Fox to stop worrying. She called a team meeting at which she planned to discuss *Sendak*'s vision again, and at which she wanted Ballinger and Smith to show the rest of the team their latest work. "This is my last push," she said to me. "If they don't believe in the teamwork thing now, if this renewed push doesn't help, I'll just think they're a bunch of obnoxious people. I don't feel like a team with them anymore."

When the meeting was convened next day, Bjerke distributed a new schedule of core team and design-editorial meetings—to be held more often, she said, in an effort to facilitate greater communication. She exhorted her teammates to believe in what they were doing and to try harder to believe in one another. She told them what Bartholomew had told her—that they were closer than ever to getting off the ground and manufacturing a marvelous product. She confessed that she "hadn't been hearing" them, and asked that they speak more openly about their concerns. Then she asked if anyone had anything to say, and was greeted by silence.

"All right," she said. "Bryan?"

Ballinger took the floor and began typing commands at a computer hooked up to a large screen at the front of the room. Suddenly, on the screen, there appeared a mountain scene, with a volcano and two other mountain peaks in the background, and a variety of creatures scattered through the middleground and foreground. Most arresting was a mournful panda who sat in one corner, chewing thoughtfully on a piece of bamboo while looking out at the audience. Like Ballinger's bear, the panda was marked by a hypnotic charm, a feral charisma, and there were ooohs and aaahs all around the room. Next, he displayed a grasslands scene centered around a kangaroo, with a hole in the foreground for "this wombat"—Ballinger opened another, smaller window on the screen, displaying a yet another endearing creature—"who will go in this hole here."

"Oooooh!" someone cooed. "He's so cute!"

The mood in the room had changed entirely. Ballinger's teammates looked like young children looking at a movie screen for the first time in their lives. They were particularly enchanted by his last picture, of a jungle scene. Peering out from a halo of foliage was the evocative face of a great ape. It stared out at the room with a resigned and confused expression. "My God," someone said. "I can't believe how beautiful these things are."

"Well, don't get too excited," Ballinger answered diffidently. "These are in 24-bit . . . although they look good in 8-bit, too."

A few minutes later, his teammates filed out of the room, leaving him behind to shut down his computer and retrieve his discs. Down in her office, Bjerke sat in her chair, perplexed. She had been bowled over by Ballinger's scenes and didn't know what to make of them. Did they attest to the worth of his stubbornness or of hers? It was a good question: he was working against his will in a style Bjerke had forced on him; and he still professed to believe his original work was better. Nevertheless, both of us could see that his pictures now were far superior. "Why can't he see how much better his work is in this style?" Bjerke asked. "I mean, that kangaroo, the texture of it . . . and that gorilla's face! It's so powerful!"

Ballinger had a way of being impenetrable, and I had to admit that I was confused by his apparent disdain for his own work. Sympathetic as I was to his plight, I thought that he was stubbornly resisting praise out of a childish urge to refuse to admit that he had been wrong. He was so wounded by Bjerke's treatment of him that he could not acknowledge even the possibility that she may have forced things to turn out for the best. From the creative energy that he was pouring into his scenes, it was clear that he was thrilled. But for him to admit that would be to acknowledge that Bjerke had been right—a point he could never bring himself to concede.

When I looked at Ballinger's pictures, the question that came to my mind was, "How could such splendid work have come out of such a dismal process?" It was a tribute to Ballinger's genius and resiliency that he could produce anything at all—particularly such marvelous images —after what Bjerke had put him through. When Bjerke looked at the pictures, though, she saw vindication for herself. How, she wondered, could everyone's morale hit such a low and everything seem to be going so poorly when the actual work on *Sendak* is so wonderful?

This, of course, was the same question Bartholomew had been asking himself for weeks. And the more he considered it, the more convinced he was that the problem lay with Bjerke. "With design problems, scheduling problems, budget problems, she's a very confident person," he said. "Give her a problem, she'll deal with it. But people problems are another story. She doesn't like to have a dialogue. A lot of times she comes to people already having a solution." He felt that events were forcing him to take action. "The way things are going now," he said, "they won't make their dates."

It was now the end of September, and *Sendak* still was going nowhere. Bartholomew, Bjerke, and Ryberg were leaving on vacations. Bartholomew was to spend his trying to decide whether to find a new program manager, change Bjerke's role on the team, or somehow inspire her to be a better leader. For the time being, he said, he was going with the third option—but only because he felt he had no other choice. He had come within a hair's-breadth of removing Bjerke from the *Sendak* team, then balked because "I don't have anybody to replace her with. Given the option, she would jump at the chance to get off the team. I can just tell she's not engaged. It's very, very obvious that she's not enjoying it. She's not doing her best work right now. When she goes on maternity leave, we'll probably bring someone in on an interim basis. Then when she comes back, she may go onto another product. I feel like I'm asking her to do something that doesn't come naturally to her."

"Are You Afraid? Are You Scared?"

Bjerke was first to return from vacation. After spending a week thinking and fishing off the Oregon coast, she had decided that *Sendak*'s only problem was a lack of optimism. Somehow convinced that Spencer and his SPAM team were doing good work and that they were determined to deliver for *Sendak*, she felt it of critical importance to get Ballinger and Smith believing in SPAM. "They don't think Phil cares about our needs," she told Gammill, "and I don't think that's true. The SPAM stuff is going to be *great*—they just have trouble believing in it." She set up a schedule of meetings between Spencer and Ballinger to allow Spencer the opportunity to explain SPAM, detail its progress at regular intervals, and get Ballinger psychologically invested in it.

During a conversation she and Bartholomew had had a month before, Bartholomew told Bjerke that she was underestimating Ballinger's contribution to *Sendak*. "A lot of the coolness of *Sendak* that everybody reacts so well to," he said, "are cool things he drew in there." Later, when she saw Ballinger's new scenes, Bjerke realized with a shock that Bartholomew was right. She decided now to bring Ballinger back into the *Sendak* fold. After having excluded him from core team meetings for the last eight months, she went to his office and asked him to start attending them again.

"Why do you want me there?" he asked, justifiably suspicious.

"Because you add value."

"Do people argue at these things?"

"Yes . . . but they know when to stop. They understand we're all working together to solve problems—that we're a *team.*"

From there, Bjerke went on a morale-shoring binge. "I'm rebuilding the *team,*" she said, "getting the focus on the light at the end of the tunnel." She designed and sent off to be printed a full-color *Sendak* poster that included some of Ballinger's animals and the *Sendak* mission statement. She wanted everyone on the team to have a copy in his or her office. She went around to every team member except for Gammill to talk about how wonderful *Sendak* was going to be and how important it was to focus their minds on their goals for the encyclopedia rather than on personal problems or crises of the moment, as they had been doing for the past year. "Everybody's been so focused on our problems that they've forgotten the *problem,*" she said. "We need to get back to solving our *real* problem: getting this done. Making it cool." She didn't bother with Gammill because of his chronic cynicism: "Kevin's useless as a brainstormer. He's basically against *any* new idea."

More likely, she sensed that Gammill would see through her facade of good cheer to the flaw lurking behind it. Bjerke was not necessarily bucking up her teammates because she believed things were going well; rather, she was choosing to believe in *Sendak* because she had no other choice. The only alternative was to insist on a later deadline—a political impossibility. She had to delude herself into thinking the current deadline could be met, then turn around and delude everyone else as well.

Bjerke came up with a new team structure that she professed to feel would be more coherent, and would give her and her teammates more rigorously defined responsibilities. She assigned to herself the functionality of design—making sure that each element designed by her teammates could be implemented, worked as it was intended, was intuitive, and did not conflict with any other elements of design. Smith was to take charge of the interface—the dialog boxes that offered users choices and preferences from among a variety of options, and the tools that helped them navigate through the product or perform such tasks as printing and copying. Ballinger was to take charge of what Bjerke called *Sendak*'s entertainments—the sprites, the gadgets in the ship, and anything else he could dream up, within Bjerke-imposed limits, that would make *Sendak* fun for kids to use. She also decided to have a single artist assigned to each disc, drawing all of its scenes and ship interiors. A fifth artist would draw the guide character, who would be on all four discs. Not only would this strategy give each disc its own distinctive and consistent look and feel, she reasoned, it also would make the artists—particularly Ballinger, in the Nature unit—feel more completely the author of their discs.

Bjerke also prepared for Bartholomew's return. She intended to bombard him with her plans and visions so as to demonstrate that she had thoroughly taken charge of *Sendak,* and so thoroughly recharged her emotional batteries that nothing could keep her from making it wonderful and getting it shipped on time. "Craig's going to come back to quite a few earfuls," she said on the Friday after her return. "It's been an incredible week."

She was most eager to give Bartholomew an earful about Ryberg. *Sendak*'s morale problems, she decided, were almost entirely due to the failure of Ryberg to get production started. She also believed that Ryberg was undercutting her supervision of Ballinger by taking his side in their disagreements and by asking him to help on other products when he should be spending all his time on *Sendak.* In Bjerke's eyes, Ryberg had become an enemy determined to subvert her management of *Sendak.* "She shouldn't have any say," Bjerke said, "in how *I* manage *my* team."

Bjerke resolved to take Ryberg off of all *Sendak* e-mail aliases and to ban her from team meetings. From now on, she said, Ryberg was to be a functional lead who had nothing to do with *Sendak* other than to fulfill its requests. She was no longer to be involved in any *Sendak* decisions. Since Ryberg had been training a contractor, Meg Nyland, to take over her responsibilities during her maternity leave, Nyland might just as well take over *Sendak* production now, thereby further distancing Ryberg from Bjerke's project.

When Bartholomew returned, he took in his earful in silence. He was amazed at the depth of Bjerke's fury. During his vacation, he had all but decided to replace her as *Sendak* program manager and start her on a new project. It would be better to put her in charge of a small product and let her build it more or less alone, without supervision. Still, he balked at removing her immediately. Whatever her failings, he had no one to replace her. So he felt he had little choice but to let her run things as she wished. There seemed no point in removing Bjerke two months before she was due to leave anyway. He could replace her during her maternity leave—most likely with a contractor—then assign her to something new when she returned the following March.

Although he had supported her in the past, particularly in her management of Ballinger, Bartholomew now believed that Bjerke had taken a can't-miss project and derailed it by virtue of her insensitivity and insistence on over-control. "Look at Bryan," he said. "He's incredibly talented. He owned the vision for the product early on. He kept people interested in doing good things. Then Carolyn kind of took over the vision and cut him out. Six months ago, he was persona non grata. Now that they've come back to his original idea, he's vindicated and bitter. I feel like with a little more diplomacy, a little more leadership, things could have been handled a lot better."

Feeling her position secure, Bjerke next called her troops together for a morale-building and rescheduling session. "I thought it was important," she began with great gusto, "that we see where we've been, where we are, assess where we're going and how we're going to get there." Her audience laughed. "We are committed to this date," she continued, "and can achieve it if we all are committed in our hearts. We're at milestone four, but before we look at that, I wanted to show the other cool stuff."

Ballinger followed with a display of his newly completed lakeshore scene, which dazzled his teammates no less than the scenes he showed a few weeks before. Fox followed. Standing at the front of the room with Debbie Annan, she read a brief line of pop-up text: "Have you ever heard a parrot 'talk'? Parrots may seem clever, but they can only say what you teach them." Then, after asking her audience to "imagine us as parrots," she and Annan, reading alternate lines, recited the script for a parrot animation, with Fox—parrot one—leading, and Annan—parrot two—following:

> *Parrots are excellent mimics*
> *Carrots or petulant spinach.*
> *They can't make sentences on their own.*
> *Grey ants take ten pencils under phone.*
> *But they're very good at copying your voice.*
> *Nut pear berry could get rock-slinging boys.*

Fox and Annan sat down, to applause. Passing out a new pop-up schedule that called for the entry into Merismus of 240 pop-ups per week through mid-July 1994, Bjerke exhorted her troops to stop worrying about day-to-day problems and "just do it." Then, with the hour drawing to a close, she asked if anyone had any questions or concerns and was greeted by silence.

Back in his office afterwards, turning toward his terminal, Gammill laughed. "Wasn't that meeting a little . . . *jolly?*" he asked rhetorically. "But that's okay—it's her job to do rah-rah bullshit."

Down in her office, Fox sat at her desk with an eerie, enthusiastic gleam in her eye. "I really think we're back on track," she said, "that all our problems are solved, that things are great again!" She stopped talking and stared at her wall for a moment. "Of course, Jayleen's on vacation. Wait until she gets back. Things always seem to get better when someone's on vacation."

Things finally had reached the point where Gammill felt he could begin work on what he saw as the most important component of the product: the display of pop-ups and their content. Although he still regarded the pop-ups as "undefined"—every time he looked at Smith's drawings and written descriptions, he saw inconsistencies and unfinished work—he decided that the pop-up design was close enough to completion to allow him to begin writing its code.

Now that he was working on the heart of the product, Gammill's mood improved markedly. For the first time, he felt he was gaining a measure of control over *Sendak*'s fate. He began arriving for work an hour earlier in the morning and sitting for hours at a time at his desk without turning away from his terminal even to answer the phone. On his schedule, kept on the computer network in a program called SchedulePlus, he blocked out the hours from 8:00 A.M. to noon, Monday through Thursday, for the next nine months, so that no one would schedule meetings for him during those hours. Every morning he came barging into his office, can of Diet Sprite in hand, popped a compact disc into his music system, cranked up the volume, sat down at his desk, scanned his e-mail, and immediately began working.

Gammill's routine was invariable, altered only by two brief interruptions each day: one at midmorning to bring up the on-line lunch menu for all Microsoft cafeterias and the other at midafternoon to check Microsoft's stock price, also available on line. He always began his day by clicking on his *Sendak* icon—a round yellow face with a tiny downturned mouth and a bloody bullet hole in its forehead. His morning then would consist of staring intently at a window full of his *Sendak* code, tinkering with it, writing new lines in it, moving lines around, scrolling through it, making tiny adjustments—here a new >, there a −>, here changing a == to a ! =, here changing "HFONTBIG" to "HTITLEFONT," and so on. He constantly was switching out of that window to compile his rewritten code, then to test his "show a stack" function, which would act on his code by trying to bring a pop-up window to the screen. All the while, he kept up a running, muttered monologue: "Fuck . . . Arrrrgh! This is a pain in the ass! . . . Come on, Kevin. . . . Fuck you, Lindsey. . . . Why is it doing that? . . . Where is it . . . where is it. . . . Shit! A bug!"

Gammill's mood was further improved, and his powers of concentration heightened, by his wife Nicole's sudden decision to resign after seven years at Microsoft. Having made her way through a variety of assignments and departments, and having spent the previous year as a program manager, she finally attained what Gammill called "normal Microsoft burnout." Now she planned to stay at home for the foreseeable future, "spend more time with my family"—as her e-mailed resignation announcement put it—manage their money, and decide what to do with the rest of her life. Among the options she was considering were law school, starting a company of her own, and helping design and market new multimedia products for any one of a number of startup companies. "This is great!" Gammill exclaimed. "Now she won't work until eight every night!"

His wife's new freedom would allow Gammill to focus completely on *Sendak*. He no longer had to linger at home in the mornings, caring for his daughter between his wife's early departure for work and the arrival at eight of their nanny. He no longer had to be home by six, when the nanny left. Now free to spend as much time as he needed at work, he cut himself off from distraction as much as possible, attending far fewer meetings than before and virtually never leaving his desk.

From October until mid-February, the Northwest is bathed in constant darkness that is relieved only by gloom. It is a dim condition that brings out an odd, often manic cheer in Northwest natives. The winter months saw Gammill at his most alert, alive, and irascible. He arrived at work in the dark, left in the dark, and dressed in darker clothing. The murk enhanced his self-styled antiheroism. He began exuding the air of a gritty gunslinger, a creature of the night. He talked incessantly about Clint Eastwood films, often quoting Eastwood verbatim. "My nanny saw *In the Line of Fire* last night," he said one morning as he arrived at work. "Then she said to me, 'You're just like Clint Eastwood. The way you talk, the way you treat women. . . .' I didn't know if it was slam or a compliment, but I chose to take it as a compliment . . . because I love the man!"

Gammill always begins a code-writing project by scrutinizing a detailed drawing of the window he is to create. "The first thing I do when

I look at something," he said, "is divide it up into objects. Then when I write code, I basically handle an object at a time. And without forgetting the big picture, I look at each individual object and see, 'Can that be done, and will the performance be okay?' And I keep breaking things down. Sometimes an object has subobjects, and they in turn may have other subobjects."

In the case of *Sendak*'s pop-up stack, the array of objects and objects-within-objects was overwhelming. When a stack was brought to the screen, the user would see a window with a caption, text, and illustrations occupying nearly all of its space. A gray strip along the bottom would contain one or two overlapping rows of dun-colored, numbered tabs, on each of which would be an icon, next to the number, representing what sort of medium—music, video, animation, and so on—could be found, in addition to text, on the corresponding pop-up in the stack. If pop-up number four, for example, contained a song, tab number four would have two musical notes next to its 4.

To the right of the tabs was the topic title ("Sand"; "Evidence for Evolution") for the whole stack of pop-ups. Next to that was the icon of a speaker on which the user could click to hear the topic title pronounced. And next to that was the Close window—a picture of a window with its shade drawn up. When the user clicked on that, a hand would rise up to the shade and pull it down, and the window containing the pop-up stack would close, or vanish.

Each item in this arrangement—the window containing text and graphics, the row of tabs, the topic title, the audio icon, and the Close window—were separate objects to Gammill. Subobjects included the text itself, its caption, the accompanying illustration, each tab, each number on each tab, and each icon on each tab. When it came time to writing code, Gammill would write separate blocks for the retrieval and placement of each of these parts of the whole window. One block of code would call on Windows to create the window for the stack, another would call upon MediaView to retrieve and display the appropriate text, still another would arrange the row of tabs at the bottom, and so on.

The numbered tabs presented Gammill with an assortment of problems. He would write five hundred lines of code—taking nearly a month—to create and display this simple, barely noticeable section of the window and make it respond properly to the user's mouse-clicks.

As an artistic device, the tabs were a clever solution to the complicated problem of presenting a window full of information to the user and allowing him or her immediately to understand what was contained in the window and how to get at it all. When the user clicked on an object in a scene, the pop-up window would appear with pop-up number one on top, and with the tab numbered one highlighted and in the foreground of the array of tabs. By looking at the tabs, the user could tell immediately how many pop-ups were in the stack, which pop-up was currently on top, and what sorts of media elements—video, animation, music—were on which pop-ups. There were never fewer than six and never more than twelve tabs, except in two cases: if information related to the topic of the stack on display could be found elsewhere in the encyclopedia, an extra tab, called a See Also tab, on which was drawn a pair of spectacles in lieu of a number, was positioned on the right end of the row of numbered tabs; and if there was information elsewhere related to the subject of a given pop-up, a Related tab—a tab with two books drawn on it in lieu of a number—would appear to the left of the row of numbered tabs whenever that particular pop-up was brought to the top of the stack.

Visually, the tab arrangement was a clear and direct way to deliver a wealth of information to the user. But the mathematical rendering of the visual effect called for a complicated series of detailed procedures and calculations that looked, to the nonprogramming mind, like an eccentric, perverse, deliberately difficult answer to a simple question. It was as if Gammill, asked for directions to a grocery store two blocks away, explained in demented detail how to raise each leg in turn over and over again, and described the optimum behavior of the leg muscles, the motion of the joints, the swinging of the arms, the interaction of all these body parts with the brain, the beating of the heart, the direction of the gaze, the speed of forward motion.

Looking at the tabs, Gammill calculated that there were 624 different possible combinations, or separate tabs. A tab could have any one of twelve numbers on it, or could be unnumbered. It also could have any one of eight media icons on it, and it could have one of six different looks: the look of one in the front row with a shadow on its left edge cast by the preceding tab's overlap of it; the truncated look of a tab peeking from the second row beneath the front-row tab partially concealing it, with a shadow on its left edge cast by the tab immediately preceding it; the look of the first, unshadowed, tab in either row; the highlighted look of an active tab—the tab corresponding to the pop-up currently called to the top of the stack; and the occasional tab, two rows long, that sat alone at the end of certain odd-numbered combinations.

To have stored 624 separate tab bit maps would have taken up too much of *Sendak*'s disc space and made the painting of pop-up windows painfully slow. So Gammill instead stored the twenty-seven different tab subobjects at three separate addresses in memory. He stored a row of bit maps for each of the six possible blank tabs at one address. At another, he stored a row of bit maps for the twelve numbers. And at a third address, he stored a row of the eight media icons.

Next, he wrote code directing the computer to commence a frenzy of calculations when painting the tab rows in a pop-up window. The computer was to paint the tabs one at a time, from right to left, doing the back row first. To that end, it first searched a file of information on the pop-up stack's attributes—all of the information about how many pop-ups there were in the stack, what media were assembled on each one, and so on—to see how many pop-ups, and therefore how many tabs, there would be. Then, having determined whether or not there were more than six tabs—the first row always was to contain six numbered tabs, and the See Also tab when the stack had one—the computer would subtract six from the total amount of numbered tabs and multiply the result by 30 pixels, the width of each tab, in order to calculate at which position to place the rightmost tab in the back row. Once that was established, the computer would ask itself a series of questions about the tab it was about to paint. Is it the active tab? Is the tab to its left active? Does it have a related tab? With each question, it was to proceed one way if the answer was yes, another if the answer was no. Then it would fetch the appropriate tab bit map from its address in memory and place its upper left-hand corner on a designated pixel, every pixel on the screen being identified by two numbers, one of which, X, measures its distance, in pixels, from the side of the window, the other of which, Y, measures its distance from the top of the window.

This rather long and tortured explanation, in English, for painting the row of blank tabs was rendered far more efficiently in Gammill's C++:

```
iStartX = (lpTabPos->iTabPos<8) ? lpTabPos->iTabPos : lpTabPos->
    iTabPos - 8;
iStartY = (lpTabPos->wFlags*TAB_FTOP) ? TAB_ROW1_Y : TAB_ROW2_Y ;


iStartX *= TAB_AREA_DX;
```

```
if ( lpTabPos->wFlags & TAB_FACTIVE )
    rSource . left = TAB_ACTIVE;
else if ( (lpTabPos>iTabPos == 1 && ! fRelated) I I (lpTabPos->iTabPos == 0 ) )
    rSource.left = TAB_TOP_LEFT;
else if ( lpTabPos-> == 9 )
    rSource.left = TAB_BOT_LEFT;
else if ( lpTabPos->wFlags & TAB_FTOP )
    rSource.left = TAB_TOP_RIGHT;
else if ( lpTabPos->wFlgs & TAB_FLONG )
{
    rSource.left = TAB_LONG;
    iStartY = TAB_ROW1_Y;
}
else
    rSource.left = TAB_BOT_RIGHT;

rSource.left *= TAB_DX;
```

Once each blank tab was in place, the computer would check the attributes of its corresponding pop-up to determine what medium was contained in the pop-up, fetch and place the appropriate media icon, then determine what number was to be painted on the tab, and fetch and place the appropriate number bit map from its address in memory. Once the tab was completely painted, *Sendak* would move on to the next tab to the left and repeat the process, moving through the process tab by tab, leaving a blank space where the active tab was to be, then painting that when all the other tabs were completed.

The bit map of tabs had to be repainted not only every time a pop-up window was opened, but every time a new tab in the row was clicked on, bringing a new pop-up in the stack to the surface. If a user clicked on a hippopotamus, for example, the pop-up window for that topic would open with pop-up number one showing, and tab number one highlighted. When the user then clicked on tab number two, *Sendak* would divide the pixel position of the click by the tab width and depth to determine which tab had been clicked on, then would bring pop-up number two to the surface while repainting the tabs' bit map to show two as the active tab. If the user clicked on a tab in the second row—number eight, say, in a ten-tab arrangement—the bit map would be repainted with tabs seven through ten in front, one through six in back, and tab eight highlighted.

Gammill spent a week getting the engine for painting blank tabs in working order before moving on to the painting of their icons and numbers. Test after test would call for new calculations. He would spend an hour refining his code, then test the show a stack function only to see that there was a gap between the tabs, or that they were too far overlapped, or that too many tabs were showing, or too few. When finally he got them properly aligned, he worked on hit detection—the way the computer calculates which tab number has been activated by locating where in the array of tabs a given clicked-on pixel position happened to be. Because the tabs overlapped and because their corners were not square, there was an uncommon number of gray areas for users to click on—areas that could be either one of two different tabs, or sometimes one of four—and the resulting confusion had Gammill muttering constantly: "Why am I getting tab eight here when I'm clicking on two? . . . Gotta do the math again by hand . . . see where I'm fucking up . . . the math is correct, but my formula is incorrect . . . math is *always* correct!"

After days spent getting all of the glitches sorted out in his hit detection code, Gammill was testing the function for bringing a tab from the back row to the active tab's foreground position when he encountered the first significant error in Smith's design.

"Fuck!" he screamed. With an array of ten tabs, he had clicked on tab number ten. The bit map was immediately repainted with tabs seven through ten in front, and one through six in back. The arrangement looked peculiar. "The behavior of this thing is screwy," Gammill said, looking at a bit map so ugly it offended even the sensibilities of a software developer. "This can't be the way Lindsey wants it to look." After he informed Smith of the problem, she changed her design to have equal numbers of tabs in the front and back rows. An eight-tab array, then, would have four tabs in front and four in back, rather than six in front and two in back, as before. In cases where there was an odd number of tabs, the second row would contain one more tab than the first; the last tab would be two rows long when the first row was in front, and a standard tab size when the second row was in front.

The changes forced Gammill to add several lines throughout his code, to make numerous small changes elsewhere, and tinker with the new mix over and over again to get everything working properly. Disgruntled, he complained to anyone who would listen that "this adds two days to my schedule." Finally, in its new configuration, his program could calculate the total number of tabs for a given pop-up stack, divide by two, then mathematically work out the pixel positions for each tab.

Gammill no sooner got the new tab arrangement working than he ran into a second, knottier problem. In painting the media icons and numbers on the tabs, he noticed that two-digit numbers overlapped the icons. "What do I do with the situation described below," he asked Smith by e-mail, sending along a bit map of a tab in which the number twelve concealed half of a media icon. "NONE of the bitmaps you guys did show this, and this probably happens all of the time." Privately, he was less civil. "I'm pissed at myself for not catching this myself, but it's not my job!" he said. It was typical of designers, he went on, not to consider every possible scenario when sketching out a design. Because Smith, in designing her tabs, had looked only at one-digit numbers next to media icons, she had not made the tabs wide enough to accommodate icons and two-digit numbers. "Lindsey didn't think through all the implications of the tab design," Gammill said. "She didn't check all her cases." An unforgiveable lapse in a developer, it was a predictable one in a designer.

Although angry—the lapse would add an extra week to his work schedule—Gammill also was resigned. It was the sort of error from designers that developers constantly encountered and that he had hoped to build into his schedule. Unfortunately, *Sendak* already was so far behind that there was no buffer left to allow for such mistakes.

Smith, who ordinarily bristled at Gammill's criticisms, was mortified. "Kevin, I'm just really, really sorry," she said when she saw him next.

"Oh, that's all right," Gammill answered, with a laugh.

"No . . . no . . . I mean it. . . . I really feel bad about it."

Thoroughly undone by Smith's display of emotion, Gammill fled back to his office.

A week after Bjerke's conversation with Bartholomew, Ryberg returned from vacation to be told by Meg Nyland that Bjerke had scheduled a visit to the Center for Multimedia—a Seattle-area multimedia graphics company—to evaluate it as an art production resource for *Sendak*. "Wait a minute!" said Ryberg. "That's not a program manager's responsibility —that's the producer's!" She intended to clear the air with Bjerke as soon as possible.

Not long after, Bjerke came to Ryberg's office. Ryberg had hardly greeted her before Bjerke began detailing her grievances. She told Ryberg that the *Sendak* team had lost faith in production because Ryberg was blocking everyone at every turn. She accused her of undercutting the project whenever she had the opportunity. She explained that in Ryberg's absence she had restored the confidence of her teammates and gotten their project back on track. "We're a team now!" she exclaimed. Were it not for Ryberg, she continued, *Sendak* would be on schedule and the *Sendak* team would be happy and confident. So in order to get things moving forward again, Bjerke said, she had decided to remove Ryberg from the *Sendak* team and from all team e-mail aliases. "Craig and I have redefined your job. You're not on the team anymore," she said heatedly.

Stunned, Ryberg stammered, "I'm on every team."

"No you're not!"

There was a long pause. "Craig should have already told you all of this," Bjerke said.

Craig would never tell me this, Ryberg thought, because he doesn't believe it. After Bjerke left, Ryberg sought out Bartholomew, who tried consoling her. He told Ryberg that he did not attribute any of *Sendak*'s failings to her or to her production department, and he asked her to go along with Bjerke for the time being. "Don't worry," he told her. "You're job's the same—we haven't redefined it." Then he went around to others in Multimedia who, like Ryberg, did work for *Sendak*, to tell them that "Carolyn is biting the bullet" on *Sendak*, that he had decided not to remove her as program manager, and that "she is going to walk all over people to get the product done."

Ryberg went home that evening demoralized. "It's political," she said of Bjerke's action. "It's about power." She pointed to her shoulder, saying, "I felt like I had my stripes ripped off. The hardest thing to deal with is this feeling that I've been kicked off the team, that no one had any confidence in production. Although Craig told me that that part wasn't true." She was convinced that Bjerke was deluding herself by attributing all of *Sendak*'s problems to Ryberg and pronouncing the product cured with her excision from the team. "I told her that I felt like she got a new religion," Ryberg said. "She kept saying, 'We're a team now! We're a team now!' It really *was* like a new religion . . . it was humorous."

Convinced that Bjerke had given in to dangerously wishful thinking, Ryberg derived some comfort from the knowledge that her colleague was headed for disillusionment. "It's just not that easy to turn things around if they're this bad," she said. And on *Sendak*, she still believed, things were irredeemably bad. "For Carolyn, it's all just list-making. She can cross something off and say, 'We're ready!' But we never start when we say we're going to start. And with all this going on, she turns around and says that production is the blocking issue, that no one has faith in me. Well, that's all just in Carolyn's mind. The real problem is that *Sendak* needs a leader and a designer."

On that last point, at least, Bartholomew agreed. He told Bjerke that he decided to hire a new children's-product designer after all, and that he or she should immediately begin work on *Sendak*.

"But I really don't think we need one at this late date," Bjerke said. "Lindsey can handle it."

"How many times a day do you go down to her office to answer questions?"

"Six or seven."

Bartholomew was appalled. "You need a new designer!" he snapped.

Perhaps because both women would be gone in three months, Bartholomew decided to let matters rest with Bjerke's banishment of Ryberg. Privately, the two women blamed one another for *Sendak*'s problems, while publicly they continued working courteously together. Bjerke, trying to make some amends to her erstwhile friend, began attributing their tension less to Ryberg's shortcomings than to the shortcomings of Bartholomew's organizational model, in which some people led product teams and others led functional teams that served all products. Bjerke believed that problems were inevitable whenever the two areas of responsibility overlapped, as they did when Ballinger needed direction and got contradictory supervision from his team lead, Bjerke, and his functional lead, Ryberg. "Craig needs to clean up this functional-team problem," she said. "Jayleen thinks the producer should find illustrators. I think the designer should. I say, 'No fucking way do *you* pick the people who implement *my* things!' "

Ordinarily, Bartholomew never would have allowed a project to drift for so long and toward such peril. Particularly uncharacteristic had been his reluctance, or inability, to intervene in Bjerke's and Ryberg's conflict. Known for his compassionate bluntness, Bartholomew never hesitated to correct or redirect those who erred. Now, with *Sendak* at its most critical impasse, he did nothing.

But he could be forgiven for his bewilderment; Bartholomew had returned from vacation to find that the end of the world was at hand. The retiring Susan Boeschen had been replaced by Patty Stonesifer, a rapidly rising star at Microsoft who had headed Microsoft Press, then been general manager of Microsoft Canada, then vice president in charge of Product Support Services. Stonesifer had spent her first months on her latest job studying the Consumer Division organization and had found it wanting. Now, Tom Corddry greeted Bartholomew with the news that the division was about to reorganize into a new set of business units that would include one for kids' products. Microsoft expected that 50 percent of its Consumer Division revenues soon would come from sales of children's titles. Currently, kids' software was spread throughout the division, and Stonesifer decided that she wanted it consolidated into a single business unit so as to better coordinate development and marketing strategy. The plan, Corddry told Bartholomew, was to move *Sendak* and all other children's titles in Multimedia Publishing over to the new Kids' business unit, where they would be linked with children's software being developed elsewhere in the Consumer Division. There would be two product units in Kids'—one for content titles like *Sendak* and one for productivity titles like childrens' word-processing software. If he chose to move with *Sendak,* Bartholomew would run the content titles unit.

Bartholomew was devastated. From the time he had first started Gandalf, he had been building a home reference set of products whose components he saw as inextricably linked. He never thought of *Sendak* as a children's title so much as a reference title—one that was part of a product line, like that at World Book Encyclopedia, on which people depended their whole life long. Now the vision that guided him for most of his career at Microsoft was about to be dissolved.

Offered the option to move with *Sendak,* Bartholomew was hesitant. He saw the choice as one of three he might have after the reorganization. Although Corddry had not told him as much, he suspected that the formation of a Kids' business unit was part of a larger reshuffling. Once complete, the reorganization might present him with opportunities to work under any one of three business unit managers: Corddry, Bruce Jacobsen—currently manager of the Consumer Division's Entry business unit, which included two products, *Money* and *Profit,* which had sold poorly—or Jabe Blumenthal, who almost certainly would be promoted to business unit manager somewhere. Of the three, Bartholomew preferred to work for Blumenthal because, he said, "he's best at company politics, and we have complementary skill-sets."

In being offered the choice to move, Bartholomew also was being forced to break up a carefully constructed set of projects that would bring its product unit manager prodigious resources for years to come. *Encarta,* now just taking off in the market, would be coming out annually forever. *Sendak,* when it first appeared, would be a four-disc set, with each disc being updated, released in a Macintosh version, and subsequently released in several foreign-language versions—all of which would be continuously updated. Eventually the two titles would comprise a huge set of products calling for the rolling out of ten or more products per year. To move with *Sendak* was to give up *Encarta,* destined to be one of Microsoft's great successes. To stay with *Encarta* was to give up *Sendak,* destined to be a large and long-standing series of titles. In his bleakest moments, Bartholomew wondered whether it made any real difference which way he went. If the two products were separated, he would lose half an empire no matter where he decided to work.

The more he considered the reorganization, the more depressed he grew. A move for *Sendak* would most likely break up its team and force it to slip, demoralizing everyone who had been working on it and leaving him with another slipped product deadline on his record. By the time the dust settled, he would have lost some or all of his best people. Fox, who had come to Microsoft to do children's titles, probably would opt to move to the new business unit. Bjerke might move as well, as might Ballinger. Worst of all would be the loss of Gammill, who might already have gotten too far into writing *Sendak*'s code to turn it over to someone else. A manager's prosperity—and, for that matter, his or her survival—depended largely on the acquisition of talent. Each year, when Bartholomew rated all of his employees in a single "stack ranking," Gammill came out on top and Fox in the second or third spot. The reorganization, threatening to skim the cream off Bartholomew's roster, might leave him dangerously weakened. "Kevin's been the number-one person in my stack ranking for awhile," he said. "I can't afford to lose him. And you don't go find another Sara."

Although directed by Corddry to discuss the reorganization with none of his employees, Bartholomew went immediately to Gammill, told him what was coming, and asked what he would do if given a choice. "I'd rather stay put," Gammill answered. "But I might have to go, because no one over there knows the technical aspects of doing content titles." After Bartholomew left, Gammill sat glumly considering his options. "If Craig goes, I'll go," he decided at last. "He's a good manager. But shit, Sara probably will quit . . . Bryan and Lindsey probably would leave . . . there's no way we could make our deadline."

Too distracted to work, he got up from his desk, put Rage Against the Machine's "Bullet in the Head" on his compact-disc player, and turned the volume up loud. "I feel like blowing off the whole afternoon," he said. Now his office was reverberating to the deafening growls of Zack de la Rocha, who was ranting against complacency and blind obedience. Gammill sat through the afternoon in this fashion, staring now across the room, now at the screen, now at his door, now at the floor, now at his blinds. He had stopped working entirely, getting up only to start his compact disc playing again. Occasionally, he would mutter something: "This is a bad one, that's for sure"; "I need a Redhook"; "You get used to reorgs. But this is gonna be a bad one"; "It'll have a serious impact on us"; "Ahhh . . . Rage Against the Machine . . . now I want to go out and kill someone."

Bartholomew, meanwhile, was fighting to keep *Sendak* from moving. "I would like *Sendak* to be a part of an *Encarta* line of products," he said. "Now, if it moves, I won't be able to control that 'steppingstone' idea." He also was determined to keep his product unit intact. He regarded it as Multimedia Publishing's most productive group. "Other than the Jayleen-Carolyn thing, nothing here is broken," he said. And he had decided that that problem could easily be fixed.

When he first had heard the news of the reorganization from Corddry, he e-mailed Stonesifer, arguing for his reference-series model of organization and against her segmentation-by-age model. He won a reprieve when Stonesifer agreed to meet with him before making her decision on *Sendak*'s fate.

Shocked as he was by the reorganization, Bartholomew also was philosophical. Reorganization was a fact of life at Microsoft—it reorganized every eighteen months, on average—and he understood that the key to his company's success was its relentless adaptability to change. "There won't be an MM Pubs in the future," he said, commencing a mournful monolog. "Everything we do on CD-ROM will be multimedia. . . . Whatever decision Patty makes has to be what's best for the division. . . . You get used to this kind of stuff. . . . If you can't deal well with change, you shouldn't be at Microsoft." Even so, he felt wounded. "This always happens when you go on vacation. When I went on my honeymoon, I came back to see that the entire CD-ROM division had been eliminated."

Stonesifer was not to render a verdict for another three weeks, during which time Bartholomew's subordinates went about their business unaware of the drama overhead. Through e-mail and meetings, Bartholomew carried on his argument, gradually winning Stonesifer over to his side. The *Sendak* team, meanwhile, busied itself with issues ranging from whether or not to copyright the terms "IgnorAnt" and "IntelligAnt" to how to go about deciding on *Sendak*'s guide character. Only one issue approached resolution during those weeks: at the end of October, a portfolio of artwork by Kim Emery, a designer from elsewhere at Microsoft, arrived. Emery wanted to get out of product package design and into children's software. The early consensus on the team was that *Sendak* had found its new art director in her—a circumstance that delighted everyone but Lindsey Smith, who was crestfallen at her teammates' happiness.

Three weeks later, after meeting and exchanging more e-mail with Stonesifer, and after a series of meetings between her, Corddry, and Jacobsen, Bartholomew was told that *Sendak* would stay in his product unit. He was elated. He had won a huge victory not only for himself but for Bjerke, Fox, and Gammill as well. He was particularly happy for Fox, who had been airing her fears of a reorganization ever since the *Sendak* project began.

When the reorganization was formally announced the next week, however, Bartholomew learned that he had won just a partial victory. *Sendak* was to stay only until some indefinite future date—most likely after its first two discs were shipped. Stonesifer had decided against moving it now largely because the move would have forced her to hire at least five new people to replace those Bartholomew would lose. In the long term, though, she felt that *Sendak* should be grouped with children's rather than reference titles. Mulling over his treasured steppingstone plan, Bartholomew said tersely, "It's hosed."

On the afternoon of the announcement, all work in Multimedia Publishing ceased. Employees walked the halls and grounds outside in small groups, assessing the damage to their product units, trying to figure out who won and who lost, and trying to decipher the reasoning behind the moving or staying put of specific products. Those people whose products were not being moved were relieved—save, to Bartholomew's considerable shock, for Bjerke and Fox.

Both women felt betrayed by him. "I came to Microsoft to do kids' products," said Fox. "I only went to reference because I was promised

kids' in the future." Bjerke, too, had become primarily a children's software designer. More than half her time for the past year had been spent
helping design common interfaces for all future Microsoft children's products, along with a Kids Market Basket marketing campaign. If Bartholomew were to keep *Sendak* for another year or two, and keep Bjerke and
Fox with him as well, then let them move after *Sendak* was launched,
the two women would be left politically weakened. "I could be really
screwed," said Fox. "By the time I get over there, they'll be established
in Kids', organized. I'll just be a *peon.* Their positions will be filled and
their organization on track. I'm sad, because Craig is a good manager,
but it makes so much sense for all the kids' products to be together. It
really does. I just hope it's not like musical chairs, and I don't get a
chair." Bjerke felt similarly threatened. "I think we should move," she
said emphatically. "If we're going to move eventually anyway, why not
move now? Meg and Lindsey probably could be hired there, and Bryan
would be happier there. Sara could establish a kids' editorial department.
If we don't move, they could staff up on their own and lock us out." She
felt that Bartholomew had acted out of a selfish desire for power. "Some
people see Craig as politically motivated, wanting to keep resources,
products, headcount. . . . Craig's ambition is to make this product line
work. . . . Mine is to build a kids' family of products . . . dammit! I've
been here as long as he has!"

Bartholomew, still unaware of the women's disaffection, sent mail to
them both, explaining that they were to do a *Sendak* demonstration for
Bruce Jacobsen in order to help him understand why *Sendak* was staying
in Gandalf. He presented Fox and Bjerke with an outline of points he
wanted made. Bjerke sent him a long response, saying, "I think the product would . . . be served better in the kids product unit if the majority
of the team could go with it. . . . I feel that I should be honest about this
to [Jacobsen] if he asks and that the fairest thing I can do is to let you
know ahead of time that I do not fully believe Sendak should stay." A
horrified Bartholomew answered immediately: "Carolyn, I hope you are
not expressing these opinions to others. If you were, I would not be very
happy with the situation." Bjerke answered, "Craig, I believe I have the
right to express concerns about a decision like this to you and to others
on the team." She went on to argue strenuously for *Sendak*'s immediate
move, and with it the move of virtually its entire team. "Carolyn, I apol-
ogize if I was abrupt in my mail," Bartholomew wrote back. "However,
PattyS sent mail today to Tom, me and Bruce saying that she did not

want any politics on Sendak—no wrangling to move it or statements that it would move or anything of the sort. She made it very clear, and I probably over-reacted along these lines." Then he went off to talk with Fox.

When Bartholomew walked into her office, Fox looked up and immediately felt sorry for him. He looked stricken. Bartholomew said that he was hurt and shocked to hear that people were eager to move out of his product unit. He explained to Fox how valuable she was to him and why he had fought so hard for *Sendak*. He reminded her that if she were to stay with him, she could do original products from scratch. In the new Kids' unit, he cautioned, they would just be buying titles from book publishers and porting them over to digital format—hardly the sort of creative work she had come to Microsoft to do.

After Bartholomew was gone, Fox laughed. "He looked so *sad!*" she exclaimed. She decided that he was right to keep *Sendak* where it was. "If it had moved, it would have slipped all to hell. And they're going to be too marketing-oriented over there anyway. Here we have the luxury of avoiding that, to a degree." The next day, a Saturday, she came into her office and e-mailed her thoughts to Bjerke:

> Carolyn,
> I was pretty surprised when I learned about all the changes yesterday. But now that I've had some time to think about it, I really think it makes sense that Sendak is staying in Craig's group for the time being.
>
> When we first started on Sendak, we all wanted to create something new. None of us felt good about the idea of just putting a book onto a computer. And we really are creating something. We're doing extensive editorial development in addition to our technical development. And the importance of the accuracy of our information is a lot more key here (same with Atlas and Encarta) than for Rabbit Ears/Ink/Splat, etc. I think the creating from scratch idea (I know we're starting with something, but we're thinking it through from scratch) is what makes this group unique and I don't necessarily think it'll be as key of a characteristic right yet in the Kids' group.
>
> We really are the only kids project that is a reference—which requires a whole different level of editorial work/involvement than something like a paint program. . . .

I think changes always get people all worked up, but I don't think it's necessarily as big of a deal as it seemed Friday. I feel a lot more normal about it after a night's sleep. I hope you do too.

Just some thoughts!
Sara

With that, the matter died—save for Gammill's closing comment. Fox had talked with him about her desire to move with *Sendak* now rather than later. Now, looking with some interest at a copy of Fox's latest opinion, he exclaimed, with an affectionate laugh, "That woman is so fuckin' fickle!"

Moving painstakingly, accompanied by constant muttering and grumbling, Gammill slogged through his code, character by character, line by line, equation by equation, design item by design item. "Fuck," he would mutter while typing, if (! CreateAnimatedClose (hWnd, CLOSE_X, CLOSE_Y, CMD_STACK_CLOSE)); "Bogus. . . . Shit. . . . Unbelievably stupid," iTabWidth = iTabWidth * TAB_AREA_DX + TAB_DX; "Grrrrrrr . . . ," for i=0; i<NumPops; i++; "Get me another Diet Sprite," if ((CreateWindow (IpszTabClass, IpszTabClass.

After getting his tabs in working order, Gammill moved on to the content of *Sendak*'s pop-ups. First he wrote the code for fetching and placing bit maps for graphics—the photographs and drawings that accompanied pop-up text. Next he wrote the code for fetching and placing pop-up captions. Then he added to code written by Bill Sproule for interfacing with MediaView to fetch and flow text into the pop-up, around its graphics. Then, working more or less on one device each day, he wrote the code that checked each pop-up's attributes to see whether it contained any of *Sendak*'s eight media elements and if it did, went off to fetch and place in the pop-up the appropriate controller—a start/stop/pause button, a start-only button, a start/stop/rewind button—so the user could play the element in question.

Sproule, meanwhile, had proven himself a godsend. He was a perfect psychological fit for Microsoft: he had a great zest for programming, found the work relatively easy, and could work almost entirely without supervision, going for days at a time without having to ask Gammill any questions. His code, Gammill said, was great. Sproule had moved into an office, gone out after getting his first paycheck and bought a Porsche 944, and got down happily to work. Gammill had only to assign tasks to him, give him a deadline, then retrieve the completed code when he needed it. It was always done on time, and done well.

Much as he liked his work, though, and good as he was at it, Sproule was worried. He had completed as much code as possible for *Sendak*'s log on screen, then had to stop because "a bunch of the crap underlying it" had not yet been designed. He moved on to *Sendak*'s sights and sounds album"—an album, kept in the ship, in which users could save copies of their favorite pictures, video clips, sound effects, songs, and animations from the pop-ups and scenes.

Sproule soon found that working on the album left him alternately exhilarated and disgruntled. Gammill had given him a relatively difficult task in implementing the album. It was designed to look like a photograph album with a spiral binding. Gammill had directed Sproule to store a bit map of a single spiral rather than of the whole spine, then write code directing *Sendak* to fetch the same bit map over and over again, storing it in a series of connected locations on the screen until enough copies of it were in place to give the appearance of a complete spiral binding. It was a complicated coding task that would save acres of disc space, and Sproule completed it without a hitch. But in trying to move on to the next part of the album—writing the engine for saving copies of media elements to it—he ran into the same stone wall he had run into when working on the log on screen: *Sendak*'s designers had not sorted out exactly what they wanted. "I don't know how much more I can do on this thing," Sproule said, "because so much stuff is undefined."

Since a given copy of *Sendak* could be used by any number of kids, there would have to be a separate sights and sounds album for each one. Sproule needed to write code instructing *Sendak* to assign the name to the album, whenever it was used, of the last person who had logged on to the encyclopedia. If a child named Katie Nash, for example, logged on to *Sendak* and copied four media elements to the sights and sounds album while she was using the encyclopedia, then did not use *Sendak* again for a week—during which time three other children logged on and used it—the encyclopedia needed to bring up the album with Nash's copied elements stored in it when she next logged on. But when Sproule went to Smith to get a final log on design, he was told that the log on screen had been eliminated. How, then, was he to keep track of which users stored which elements in these albums? No one could give him an answer.

"Every time I work on something," he said, "I run into all this stuff that design hasn't thought of. And when I was going through the spec, I kept coming up against stuff that wasn't consistent from section to section. I ask questions, but get vague answers. Then I try to go on and do other stuff."

With each day, Sproule grew more desperate. "It's getting to the point where it's getting tough," he said one afternoon. "Every time I say I'm gonna do this because I can't do that yet, they say, 'Oh, the interface isn't done yet.'" This was not the way he had expected things to be done at Microsoft. "I can't understand it," he said. "There must be stuff . . . there must be stuff by now . . . there *has* to be stuff. We're just sitting here with this huge amount of work ahead of us, and it's frustrating not to be able to do anything. I've never been through one of these things before, so I don't know . . . but I'm starting to get a little worried."

Gammill fell into the habit of waving off Sproule's frequent expressions of fear with the same dubious consolation: "Don't worry—you'll get used to it." Intended to be reassuring, it had the opposite effect. Sproule couldn't conceive of working in eternal uncertainty, without defined boundaries and rules. "This," he said, "is going to be a nightmare."

Even so, Sproule managed to keep his sense of humor intact. After weeks spent working on the find gadget's thumbnails and breadcrumbs screen, he sent e-mail to Smith begging for thumbnail artwork to plug into his code, so he could test it. Time and again, he was told it wasn't ready. Finally, as Gammill had done, he dug up some artwork on his own, scanned it into the computer network, and converted it to bit maps for the find gadget. Then he e-mailed Gammill with the news that the gadget was done and that he should call it up on his screen and test its functionality. Gammill did. There, on his terminal, sat *Sendak*'s find gadget, its screen full of miniature pin-up photos.

Though Gammill appeared dismissive of Sproule's fears, he was angry. It now was the end of November, two months after he had finished his work on *Encarta 94* and turned his attention to the pop-up stack code. Now that the code was complete and working, he too wanted to use "real data"—actual encyclopedia content—to test it. But on the day 120 pop-ups' worth of material was supposed to have been completed, entered into Merismus, approved by *Sendak*'s editors and designers, and their approval registered in Merismus, there still was nothing for him to use. At a meeting in which Meg Nyland reported on her progress, she looked at the "120" on her milestone chart and cheerfully said, "We have forty in progress." Back in his office, Gammill screamed, "They have zero! Zero! I wanted to say, 'So that means zero, right?' But I didn't want to do that in front of all those people." Nyland had also shown two pop-up drawings—one of a cannon, the other of blindfolded Justice holding her scales aloft—that were of decidedly poor quality. "And that cannon looks like shit!" Gammill continued. "That Justice looks like shit, too. Sure has big boobs, though."

Every morning now, Gammill would call Merismus up on his screen and ask it to produce a report of approved elements—content ready to be built into the encyclopedia. Each day, the report showed that there was nothing. "I'm gonna run this every day until I can generate a fuckin' report!" he shouted one morning. "Actually, that's factually incorrect. . . . I *can* generate a report. It's just that there's nothing in it!" He turned back to his main terminal. "Arrrrrgh! If I start thinking how nothing's been approved yet, I'll get pissed. Because then I'll start thinking about how we're not going to ship on time."

He stopped venting his anger at teammates and supervisors now, opting instead for gruesome humor. Bartholomew, looking either for entertainment or relief, wandered into Gammill's office one afternoon and was greeted with a distracting reminiscence. "I was just remembering my high school annual my senior year," Gammill said. "I didn't have any autographs in it—I wasn't that kind of person. All I had written in it were these two Christa McAuliffe jokes."

"*Christa McAuliffe* jokes?"

"Yeah . . . I was in high school when the shuttle blew up . . . and there were all these jokes floating around . . . like, 'Did you know her eyes were blue?' 'No.' 'Yeah. One blew this way, the other blew that way.'" He chuckled. "And this one: 'What did her husband say to her before she left?' 'I'll feed the dog, you feed the fish.' There were a whole bunch of them, but those are the only two I remember."

Bartholomew was standing next to Gammill's door, his back against the wall, his wrists crossed behind his back, at the waist. He looked like someone tied to a stake, ready for his execution. Leaning his head back against the wall, gazing up at the ceiling, he said to Gammill, "It's amazing that we did this again. After *Encarta,* we said, 'Never start a product without a full team.' Then we turned around and started a product without a full team!'"

Now, nearly a year later, he finally had a full team in place. Ralph Barton, a contractor who was finishing up program management for the Macintosh version of *Encarta,* was to take Bjerke's place during her maternity leave. Due to leave in two weeks, Bjerke had seen to it that Barton understood everything that had been done and remained to be done on *Sendak.* And in Kim Emery, who had been hired two weeks before, Bartholomew now had an experienced designer with strong opinions and a proven ability to thrive in Microsoft's culture. Bartholomew had been particularly impressed during her interviews with her ability to dissect the "flatness" and "inconsistency" she saw in *Sendak*'s emerging look and feel.

Emery's arrival coincided with a product unit meeting at which Gandalf's three teams showed one another their current prototypes. After the meeting, Bartholomew sent e-mail that reduced everyone on the *Sendak* team, save for Gammill, to a state of shock. "My sense right now," Bartholomew's mail began, "is that we're tracking toward a solid but not yet exceptional product. . . . I don't think the product 'works' across the board yet as the kind of multimedia 'experience' that's going to get teachers and kids telling parents 'I just saw the *coolest* product today.' " Bartholomew went on for two full pages, noting that he wanted *Sendak* to be "not so much of a 'text/pictures' product," and listing improvements he wanted to see.

After reading the mail, Bjerke, who had now developed an amused detachment toward *Sendak,* said, "If we start making these kinds of changes, we'll have to cut content, which will completely freak Sara out. Craig thinks he's improving the product, and maybe he is . . . but it's at the expense of the *people.*" One of those people, Ralph Barton, came storming into Gammill's office after reading Bartholomew's mail. "It's too late for this kind of stuff!" he shrieked. "Relax, it's just Craig," Gammill answered. "He always does this kind of stuff in the late going. You'll get used to it." Having gone through *Encarta* with Bartholomew, Gammill saw his mail now as a simple push for harder work on those design elements not yet completed. Because of Bartholomew's obsession with shipping on time, Gammill reasoned, he would never call for redesign of anything that had already been coded. Normally panicked at anything calling for changes in design, Gammill was thrilled to see that Bartholomew finally was putting the screws to someone other than a developer. From his point of view, the worst that could happen was that his teammates finally would focus on their work and get him some completed features to implement.

While waiting for that unlikely turn of events, Gammill busied himself with optimizing his pop-up stack code—making it run faster—and integrating decompression into the retrieval of text and other media. At least twice each hour, he would run his show a stack function just to watch the window open, the tabs take form, and the text and images flow into place. To him, it looked terrific—and it was tangible proof that things in *Sendak* actually could be done, and be made to work, and that the whole thing really could be finished on time. Now, instead of grumbling fatalistically whenever friends asked him how *Sendak* was going, he would exclaim with great good cheer, "The pop-up stack's done!"

Its decibel level notwithstanding, Gammill's office now was the calmest corner in *Sendak*'s domain. Outside it, largely unbeknownst to him, there was a roiling series of impromptu meetings between Emery and her new teammates as she cruised around now to Bjerke's office, now to Fox's, to Ballinger's, to Smith's. Carefully avoiding Gammill's lair, she peppered the rest of the *Sendak* team with questions about why and how the design had evolved to the point it had, why it had stopped, and why this or that detail had been incorporated. Her lone encounter with Gammill had come outside a conference room after the two attended a team meeting. "Were you pissed off in there?" Gammill asked.

"No," she answered, "when I'm pissed—believe me, you'll know it."

"We'll get along good, then."

Although Bartholomew's mail had the effect on Emery that he intended—he wanted, he said when outside the hearing of *Sendak* team members, to let her feel that she had a free hand to do anything she wanted with *Sendak*—she still proceeded gingerly, taking care during her first two weeks not to criticize any of the completed design work. She got from Smith all the old *Sendak* layouts and studied them in order to "learn the whole process, how they got to this point." Then her own ideas began to take form. "Last week," she said in mid-December, "I first began to understand what I want to do." She had proceeded with care, she said, because "the company is full of people with their own personalities, ideas, and agendas. You have to read people's psyches and treat them carefully. You get a number of smart, ambitious people together—it causes a lot of problems."

She had seen almost immediately, though, that *Sendak* had "a horribly inconsistent design. There were a lot of 'disconnects' with the story behind it. It's too cute. All the animations and sound . . . you forget that it's a content product. I mean, we have to sell it to parents. Information is what is important—that's what we're about." She also felt that the overriding metaphor of exploration was confused. "I don't get the ship," she said. "Why would kids get in a spaceship to visit their own planet?" Having seen Ballinger's original drawings and compared them with his current work, she felt that "the original ones were better. I can tell by his current work that he doesn't want to do it this way." She believed that *Sendak* had been over-tested and skewed too much toward marketing. "If Disney had focus-tested Robin Williams's Aladdin character," she went on, "they would have cut it right away. Sometimes testing is bogus. You need to be instinctive and reactive—sometimes you need to go from the gut."

Emery had not yet decided exactly what in *Sendak* she wanted to change. "I want to look at the content and how it's presented," she said. "That will drive any major changes."

As it happened, she was focusing on the presentation of content during another of Fox's crises of confidence. After reading Bartholomew's mail, Fox decided that he had brought up "a real problem. Our stack is too linear. There's no exploration. Kids just go through them in order." She had been looking at the Dorling Kindersley book upon which *Sendak* was based, and had been shocked to see that the book allowed browsers more freedom to explore at random than did the computer. Yet the computer was supposed to be this grand force of liberation from the strictures of the printed book. In the book, she pointed out, the text flowed freely around pictures, and readers could browse through it at their leisure, taking in volumes of content at a glance. In *Sendak*, they would be funneled through the pop-ups in numerical order, allowed only a few sentences of content at a time. It was a hideous paradox: the computer actually would be more restrictive than the book. "DK did the opposite of what we're doing," she said at a core team meeting, "and we turned into gatekeepers. Maybe we should have the pop-ups come up randomly or something."

Ballinger's head was spinning after this pronouncement. He had been trying for three weeks now to get his bearings under a new art director —an unknown quantity, she was effectively the fourth director put over him in the last year. He had been constantly frustrated in his efforts at getting *Sendak*'s fifteen Nature scenes finished by December 22. Fox and her assistants made changes in every scene he completed, forcing him to redo them again and again. In addition, they had added a new Nature scene, a farm, moved from the Civilization disc. By his deadline, he would have only nine of sixteen scenes completed. Since no artists had been hired to draw the character or the ship, or to do *Sendak* animations, there was every possibility that he would be called in at the eleventh hour to work on those as well. And now Fox was all but proposing that they start everything over again. Asked for an assessment of his mental state after meeting with her, he answered, "Fried. For today and for 1994."

The only people at peace on the project were those who were leaving. Bjerke would be gone in a few days—her leave was to begin on December 17—and Ryberg a month after that. Both had so thoroughly briefed their replacements that they were all but disengaged from the project. Smith, whose husband had just landed a job in the Silicon Valley, would be leaving in a few days. While there were palpable signs of relief on the faces of Bjerke and Ryberg, Smith fairly screamed her happiness in the face of anyone who came near. "Man," she exulted after the meeting at which Fox had aired her latest concerns, "if I wasn't leaving, I'd *die*. There's so *much* going on . . . and coming down. . . . This is *way* worse than *Encarta*, way harder."

Of those remaining, Gammill was happiest. Although still frustrated with his teammates' irresolution, he had, by completing the pop-up stack, solved the most complicated problem—or, at least, the most complicated problem over which he had exclusive control—in all of *Sendak*. There would be horrible time crunches during the building and testing phases of the project, but he was well prepared for those. In having completed the pop-up stack and the find gadget's thumbnails and breadcrumbs features, he and Sproule had dealt with the core of the product: access to its content.

Gammill was idly tinkering with his pop-up stack code when Kim Emery suddenly came into his office without knocking, closed the door, sat down facing him, and turned down his music. A blond, outspoken woman with a faint sneer perpetually on her face, she was an anomaly: someone with the gender and face of a designer, and the facial expression and attitude of a developer. Gammill had taken an instant liking to her because she was nearly as blunt and insensitive in meetings as he was.

Now, though, he looked at her apprehensively.

"Are you afraid? Are you scared?" Emery asked, laughing.

"That depends," Gammill answered.

She followed with a series of concerns and questions, only occasionally waiting for Gammill to answer: "People can't see the depth of content. . . . The buttons are inconsistent all the way through. . . . That's as big as the pop-ups can be, right? . . . I have a question about the find thing . . . those pictures by the words? I don't understand that at all. *At all.*" She told Gammill that she had decided to redesign the find gadget. Then, by way of trying to assuage Gammill's fears of wholesale design changes, she said, "Don't worry about big changes . . . probably one of the biggest thing's that gonna change is the pop-ups."

Suddenly Gammill, a habitual twitcher, was sitting perfectly still. A subtle slackening settled over his face, as if he had abruptly been drained of consciousness. "O-kay," he said, his voice barely audible. "Because . . . those are like . . . about done now. . . . I'll have to cost out the time."

Emery chatted on cheerfully, Gammill not quite managing to take in her words. "The whole concept of a stack . . . kind of from scratch, really . . . the visual's not gonna change . . . the content's not gonna change." Since Gammill gave no sign of having heard her, she finally thanked him for his time, said goodbye, and fled.

Gammill sat perfectly still for several more minutes until finally life and motion returned first to his fingers, then to one of his feet, then at last to his head. "Now I don't know what to work on," he said in a muted voice. "Fuck . . . I don't have the heart to tell Bill that the thumbnails are gonna be nuked. . . . But it's my job! . . . I'm sick!" He turned to his terminal to type and send an e-mail message to Sproule, telling him to come down to his office. "I guess I'll concentrate on my *managerial* responsibilities!"

Waiting for Sproule, he typed an algorithm into his computer and kept up a running monologue while tinkering with it. "Carolyn keeps calling this the Project from Hell," he said, "and Craig's always talking about how he's never been through anything like this. But Craig's also always talking about how we made this mistake and this mistake and this mistake on *Encarta* and now here we are making it again. And Sara always says, 'A product cycle is so . . . *cyclic.*' Every project here is like this! We keep saying that we learn from our mistakes . . . but we keep going through the same shit over and over again."

Sproule came in and sat down. "They nuked your thumbnails," Gammill said.

Sproule, shocked, began writhing in his chair, lolling his head back and forth. "I mean," he said, "I mean . . . I spent all this—"

"I know, I know," Gammill interrupted. You'll get used to it. . . . You'll get used to it—trust me. It just takes two years or so."

He waited for an answer, but all Sproule could manage were some strangled choking sounds.

"Don't feel bad about it," Gammill continued. "You're still getting paid."

"Oh . . . it doesn't bother me."

"It *does* kind of suck. . . . Here, look at this!" Pointing to his screen with one hand, he motioned with the other for Sproule to come around his desk. In the middle of the screen sat the algorithm Gammill had been typing:

```
DWORD dwSum = 0;
LPNODE lpHold = lpNode;

while ( lpNode != NULL )
{
        dwSum += lpNode->dwValue;

    if ( lpNode = lpNode->lpNext) == NULL)
        lpNode->lpNext = lpHold;
```

Gammill smiled. Sproule laughed, then left, closing the door behind him. Gammill got up and put a disc in his CD player, then turned the volume up to unprecedented levels. "I'm always fucked!" he screamed. "Fucked! It's the plight of a developer! You get really used to bending over in this job. . . . 'Grab your ankles!' "

With a tremendous electronic crash, the voice of Layne Staley was ushered into the office, alternately roaring, moaning, and growling:

> *Down, down, down, you're rollin'*
> *Watch the blood float in the muddy sewer*
> *Take another hit*
> *And bury your brother.*

Gammill sat tapping his foot and fingers in time to the thundering melancholy. He was amazed at how accurate the unwitting aim of his new teammate had been. Emery had zeroed in on precisely those features in *Sendak* that already were coded, leaving the rest, as far as he could tell, untouched. "This product is doomed!" he shouted. Then he started cleaning up his desk. He threw out Smith's "Final Pop-up Spec." He threw out the paper copy of his schedule. Drawings, sketches, notes, equations, printed e-mail messages, all of it—a year's worth of work and planning—went soaring into the recycling box he kept behind his desk. Then he sent e-mail to Bjerke asking to borrow her laptop computer. In a few days, he would be taking his family to Vail for the Christmas holidays. Bjerke wouldn't be needing her laptop for months. He could use it during his vacation to write a new development schedule.

Aftermath

On December 20, 1993, Multimedia Publishing received the news via e-mail that it no longer existed. Multimedia's former product teams were to be broken up and their members sprinkled throughout the revamped Consumer Division, which now would number eight business units. The only multimedia unit remaining intact was Gandalf, which became part of a new Reference business unit, to be headed by Tom Corddry and to include—along with Bartholomew and his line of titles—*Bookshelf*, a medical encyclopedia, Merismus, and MediaView. Jabe Blumenthal, at Gates's personal request, agreed to be named manager of a new business unit developing personal financial management software and on-line financial services. His first act was to take Phil Spencer with him, thus absolving Spencer of his SPAM responsibilities. Most of the Jurassic and Mercury titles and their teams were moved to a new Personal Interests/Lifestyle unit, and SPAM moved to the Kids' business unit.

Spencer viewed moving with Blumenthal as a form of deliverance, as he no longer would have to bear the burden of SPAM's impossible deadlines. Nevertheless, he was appalled at the turn SPAM took immediately upon its move to Kids'. "All they talk about in meetings now," he said, "is how to ship the Kids' titles." Although SPAM was supposed to be a "cross-unit" Consumer Division resource, its move to Kids', Spencer believed, was a political disaster for *Sendak*. SPAM's loyalty now would be to the titles in its own unit; the children's encyclopedia would move below the bottom of its list of priorities.

Brenden Sawyer Bjerke was born at 10:45 P.M. on January 2, 1994, at nine pounds, twenty-one inches. Bailey Annabelle Ryberg Moritz was born at 8:30 P.M. on January 17, weighing in at eight pounds, seven ounces, and measuring twenty and one-half inches.

Ralph Barton and Kim Emery, the new program manager and designer for *Sendak*, melded with their new teammates with surprising ease at first. Emery and Fox, inspired by the design of Fox's digital wristwatch, redesigned the pop-up, find gadget, and sights and sounds album windows to look like space-age information devices. The new design allowed Emery to eliminate the guide's backpack, as all of the tools' functionality was moved to the margins of the window. The new pop-up window was a grayish gadget that displayed text and pictures in a space framed by rounded sides and squared corners. Various buttons and icons were arrayed around the edges of the gadget, and one row of brightly colored numbered buttons down its right side served the function previously served by the numbered tabs in Lindsey Smith's notebook design. Each of these buttons corresponded to a pop-up. As rendered by Ballinger, each one, before bringing up its pop-up, behaved differently when clicked upon. One button fell through the gadget, to the sound of breaking glass, leaving a hole where it had been; another turned into a dilating eye; another flattened out and spun around like a coin on its edge. Under the last numbered button was an extra credit button that appeared only when a topic had more than six pop-ups. Clicking on it allowed the user to move deeper into the stack. Under that was a See Also button that brought up a list of related topics.

Fox vacillated greatly in her feelings about Barton and Emery. "They're blaming everything on the old team," she said one day, gloomily. Barton refused to allow her to tinker with Ballinger's scenes once they were completed, and he began eliminating feature after feature in *Sendak* for the sake of the schedule, cutting off Fox's questions and protests. Emery tended to insist on guiding discussions with Fox, treating her as a subordinate rather than an equal. Compared with these two, Fox thought, Bjerke had been positively indulgent.

But Fox also noticed that *Sendak* began moving forward and that design issues, once resolved, generally stayed that way. And she was most impressed with Emery's handling of Ballinger. When Fox and Emery would work out the concept of a given feature's new look, Emery would make pencil sketches, then show them to Ballinger, describing in broad outline what she and Fox hoped to see. Then she left Ballinger alone to execute the designs without further direction. "She lets him work things out on his own," Fox said, "and his stuff is so much *better* now."

Under Emery, Ballinger's responsibilities grew almost back to the proportions planned for him at the beginning of *Sendak*. With each of her attempts to find solutions from artists and researchers outside of Microsoft, Emery grew more and more disappointed, and came to rely increasingly on Ballinger. Eventually, she turned completion of *Sendak*'s last two scenes over to a contract artist so that Ballinger could devote more of his time to the encyclopedia's interface, the ship's interior, and the guide character—those parts of the product that first engaged the user and set *Sendak*'s tone.

Left to his own devices, Ballinger began adding more playful elements to the encyclopedia. Among the team's favorite was his customization feature, which allowed users to change the interior of the spaceship. A click of the mouse key covered the ship's walls with any one of the following motifs: a swamp scene, insects (most of them cockroaches), a plaid pattern, little yellow smilefaces, a stone wall pattern, a lush nature scene with a stream running down the middle of it, hundreds of little frogs' heads, or a honeycomb pattern.

Emery was to turn in particular desperation to Ballinger after making what she would later regard as a hilariously misguided move. She had consulted with a California company, Youth Market Systems, when she first began working on *Sendak*, asking YMS to come up with a guide whose appearance and behavior was buttressed by a sound marketing philosophy. YMS concluded that there should be two characters—a guide and a sidekick—with the sidekick providing "the needed elements of comic relief, unpredictability, dual gender appeal, and fun in great part through the character dynamic." In order to "transcend ethnic perceptions," be "credible, powerful and trustworthy," and fulfill other objectives, the characters, YMS suggested, should be "JAXX, a CyberWiz, and his Pet-Bot." "From an archetype perspective," YMS wrote, "JAXX represents a fallible aspiring hero with warm and personable personality qualities."

Jaxx was to be "a futuristic cyborg wizard/magician. This means he would have a combination of robotic elements and human ones. For maximum personality identification, the recommendation is to make sure that his head be handsome and mostly human in its appearance." He was "not the male macho hero archetype, but a softer, more emotional, and sensitive type of hero." Then, in a line that cost YMS the vote of Fox, the document read, "In addition, it has been proven again and again that while boys strongly resist lead female characters, girls much more readily accept male leads."

Pet-Bot, the force of randomness, was "an unusual yet 'cute' robotic sort of dog," who, on a scale of one to five—one being "femaleness" and five being "maleness"—was a 3.5. His "predominant emotions" were "Love, Enthusiasm, Fear," and his "Needs"—a bit risque, it seemed to me, for a children's product—were "insatiable curiosity, love . . . , physical, Stimulation, Release."

Drawings by YMS and freelance artists of possible Jaxxes were of young Aryan figures in anatomically correct armor. They ranged in look from adolescent superheroes to happy little superheroes who had not yet reached puberty. They provided a source of considerable comic relief to Gammill, who papered his office walls with the drawings and gave them names: "Condomboy," "Homoboy," "Catamiteboy."

It was a good lesson in the perils of turning to science to create art. Deciding that the heart was more reliable than the head, Emery asked Ballinger for character sketches, and he spent two feverish days coming up with four guides—an armored owl, a toad, an ant in a spacesuit, and a legless robot—and with an animation sequence of each one traveling from ship to scene and back. The sequences were highly entertaining. Fox's favorite, and the favorite of kids in usability tests, was Ballinger's Turbo-Toad, which eventually became *Sendak*'s guide. The creature's head was encased in a transparent glass bubble and it traveled through *Sendak* on a rocket-powered lilypad, steering with uncertain skill by means of a joystick. It introduced itself to the user by proclaiming, "Hi! I'm Thaddeus Pole. . . . You can call me Tad!"

At first, it seemed that only the mood on the *Sendak* team changed, while actual progress remained at a standstill. What little art had been completed for pop-up illustrations had to be replaced. Drawn to meld with Smith's pop-up design, it did not fit with Emery's. Then, after Emery redesigned the pop-ups, Fox noticed that there was too little space in them to display text and illustrations properly, so they had to be redesigned again. As a result, *Sendak*'s first proofing build, scheduled for February 9, had to be moved back to mid-March, as there were no completed pop-ups for Gammill to build into *Sendak*, and Merismus still wasn't working.

As each design question was settled, Gammill and Sproule immediately got the features coded and implemented. By the beginning of April, the pop-up window, sights and sounds album, find gadget, and a host of other interface elements were finished and working. By month's end, though, pop-up production was dangerously behind schedule. Near the deadline for their completion, they were only 40 percent done. Time and again, while exploring *Sendak*, its manufacturers would get a huge "NOT COMPLETE" in the pop-up window when they clicked on a topic title in the Find window.

Sprites presented an even knottier problem. Before departing for her maternity leave, Ryberg had tentatively contracted with Waaahoo Productions, an animation studio in Las Vegas, to draw and color all of *Sendak*'s scene sprites. The plan called for Waaahoo to produce the sprite art on Macintoshes and for Microsoft employees to port it over to the PC, where the animations could be scripted in SPAM. Unfortunately, the first drawings sent in by Waaahoo were crudely colored, the animators unable to duplicate Ballinger's realistic detail. Using MacroMedia Director, *Sendak*'s producers spliced together one of Ballinger's creatures with the studio's drawings in an animation sequence. When a mouse-click triggered the animation, the creature's appearance changed entirely, then reverted to its original form when the animation was finished. Ryberg's replacement, Meg Nyland, decided to have Waaahoo do line drawings for the animations and for contract artists at Microsoft, closely supervised by her and Ballinger, to do the coloring.

The coloring proved painfully slow. By the beginning of April, only one *Sendak* sprite was finished. A sleeping koala falling out of a tree, the sprite consisted of seventy-seven frames and ran for ten seconds. Nyland estimated its total cost at $145 per second for the drawings, another $300 for the coloring. She calculated that there were 12,000 frames of scene sprites in *Sendak*'s Nature and Civilization discs, and that the team of seven animators available to her could draw three scenes' worth of sprites per week. Six colorists, though, could only do three to five sprites per week. Near the end of April, in an attempt at reducing the workload, she and Barton decided to simplify the animations, reducing the total number of frames to nine thousand.

These problems in themselves would have caused *Sendak* to slip by at least a month. However, once SPAM began slipping dramatically, they proved to be inconsequential. SPAM would have caused *Sendak* to slip even if the *Sendak* team's own work had been ahead of schedule. A preliminary and incomplete version of the SPAM authoring tool, given to *Sendak* early in April, proved unreliable and almost impossible to learn. By mid-April, SPAM was three months behind schedule. Worse, it lacked features and behavior critical to *Sendak*. The SPAM team planned to play animations in a manner impossible on most standard personal computers. If a *Sendak* user clicked on an object, for example, SPAM, as designed, would retrieve the animation from the compact disc, move it to virtual memory—a portion of the user's hard disk set aside for temporary storage of data on its way to the screen—then play the animation from there. For *Sendak*, this was a disaster. SPAM's plan would require a user to have 40 megabytes of hard disk space free to dedicate to virtual memory, while a standard machine generally allowed only 4 to 8 megabytes. And by moving animation data from the compact disc to the hard disk, SPAM was making the wait between a user's mouse-click and the playing of an animation intolerably long. "This is completely brain dead!" Bartholomew said. "We need to stream animations directly from the CD! They *have* to change that!" But the new SPAM lead, Anthony Cockburn, was not encouraging. "OK," he wrote in e-mail, "we will look into it but anything we do will likely cause a slip in the schedule."

A concerted whispering campaign against *Sendak*, directed at Patty Stonesifer, broke out in the Kids' business unit. The whispers had it that *Sendak* was "broken" and "screwed up," and that it would never fulfill the original hopes for it. Bartholomew, outraged, believed the rumors were orchestrated by Kids' managers, who were determined to get Stonesifer to reverse her decision to keep *Sendak* in Bartholomew's business unit. "No way," Bartholomew said determinedly, "are they going to take kids' reference away from us. This is pure arrogance—people here always want more control, influence, responsibility." He had heard exactly the same sorts of whispers when working on *Encarta*, he said now with some heat, "and now it's the number-one application in the whole country. But back then, people here were saying, 'It sucks . . . it's too complicated.' " Taking a glum Barton aside one day, Bartholomew said, "The best way to beat all this is to ship a great product!"

The rumors elicited sympathy rather than alarm from Stonesifer. Calling Bartholomew into her office, she noted that *Sendak* had been subjected to enough turnover in personnel and enough trouble from the SPAM team to justify moving back its deadline. Bartholomew turned her down. "It just doesn't make any sense to ship later," he said. "We won't be as competitive later."

For Tom Corddry, the elimination of MM Pubs was tactically brilliant and psychologically devastating. Management of the division had consumed him for the previous four years, destroying his personal life and bringing him to the brink of divorce. Then, as a reward for his labors, he had to spend the last four months of 1993 taking what was effectively his life's work and "carving it up like a Thanksgiving turkey."

Intellectually, Corddry saw the breakup of Multimedia Publishing and its spread throughout the Consumer Division as the necessary fulfillment of his own original vision. He had always planned for the Multimedia division to be only temporarily separate from the rest of Microsoft, as eventually all personal computers would be multimedia machines equipped with compact disc drives. But now that the time had come, he found himself emotionally unable to cope. After finishing his work on the reorganization, he had taken a few distracted days off for Christmas, then returned to begin work immediately on a new three-year plan—an annual exercise at Microsoft. "I went through this emotional letdown at Christmas," he told me later. "I was having trouble concentrating. My body and mind were rebelling. I was so tired, I felt physically heavy, and finally I realized I was in denial over the loss of MM Pubs."

He went about his new three-year plan in his typically random fashion, working on it up to the minute he walked in to present it to Gates. It was an approach that Susan Boeschen, his previous manager, had tolerated. But Stonesifer, who was caught by surprise by Corddry's projections, was caught even more by surprise by Gates's endorsement of them. Corddry was planning for Family Reference, the new business unit he was to manage, to grow so fast that in three years it would be bigger than MM

Pubs had ever been. A week before, at a management retreat, Stonesifer had asked for scarcely half of what Corddry was requesting, and Gates now added resources in excess even of Corddry's numbers.

After the meeting, Stonesifer took Corddry aside and laid down the law to him, explaining that his days as a managerial anomaly were over. He was to become much more of a disciplined, buttoned-down manager and less of a visionary. Before he realized what he was doing, Corddry, an extremely mild-mannered man, began shouting at her. Then he told her that he probably would leave Microsoft.

The next day, Gates called Corddry and asked him to stay. He suggested that Corddry work three more months, take three months off, then come back and define a job for himself. For the time being, they could call the job Creative Director. Corddry was enormously gratified. "The title 'Creative Director,' he said, "is a blank check. And having Bill call me and say that I'm valuable, that they don't want to lose me. . . . I've been getting the red-carpet treatment ever since."

Bartholomew did not fare as well. He wanted to replace Corddry as business unit manager of Family Reference. Corddry lobbied hard with Stonesifer on Bartholomew's behalf, and Bartholomew himself argued strenuously for the promotion. While promising to consider Bartholomew, Stonesifer chose instead to hire Richard Tait, a standard Microsoft managerial type, to succeed Corddry. The acquisition of Tait, a protege of Steve Ballmer—Gates's right hand—was a coup for Stonesifer, and even Bartholomew, angry as he was at Stonesifer's treatment of him, concurred with her decision. "She went for the best available athlete," Bartholomew said. "She looked at her options, weighed getting this guy against the risk of me leaving, and decided it was worth the risk. This place is like the San Francisco 49ers—they just keep moving people, no matter how good they are, in the hope of getting someone better. In a way, I have to respect them—it's a good gambling mentality."

Still, he was furious, particularly at Stonesifer's invocation of the Peter Principle in telling Bartholomew he would not be promoted. When she asked him to commit to Microsoft for another four months, he refused, and when company vice president Mike Maples later asked him not to leave, he angrily refused to discuss his plans with him.

In private, though, weighing his alternatives, Bartholomew saw that he had no choice but to stay. Software tools had not developed to the point where he could start his own company and do decent titles. "It still costs millions to do these products," he said, "and Microsoft is the only company that can spend millions up front." Approached by Knowledge Adventure, another software company, about a vice president's position, he declined. "You can see by their products," he said later, "that they have to cut corners to save production costs. You never have to do that here." In the end, he decided that Microsoft was "still one of the better places to work." Then he laughed. "I sat down and looked over my stock options. It just wouldn't be very smart for me to leave right now."

The "why" of staying at Microsoft was more complicated for Corddry. For him, as for thousands at Microsoft, it was no longer a matter of money. "I remember Mike Maples saying once," he recalled, "that everybody at Microsoft at a certain economic level are volunteers. Because they're rich. I mean, here, there's thousands who can retire. In a normal Fortune 500 company, there might be two dozen." There was something fatal about the allure of a company that kept you at virtually a self-destructive level of dedication long after it was economically necessary. "It's silly to keep a job," Corddry said, "so you can make a million dollars then go through a divorce and lose half of it."

Yet everywhere he looked, including within, he saw people who kept on working whatever the costs, as the excitement at Microsoft was irresistible. "The intelligence level here is addictive," he said. "Even my wife understands that—she's jealous of all the smart people I spend my days with."

There also was the matter of impact on the world. Corddry had taken an idea in Bill Gates's head and turned it into a financial juggernaut. Just as Corddry had predicted, the multimedia market was surging dramatically and Microsoft was better positioned than anyone else in the world to ride the wave. Sales of multimedia computers in 1993 had reached 4.8 million, triple the sales in 1992. One in ten personal computers sold now was a multimedia machine, and prices had dropped to the $2,000 level—less than the cost of a standard personal computer a year ago. At the end of March, looking ahead three months to the end of Microsoft's fiscal year, Corddry predicted that the "old MM Pubs" would bring in $60 million in sales. "We went from $2 million in revenues to $12 million to $60 million in three years," Corddry said proudly. "That's 600 percent growth per year."

Encarta alone, which finished 1993 as the world's best-selling encyclopedia on CD-ROM, had racked up sales of 350,000—400 percent over projections—worth $25 million in revenue. (By October 1994, *Encarta* sales would have topped 1 million copies.) Compton's, *Encarta*'s leading competitor, had totaled $9 million over the same period. Three of 1993's top-ten selling multimedia titles were Microsoft's: *Encarta, Cinemania,* and *Dinosaurs.*

I remembered then the most oft-stated fear among *Sendak*'s creators: "that this is *Encarta* all over again." And I began to wonder if for the past sixteen months I had been chronicling not a futile and inept false start, as I had believed, but an effort certain to succeed, and whose signs of success had been there before me all along.

Corddry looked back over the accomplishments of MM Pubs with a pleasure and pride he took pains to conceal from those under him. He had taken on the role of visionary at Microsoft, building a business enterprise out of what struck the rest of the company as incomprehensible fantasy. In the process, he had fashioned a dreamers' corporate culture that now, of necessity, had to be eliminated. Corddry and those like him were stepping aside for the human spreadsheet types who generally ran Microsoft business units. "All these good people who built this enterprise," Corddry said, "see these traditional Microsoft managers coming in, they're resentful and bitter." But he felt now that multimedia had advanced from concept to reality and that it needed harder-headed managers. "So I'm actually enjoying myself right now," he said, relieved of his responsibilities. "Multimedia took off, it worked!"

As Corddry had predicted, companies throughout the computing and entertainment industries were jumping on the multimedia bandwagon. WordPerfect, long a force in corporate word processing, was launching a multititle series of products for the home. Paramount, Dorling Kindersley, Disney, Time Warner, Sony, and hundreds of other companies, many of them start-ups, were coming out with new CD-ROM titles. And Corddry, having been there from before the beginning, was exuberant and exhausted from the sheer drama and excitement of it all. Even with all these competitors joining in, Multimedia still struck him as a thrilling terra incognita, fraught with peril. "We could be building a Ferrari for a country with no gas stations," he said excitedly. "Because we don't own content."

He was enchanted by the high irony of Gates's decision to eliminate Multimedia Publishing just as the multimedia industry was entering the cultural mainstream. "Here Microsoft is planning to get rid of the name 'Multimedia' as an entity just when the rest of the industry is getting started," he said. It was a classic example of the company's constant determination to stay ahead of its competition—an ethic that made working at Microsoft, Corddry added, "like doing open-heart surgery on a runner in the middle of a marathon."

By mid-May, the *Sendak* project, once planned as a four-unit, one-disc encyclopedia to ship simultaneously on the Windows and Macintosh platforms in August 1994, had become a four-disc series shipping in increments first on the Windows platform, then on the Mac at some undetermined, distant future date. The first Windows disc was to ship on September 30, 1994, the next a month later, and the other two early in 1995. The mood on the *Sendak* team shifted from anxiety to despair.

The Consumer Division was moved from Building 10 to the just-completed Building 18, and the onset of spring saw a flurry of change in the professional and personal lives of many of those connected with *Sendak*. Gammill, Bjerke, and Bartholomew all bought new homes. Ballinger, who had resolved to "get a life" outside of Microsoft, did so with a vengeance: he bought a new home, got engaged, and began planning an October wedding.

After spending her maternity leave exploring every conceivable alternative to returning to Microsoft, Bjerke came back to the company as a design lead for "Zack," a Microsoft joint venture with Lego. "I am fortunate," she said in e-mail to her old teammates, "to have worked with such a warm, and talented group as you are." She had hardly begun her new job before she decided to give up her employee's position and work as a contractor both for Microsoft and for other companies. "I'm willing to lose the stock stuff," she said of the benefits she would be forsaking, "because I have the house I want anyway." By the end of that summer, she had launched a new digital design venture—an electronic artists' co-op called VisionMakers—with three partners: her husband, a musician and sound engineer; a television producer and director; and an artist she had met while working on Zack.

While at Intermedia, Gammill was offered a $100,000-per-year position by Grolier's, manufacturer of another multimedia encyclopedia. He turned it down. He was directed in e-mail to sign up for a management seminar on interviewing and supervising development level 12 and above employees. Looking over the list of his classmates, Gammill was impressed and confused. All were long-time Microsoft employees who occupied significantly higher rungs on the corporate ladder. His inclusion on the list was an indication that his status was changing. "Holy shit," he muttered, pointing to the first name on the list. It was Melinda French—Bill Gates's wife.

At the end of August, as the ship date for *Encarta 95* drew near, Gammill and testing lead Len Dongweck were moved over to help finish *Encarta.*

After convening focus groups in Chicago and in Walnut Creek, California, *Sendak*'s product name was chosen in May. It would be called *Explorapedia.* The nature disc was dubbed "The World of Nature," and the Civilization disc, "The World of People." Names for the Geography and History discs were to be determined later. At the end of June, the ship date for "The World of Nature" had slipped to October 15, with "The World of People" due to follow on November 2. Shipping on those two dates, Bartholomew assured Patty Stonesifer, would get both discs into stores in time for the peak of the Christmas shopping season.

Near the end of August, though, the ship date for "The World of Nature" was moved back to November 15, with "The World of Civilization" due out on December 13. The team had formally given up on Christmas, a defeat that hit Ralph Barton particularly hard. Pointing out that the two most senior and experienced employees working on *Explorapedia,* Gammill and Dongweck, had been taken off the project at its most critical time, Barton swore never again "to commit to a deadline if management won't commit to giving me resources."

In truth, these slippages were caused by SPAM rather than by anything specific to *Explorapedia.* By early August, SPAM's problems were acute enough for Bartholomew to send mail to Richard Tait outlining them in detail. After cutting back on the quality and quantity of sprites as far as possible, Bartholomew wrote, SPAM performance still was unacceptable. When testers clicked on some pictures to activate sprites, they had to wait forty-five seconds for the sprite to begin moving. One transition from the spaceship to a scene took forty-four seconds, and the return took thirty-eight seconds. Another sprite took ten seconds to begin, at which point SPAM would drop all but one of the animation's frames.

Gammill and Bartholomew considered dropping SPAM altogether, and employing a different animation engine, two more of which emerged elsewhere at Microsoft—one developed by a Russian emigre working there, the other purchased when Microsoft bought another software company. Finally, though, Bartholomew decided to stay with SPAM, pressure its developers to deliver on the features he needed, and slip his ship dates for "The World of Nature" and "The World of People" into 1995. "I can't see compromising Explorapedia," he wrote me in e-mail in September, "we've worked too hard and have too cool a product to rush forward, burn the team out, deliver something below our expectations. . . . It's better to be realistic and shoot for simultaneously RTMing Nature and Modern Civ on 2/1/95. . . ."

I remembered then that that was the date originally scheduled for *Sendak* by Jayleen Ryberg in December 1992, when she first had sketched out a product plan. And there shone round about me then a blinding light. Trembling and astonished, I stood up and made my way outside. I walked across the Microsoft campus until I came to the strip of concrete that Gammill so long ago had pointed out to me. I stopped and stared up in wonderment, through a bank of windows, to where the Gates of Wrath was stored.

Postmortem

My intent in taking on this project was to observe and describe from inside Microsoft the perilous magic of its success, to capture as accurately as possible the working conditions and emotional state of the Microsoft worker, and to replicate the workers' pride, tension, and angst in the mind and heart of the reader. To those ends, I immersed myself in the physical and psychological environment of the people who design and develop Microsoft products, and devoted considerable energy to researching the question of how typical the team in question was.

I was assured by Kevin Gammill and many others at Microsoft that the *Sendak* experience was common. I also found ample supporting evidence in Microsoft portmortems—reports, written by program managers, detailing the successes and failures of their recently completed projects.

Every Microsoft project has its postmortem report; without exception, these reports read like the recountings of disasters. If all product names were removed from them, the reader would assume they were investigations of failed projects. In his *Encarta* postmortem, Craig Bartholomew described his team as having "lumbered at breakneck speed" through the project, and the list of "things that went wrong" runs to several pages. Other reports cited endless mistakes in judgment, blind alleys, power struggles, bitter personal battles, hospitalizations from stress, abrupt resignations, and many other bad breaks—it seemed miraculous that any of these products ever made its way into the marketplace.

Yet make their way into the marketplace they did, and nearly all of them proved to be among the best-sellers in their category. However dismally they may have been regarded by their creators, they can only be viewed from the outside as successful.

It never occurred to me when I first approached Microsoft that I might end up chronicling a failed project. Yet from almost the beginning until near the end of my stay there, I believed that I was indeed observing an object lesson in how not to develop a product. Since everyone connected with *Sendak* was so miserable, so angry, and talked so incessantly about frustration and disappointment, I could only assume that chance had hooked me up with a catastrophe.

But in fact the *Sendak* project was an unqualified success. While each particular feature in *Explorapedia* is a pale version of the feature first envisioned for *Sendak,* and technical limitations turned it into a series of products rather than a single one, the encyclopedia nevertheless entered the marketplace as the sole product of its kind: a children's reference work that ran reliably on a broad number of personal computers, that was easy to use, whose text could be both read and heard, that melded games and other forms of entertainment with impressive depth and breadth of content, and that broke new technical ground. "The World of Nature" disc alone had 4,000 paragraphs of narrated text; a Wise-Cracker feature (the IgnorAnts, alas, never materialized) with 400 questions configured into 80 different games, 17 hours and 42 minutes of audio, 55 video sequences, 265 animation sequences, 52 activities, 9 songs, 923 photos, 915 other illustrations, and 142,135 words.

It also succeeded in one other important respect. Finally shipped on November 23, 1994—three months earlier than Bartholomew last predicted—the first of its four discs was brought in ahead of the schedule its first program manager, Jayleen Ryberg, planned for *Sendak.* To have designed a product the likes of which had never been seen before, to have built many of the tools required to create the product as it went along, and to have finished it on time was a remarkable achievement for the *Sendak* team. Yet if you were to ask any of them now how they felt about the end result, they would profess to be disappointed, citing the failure to get onto stores' shelves in time for that year's Christmas, and the failure to have completed all four discs, as originally planned.

It is instructive in this respect to compare *Explorapedia* with the first version of *Encarta.* The design cycle described in such excruciating detail in this book took almost exactly one year; the same design cycle for *Encarta* took four years. And everything about *Explorapedia* was more challenging. It incorporated a metaphor of exploration that afforded an additional, entertaining means of access to its content, and all of its technical features were more ambitious and more complicated than those in *Encarta*.

The faster pace of design and development and the greater level of complexity in *Explorapedia* testify not only to the rapid rate of progress in the development of multimedia products and tools generally, but also to how much the creators of *Explorapedia* learned from their experience on *Encarta*.

I came away from my time at Microsoft convinced that the long and tortured search for answers to questions of aesthetics is inevitable in the development of any new medium or art form. The quest should be particularly tortured in multimedia computing: an art form, developed by engineers, of unknown value and interest to an undefined set of consumers. By comparison, film, following theater, or television, following radio, had ample information on what audiences were likely to want. In the early days of multimedia computing, the search for interesting, useful, entertaining, and profitable products was at best a *Myst*-or-miss proposition. What is remarkable about the *Sendak* experience is not how long it went on, but how quickly it ended.

I asked Bill Gates once why he thought his company had become so successful and so dominant. He brushed aside my question by saying, "We're always trying to figure things out, look at our mistakes, give ourselves a hard time. I've always been fairly hardcore about looking at what we did wrong. We're not known for reflecting back on the things that went well."

Looking back at *Explorapedia* and its creation, I can see now that Gates and his managers had cunningly set goals and standards that would prove impossible to meet. By arbitrarily shortening *Sendak*'s schedule, they guaranteed that the eventual success of its team would be seen by team members as a failure. It was exactly what Gates had done to them on *Encarta*: while giving his employees the means to win, he also ensured that they would interpret their victory as defeat. There would be no laurels for them to rest upon; instead, they would dive immediately into their next project hoping to redeem themselves.

Index